Praise for *Black Sands*

"Within the beauty of Hawaiian flowers, volcanic sands, and turquoise seas, danger lurks . . . and you won't want to miss a minute of this adventure! Reading Colleen Coble's *Black Sands* is almost like visiting the Hawaiian Islands yourself!"

—Angela Hunt, author of *The Novelist*

"An injured woman, a man from her past, and a race against time to get to the truth that could change their world forever. With her usual flair, Colleen Coble has created a story rich with memorable characters, blockbuster plotting, an adorable mongoose, and a Hawaiian setting so real you'll get a whiff of coconut on every page."

—Diann Hunt, author of *Hot Flashes & Cold Cream*

"Colleen Coble is an expert at taking a place and turning it into an intriguing character. This skill shines in *Black Sands* as we indulge our senses in the exotic beauty, mystery, and passion of Hawaii. Fall in love in Hawaii, *with* Hawaii, and with the people who live there."

—Hannah Alexander, author of *Last Resort* and *Note of Peril*

"Filled with the spirit of aloha and page-turning twists and turns, *Black Sands* is romantic suspense at its thrilling finest. A can't-put-it-down read."

—Linda Windsor, award-winning romantic comedy author of *Paper Moon*

"Vengeance, volcanoes, and vital clues kept me turning pages late into the night. *Black Sands* is Colleen Coble's best yet!"

—Lyn Cote, author of The Women of Ivy Manor series

"No one takes you to a setting like Colleen Coble, and what better place to be than the *Black Sands* of Hawaii? Reading the book was like a cool dip in the balmy ocean—under the lurking shadow of a volcano in shark-infested waters. Enjoy, but beware!"

—Kristin Billerbeck, author of *With This Ring, I'm Confused*

"To write about Hawai'i requires extensive knowledge and a very delicate weaving. Ms. Coble has a master's touch that separates the fine nuances and finds a balance between all cultures and their political, social, familial, and religious views."

—Malia Spencer, English major, University of Hawai'i

"This talented author combines Hawai'i, tropical nights, on the edge suspense, defined characterization, and spine tingling romance to pen a story you can't put down!"

—Lori Copeland, author of *Men of the Saddle* and *Brides of the West*

"A great story told by a master. Colleen Coble continues to shine."

—Lois Richer, author of *A Time to Protect*

"*Black Sands* is full of suspense, romance, intrigue, and everything you'd expect in a good mystery. I loved the exotic setting."

—Linda Hall, author of *Steal Away* and *Chat Room*

"As a long-time fan of Colleen Coble, I have come to expect a riveting story with characters who seem so real they remain in my thoughts long after I've turned the final page. Coble raises her own high standard to new heights in *Black Sands*, in a story that will linger in your heart."

—Carol Cox, author of *Sagebrush Brides*

"This quick-paced suspense will have you flipping pages as fast as you can."

—www.dancingword.net

"Wow! Reading Colleen Coble's *Black Sands* is like taking a romantic excursion to Hawaii's rugged shoreline. Coble brings the setting to life, draws engaging characters, and spins an intricate web of intrigue."

—Denise Hunter, author of *Saving Grace*

"Danger and romance walk side by side making for a creative contrast."

—In the Library Reviews

Black
Sands

Black Sands

COLLEEN COBLE

THOMAS NELSON
Since 1798

NASHVILLE   DALLAS   MEXICO CITY   RIO DE JANEIRO   BEIJING

Published in Nashville, Tennessee, by Thomas Nelson. Thomas Nelson is a registered trademark of Thomas Nelson, Inc.

Thomas Nelson, Inc., titles may be purchased in bulk for educational, business, fund-raising, or sales promotional use. For information, please e-mail SpecialMarkets@ThomasNelson.com

Scripture quotations are from the New King James Version ®, copyright 1979, 1980, 1982 by Thomas Nelson, Inc., Publishers.

Publisher's Note: This novel is a work of fiction. Names, characters, places, and incidents are either products of the author's imagination or used fictitiously. All characters are fictional, and any similarity to people living or dead is purely coincidental.

Library of Congress Cataloging-in-Publication Data

Coble, Colleen.
    Black sands / Colleen Coble.
      p. cm.—(The Aloha Reef series ; bk. 2)
    ISBN 978-0-7852-6043-1 (pbk.)
    1. Hawaii—Fiction. I. Title.
    PS3553.O2285B57 2005
    813'.54—dc22

2005011656

Printed in the United States of America

08 09 10 11 12 QW 9 8 7 6 5 4

For my husband, David Coble.
Your constant love gives me wings.

Prologue

The sulfur-laden air seared Adele Tagama's lungs even as the *a'a* shredded the bottom of her feet. She was inhaling the very fire of hell. They were back there somewhere. She'd escaped them, but the hopelessness that lodged in her chest slowed her down. She ran over the rough, hardened lava. She wanted to shriek from the pain in her feet, but she didn't dare betray her location. If she could hide, maybe they would run past her. She had to get to help, had to tell someone what she'd found out. Would anyone believe her?

A cough welled in her chest, and she tried to smother it. Her lungs betrayed her with a hoarse croak that caused the steps behind her to quicken. A hard hand fell on her shoulders, and she beat at the figure looming out of the darkness like Satan himself. It was no use. Something shifted under her, and then she was falling, falling into the red mouth that opened wide to receive her.

One

One Year Later

Annie Tagama squatted on the lava and examined the cracks. Vog burned her nose and eyes. She barely noticed the stink of sulfuric gases that hung in a miasma around her. The thick air was as much a part of her world as the rough lava under her feet and the blue Hawaiian sky over her head. Even though she knew she was safe here in this stable part of Hawai'i Volcanoes National Park, caution dictated her choices on this work day—her first since the accident.

"Can you bring me a new GPS receiver?" Monica Rogers called from the edge of the lava shelf. "This one is shot." The older woman's voice reminded Annie of Minnie Mouse, and it didn't match Monica's stocky frame.

Annie stood and took two steps toward Monica. She peered toward the drop-off, where heavy clouds of sulfuric mist billowed. Sweat broke out on her forehead. Her lungs constricted. *You can do it. It's safe.* She swallowed the sour taste in her mouth. Carrying the new receiver, she took a few more steps.

"Hurry up!" Monica squeaked.

"I'll do it." Annie's best friend, Fawn Trenton, took the receiver from her hand, her expression warning Annie not to cross Monica.

Annie froze, and Fawn hurried toward Monica. Thirtysomething Fawn turned heads wherever she went. Her tawny hair gleamed in the filtered wash of sunshine. Bright blue beads decorated the long braid that hung over one shoulder. Her T-shirt read SAVE THE RAIN FOREST.

Annie stepped away from the edge and sighed with relief. She had to get over this fear that turned her knees to jelly, but she wasn't sure how to go about it. The shelf out there was perfectly safe. It hadn't had a collapse in years. But her face was still damp, and her pulse still galloped. She was such a failure.

Turning her back on the other women, she returned to her task. Her pack held cans of yellow spray paint. She grabbed one and began to spray the cracks in the ground. Watching the paint over the coming weeks would tell the scientists about the earth's movement. She forced herself to focus, though it was hard not to let her gaze stray to the vog drifting up from the drop-off.

Half an hour later, Monica and Fawn joined Annie near the two all-terrain vehicles. Monica's lips were tight, and she kept shooting angry glares toward Annie. "I'm going to headquarters," she said. Her movements stiff, she stalked to her ATV and drove off.

"I hope she doesn't rat on you," Fawn said.

Annie bit her lip. "I don't think Gina will listen if she does." Limping toward her ATV, she saw a glint of metal in the sun. She stooped and picked up a delicate necklace. *What was this doing here?* The familiarity made her catch her breath. It couldn't be her sister's, could it? Surely there were many necklaces like this on the island.

Fawn peered over her shoulder. "What's wrong?"

Annie turned over the heart-shaped pendant and saw the initials A. T. on the back. "It's Leilani's," she muttered. She rubbed her forehead.

"How did it get here? Your sister wouldn't set foot on the volcano if you paid her."

Unease began to coil in Annie's chest. "She didn't come home last night. I figured she was out with her friends and didn't think much about it. You know how she is. I'm sure she called Father after

I left the house this morning." But that didn't explain the necklace's appearance out here.

Fawn's gaze followed hers. "Maybe she loaned it to someone? Did you borrow it a few days ago and forget about it?"

Annie shook her head. "She never takes off this necklace. Mother gave it to her the week before she died. Leilani even showers in it. These are Mother's initials. A. T. Adele Tagama." When their mother committed suicide a year ago, she and Leilani both had clung to anything of their mother's. Her thoughts boiled with possibilities—all of them dire.

Fawn squeezed Annie's arm. "Don't go jumping to conclusions. Maybe it broke and someone found it."

It was hard *not* to jump to conclusions, not after her mother had died out here. She'd thrown herself into the lava, leaving only her Surfah flip-flops behind. Blue ones that Annie kept on her dresser. She shuddered. Trouble had been Leilani's middle name since then. Annie was ill equipped to deal with Leilani's rebellious ways. Though her sister was only five years younger than Annie's thirty years, sometimes Annie felt generations older.

Annie told herself not to worry. There was likely a perfectly reasonable explanation. "You're probably right. It's not unlike her to be gone overnight. It's just this necklace." She went toward their vehicle. "I'd better check and see if my dad has heard from her. I'll call some of her friends. I'm sure there's some explanation."

Fawn followed her. "Annie to the rescue. Don't you ever get tired of being the one that everyone leans on? You'll never get to live your own life."

"I love my family," Annie said. They reached the Kawasaki ATV. "Hop on, let's go."

Fawn shrugged and got behind her. "Your family's expectations are going to kill you. I hate to see the way you beat yourself up when you can't do everything. Have you been drinking the chamomile tea I gave you? It should help with the stress."

Annie grinned. "Yes, doctor."

"I know you think I harp on this too much, but you've taken over everything for them since your mom died. They're never going to let you have a life if you make it too easy for them. They've all turned into babies. They're adults. Make them act like it."

"I know, I know. I will." Annie negotiated the *a'a* trail carefully. She didn't dare drive too fast, or the sharp bits of lava would shred the ATV's tires. The *a'a* finally gave way to black gravel, and she picked up her speed. "*Harp* is a good word. On a double-word square it would be worth eighteen points." Talking about Scrabble was better than thinking about the necklace in her pocket. Or about how accurate Fawn's observations were. Things *had* changed for the Tagama family, but there was no going back. Annie couldn't bear to see her family suffer anymore, not if she could shoulder the burdens for them and ease their lives.

"I should save my breath," Fawn said. "I was going to offer to get you an appointment at the Fairmont for a *Lomilomi* massage, but you don't deserve it."

Fawn knew how to stab her where it hurt. "Meanie." Annie turned the corner onto concrete. The long, squat building that housed the offices sat at the top of a small rise and was surrounded by lava fields. To the right of the Hawai'i Volcanoes Observatory was the Jagger Museum, containing a history of the Hawai'i volcanoes. Scientists from all over the world came here to study the geological processes that triggered volcanic activity. She parked the ATV and waited for Fawn to hop off, then dismounted.

Fawn smoothed the locks of hair the wind had teased from her braid. "You're too young to spend your life in front of a board game. When was the last time you went to the movies or even out to eat?"

Annie scrunched her forehead as she thought. "Um, the last time you and I went. I guess it was last month," she said.

"My point exactly. Five weeks ago, to be exact. I've invited you to do something every Friday since then too, and you always say you have to fix dinner for your dad. That's not normal, Annie. You're only thirty, not eighty. And you're letting him become a tyrant. I think he thinks he's a Japanese emperor from the 1800s now that your mom isn't around to keep him in line."

"I know, I know." The parking lot beside the squat brick building was nearly empty, and Annie realized it was after five o'clock. Gina's car was still in the lot though. Annie started toward her Nissan Pathfinder. A movement at the office door caught her eye, and she glanced up to see her boss waving at her imperiously.

"Annie, I need to see you," Gina called.

Annie sighed. Fawn raised her eyebrows. Their boss, Gina Sarris, turned and walked back inside. Judging from Gina's stiff back, Annie was headed for trouble. Annie limped toward the building. She didn't have time for this.

The hum of the banks of computers greeted her as she opened the door. The familiar squawk of the scanner and the click of the seismometer eased her tension a little. She went down the hall, which was lined with pictures of volcanoes in various stages of eruption. Other walls held photo essays of the various studies going on—projects like gravitational studies, electrical processes, gas geochemistry, and ground deformation. She stepped into her boss's office. It was empty. She went to the office chair by the window.

"Sorry to keep you." Gina came into the room and moved to her desk. Barely five feet tall, she still wore the heavy work pants she donned when out in the field. A stench of sulfur followed her. The cracked leather chair practically swallowed her. She pulled her glasses to her nose, then flipped open a folder.

"I need to get home right away." Annie slipped her hand into her pocket and fingered her sister's necklace.

Gina gave her a kind smile. "Don't look so scared, Annie. We're just going to talk."

Gina had taken over as Scientist-in-charge a little over a year ago. Things had run smoothly under Gina's supreme organizational skills. Her dark hair never dared to be out of place, and every paper clip on her desk was perfectly aligned. Though in her fifties, she was still beautiful with perfect, unlined skin. She had a faint accent no one had been able to figure out. With her dark coloring, she could be French, Greek, part Hawaiian, or any of the other nationalities in this melting pot.

Annie knew Gina liked her. That was the only thing that might save this interview from going south. "Okay." She moved toward Gina's desk.

"It's good to have you back. How have you been feeling? I noticed you're only limping a little now."

"Pretty good. The doctor says the limp may go with time, or it may hang around. But either way, it's not bothering me much. The pain is gone and it's just still a little stiff."

"Scars? You don't have your slippers on today. I kind of miss the designs on your toenail polish."

Annie managed a smile. "The designs are still there. I just figure no one wants to see the scars." *Especially me.* Every time she saw her right foot, she averted her eyes. "They're pretty gruesome."

Gina closed the folder and folded her hands. "Could you explain what happened today? Monica says you refused to bring her some equipment."

Annie bit her lip. How could she explain the way fear had paralyzed her? "I couldn't," she whispered. She put as much pleading into her expression as she could. "Maybe I'd better stay in-house for a while until I get my bearings. I just froze out there. All I could think about was the pain of falling into the lava." She rubbed slick palms against her jeans.

Gina shook her head. "We need your expertise in the field. Those new GPS receivers need to be planted. You're going to have to face your fears, Annie. I know how scary it must have been for you when that lava bench gave way. But you're a volcanologist. You can't study volcanoes from inside this building."

Annie nodded. Gina was right about that, but there was no way anyone who hadn't gone through it could understand what Annie experienced. One minute she had been walking on solid ground, and the next moment she'd found herself standing in hot lava. The only thing that had saved her was the fact that the stream of lava was so small. The lava in the tube had almost emptied. What if the next time a full river of lava swallowed her? And the pain had been horrific. She still had nightmares about it. Besides, her mother had died out there. Maybe she was cursed to do the same. She wrapped her fingers around the delicate chain on the necklace in her pocket.

When Annie didn't answer, Gina sighed. "You can't let this fear defeat you, Annie. Face it and go on with your life."

"Just a few weeks," Annie pleaded. "I can't go out there right now."

"You can and you will." Gina's voice hardened. "What kind of a boss—and even more importantly, a friend—would I be if I didn't make you face your fears and do what is best for you in the long run? I know it's hard. But you're stronger than you realize, Annie. I want you back on the job. You're too good a scientist to let this beat you."

It helped to hear Gina's confidence in her, but Annie cringed at the thought of going back on the lava. "One week," she begged.

Gina's face softened. "Okay. But see a professional about this if you need to. I don't want to lose you. I know I shouldn't play favorites, but I've seen myself in you so many times, Annie. Your quick mind and total dedication to your work is outstanding. You have a bright future ahead of you. Don't let this experience ruin your career. Get over it. I want my little 'volcano cowboy' back."

Annie's face burned at the reprimand. She gave a brief nod. "I just need a little more time."

"One week. That's the best I can do. I need a crew that can pull its weight. If you can't get control of this fear, you're going to need to look for a new line of work. What about your underwater research with Jillian?"

At least this was one area where she wouldn't let Gina down. "That's still ongoing. I'm okay in the water."

Gina nodded and stood, and Annie knew she was dismissed. "*Mahalo,* Gina." She couldn't talk anymore. She rose and practically ran from the room. Outside the office, she nearly mowed down Jillian Sommers. "Sorry," she muttered.

Jillian was Annie's inspiration. If Jillian could recover from the blow life had dealt when her husband abandoned her, Annie could get over a simple injury. Annie smiled. "You're here late."

"You too." Jillian's ash-blond curls lay against her sculptured cheeks. She'd lost weight since Noah left. "I was just going over the data from the seamount. Some of our bottom-pressure recorders are going bad. We're going to have to go down to replace them. What's your schedule looking like?"

"Maybe Monday?" Annie hoped to get home and find Leilani there safe and sound.

"Sounds good. I'll touch base with you then." Jillian said good-bye, and Annie hurried to her car.

The fresh, cool air relieved her heated skin as Annie passed through the rain forest. The ohia trees that grew in abundance along the road to her house pressed close to the SUV. The Tagama family had owned the hundred-acre compound for more than fifty years, though she wasn't sure how much longer they could hold onto it. When she was a little girl, she used to lay under the *hapu'u* ferns beneath the trees and pretend she was a fairy in her house. It was her way of escaping her father's high expectations. She hated to disappoint him, even as a child. Since her mother's death, his expectations had risen exponentially. She hardly recognized the demanding man as the exemplary father figure he'd been all her life.

There would be no escaping her father's anger if Leilani wasn't home. Annie had no doubt his first reaction would be to blame her.

She slipped her hand into her pocket and rubbed her thumb over the pendant. Leilani would never lose this necklace. It meant too much to her. So what did it all mean? Annie was afraid to find out.

She pushed open the door. "Father? Where are you?" Her pet mongoose, Wilson, scurried to meet her at the door. He wrapped himself around her ankles. An orange peel teetered on his back. She scooped him up and picked it off. "What have you been into?" He was almost dead when she'd found him months ago beside his dead mother and siblings. Though she nursed him back to health herself, he never gained the full size of a regular mongoose. He was only a foot long, head to tail. The warmth of his sleek body gave her courage. She dropped the peel in the trash in the kitchen, then went down the hall to the living room.

Her father scowled when he saw Wilson in her arms. "I told you to get rid of that animal, Annie, yet you continue to defy me. He got in the trash again and dumped it all over the floor. I want him gone."

Annie's fingers stilled, and she clutched Wilson closer. "I'll clean it up, Father."

Her father's jaw hardened, and he stepped toward her. "Give him to me. I'm getting rid of that creature once and for all."

"No!" Annie stepped back. She softened her voice. Harsh words would only make her father more unyielding. "I mean, please give him another chance, Father. I'm still training him. He'll learn. He . . . brings me comfort since Mother died."

Her father's face softened at the mention of her mother. He shook his head, and his frown returned. "You don't have time to be cleaning up after him all the time. I have some dictation I need you to do tonight."

"I'll have time to do both."

He harrumphed, but he didn't try to take the mongoose again. She needed to ask him about Leilani, who obviously had not returned. Wetting her lips, she tried to decide how to raise the question without bringing more disapproval on her own head.

Her father peered past her out the glass in the storm door. "Who is here?"

Annie turned. An unfamiliar car crowded to the back of her car. A pale blue Chevrolet, it looked like one of those nondescript rental cars. Maybe it was about Leilani. Annie hurried to the front door. A burly figure got out of the vehicle. She froze. Her nails bit into the palms of her hand, and she nearly turned and slammed the door.

Mano Oana. She hadn't heard from him in more than a year, not since he called to tell her about her older brother Tomiko, nicknamed Tomi. She wasn't ready to face him even now. Wilson burrowed against her neck and squeaked. She told herself to move, to go to the door. Her hand shook when she finally reached out and opened it quickly. There was nothing to be gained by delaying the inevitable.

Mano's gaze fastened on her face, and he gave a tentative smile. As always, she found herself caught by his dark eyes. If eyes really were the windows to the soul, Mano's soul was full of intensity and passion. His name meant "shark," and it had never seemed more apt than this minute. He could destroy the even tenor of her life as easily as a great white could thrash a seal.

Annie wet her lips and tried to find something to say that didn't sound inane. "Mano, what are you doing here?"

"Could I come in a minute?"

She stepped aside silently. Her father had turned his back. He looked out the opposite window toward the Japanese garden her mother had loved so much. A curl of incense drifted around him from the bowl on the table. It was her father's favorite scent: Joy, a blend of sandalwood and tea leaves that was supposed to evoke memories of happiness, though Annie couldn't remember a single happy moment since her mother had died. Without her mother's attention, weeds had choked the path to the koi fish pond in much the same way that the family's cares had begun to strangle Annie.

The bonsai had lost its shape, too, just as her family no longer resembled the perfect unit it had once been.

Mano would find them much changed.

Her father would be no help. Annie turned back to Mano, who hadn't moved though she'd stepped out of the way. "Come in."

Mano stepped inside and nodded to her. "Annie. It's been a long time."

"Not long enough." Wilson struggled in her arms, but she held on. She needed him. After a final wiggle, he went still. She stared at Mano. "What do you want?"

Annie had to wonder if his cool self-assurance was just a charade. Her gaze traveled to her father. Though in his midfifties, Edega Tagama's black hair was still thick and lustrous, but the past months had aged his face. He turned and stared at Mano with an attitude of belligerence. At one time, Mano had been almost part of the family, but he wasn't welcome here anymore.

Mano glanced at the cane-backed chair under the window. "Okay if I sit down? This may take a little while."

Her father thrust out his chin. "We have nothing to say to you."

Trying to hide her limp, Annie went to the loveseat. "I have plenty to say. Sit down." She tried to adopt a nonchalant attitude by crossing her legs, but her leg trembled and gave away her agitation, so she uncrossed them and steadied her tremors by pressing her heels into the ground. She hoped he didn't see how much his presence affected her.

Mano's U.S. Navy uniform fit him superbly. Impeccably pressed and spotless, he was the epitome of a spit-and-polish officer. His white mess jacket over navy pants hid the muscles she knew lurked under the fabric. He was a wrestler. Leilani and Annie used to go to watch his matches on the base with their brother. She averted her eyes. It was best not to think about what used to be. She swallowed and tried to compose herself.

Her father gave a disgusted snort, then moved to the sofa and perched on the edge. "I will hear this if I must. Then you are no longer welcome in my home."

Mano took a deep breath. "I'm sorry I missed Tomi's funeral, but I was—" He glanced away as his words died.

"You killed him," Annie said. Her voice trembled as much as her limbs, but she forced herself to meet his gaze. "And by killing him, you killed my mother."

"I'm sorry about your mother," Mano said. The muscles in his neck moved as he swallowed. "It seemed so out of character for her—" He stopped at Annie's glare.

"You will not mention my wife," Edega burst out.

Mano's gaze slid back to Annie, and she read the desperation in his face. She took pity on him, though she knew he deserved every bit of her father's anger. "Why are you here, Mano?" She wanted to get rid of him and talk to her father about Leilani.

He squared his shoulders. "I have your brother's belongings. I wanted to bring them to you." He hesitated. "I have something else to talk to you about too. Is Leilani here?"

An ache spread from Annie's center outward. Leilani was always the one men noticed. Annie had gone on one date in her life, a mercy date for the bash her family threw her when she got her PhD. Leilani had arranged for one of her castoffs to escort her. Mano was one of those now too.

Maybe Mano wanted to try his luck again. The pain that rippled through her at the thought surprised her. "She's not here," she said shortly. She thought she saw disappointment on his face. And why not? Leilani was beautiful and vivacious, while Annie was a brown, colorless Eurasian sparrow.

"I really wanted to talk to all of you together." Mano turned toward the door. "Let me get the stuff from the car." He went to the door and stepped outside.

As soon as she heard the door slam, Annie sagged against the loveseat. She wouldn't cry, not until she was safely in her room. Her father would demand to know what she was upset about, and he wouldn't understand. She didn't understand herself. The lump that formed in her throat was as acrid as the smoke from Kilauea. Her eyes burned. She didn't know if she was ready to go through Tomi's belongings.

"Leilani should be here," her father said. His voice trembled. "We should present a united front."

Leilani. Annie put down Wilson and her hand went to her pocket. She pulled out the pendant. "Have you talked to her today?"

"She has not shown her face since yesterday, the silly girl." Edega stood and paced. "She has been out since then?" Annie nodded. "We shall have a most stern talk with her when she gets home."

Annie sighed. She opened her fist and showed her father the locket. "I found this near the Kalapana Trail."

The anger left her father's eyes. "She never goes to the volcano. You don't think—" He gulped and choked back his words.

Annie hadn't wanted to even consider suicide, but she realized the thought had hovered at the back of her consciousness. "Surely not," she whispered. "She would never kill herself, especially not there."

"She's been acting strange since she joined that club." Her father sounded fearful. "Secretive and sometimes despondent. You should have put an end to it, Annie."

Annie exhaled slowly. She should have, but Leilani was so headstrong. She glanced out the window. Mano was still unloading the trunk of the car. He seemed to be taking his time. Maybe he was less self-assured than she first thought.

She grabbed the portable phone on the table beside her and called the shop where Leilani worked. Her sister had not shown up for her shift. Annie dialed CeCe but couldn't reach her. Annie

called the police next. The dispatcher promised to send out an officer. Annie clicked off the phone and let her eyes return to Mano as
he hefted three stacked boxes and started toward the house. She let
her gaze linger on his dark hair. In her daydreams, she used to imagine plunging her fingers into that thick thatch. No more. Mano
Oana had destroyed her family as surely as if he'd sent a cloud of
choking ash to smother them all.

Two

M ano hoped Annie would see him coming with the boxes before he reached the door. After landing in Hilo, it had been all he could do to force himself to drive the familiar road out to the Tagama house. The lava fields stretched out on all sides of the winding road, and the memories assaulted him. Things were so different the last time he was here. Regret left a bitter taste in his mouth.

Knocking on the Tagama door today had been the hardest thing he'd ever done, which was sad considering how much he'd always loved coming here. Their home blended their Japanese heritage and the American culture they'd adopted as their own. Edega had emigrated from Japan when he was in his teens and married a Japanese American girl who treasured her American upbringing. Edega had insisted on a Japanese name for his son, and her mother had demanded an American name for Annie. Leilani had been a compromise, a Hawaiian name to celebrate their new home. The conflict was typical of the cultural tug of war that went on throughout the marriage. That was what had made coming here so lively.

Edega seemed different—more remote and austere. And Annie—she seemed smaller. She'd always been withdrawn, but now she was almost like a ghost. His cell phone rang, and he set the boxes down to answer it.

"Hey, big guy, where are you?" his sister, Kaia, said.

"On the Big Island. I came to see the Tagamas."

The phone went silent. Kaia finally cleared her throat. "That's got to be hard. It's the first time since—" She broke off.

"Yeah, it is. But it has to be done." He thought about telling Kaia what he suspected but bit back the words. She was in the middle of wedding plans. No sense in dragging her into this.

"Well, guess what?" Her tone lightened. "I'm here on the Big Island too. I'll find a place to get you fitted for a tux while you're here. I came to do some planning with Jillian. And to bring Nani for a while. She followed the boat here."

Jillian was Kaia's soon-to-be sister-in-law. "Nani? What's up with that?" He hadn't thought Kaia would let the dolphin out of her sight. Since Kaia had bridged the communication gap and begun to "talk" with the dolphin via a device that translated words into clicks and whistles, Kaia had been even more obsessed with her work. Maybe the upcoming wedding had divided her attention.

"Jillian asked if Nani might help her for a few weeks. She and a coworker want to check some underwater lava flow, and it's too deep for comfortable diving. I figured Nani might enjoy seeing Heidi again too. Besides, the reporters are still hounding us, and Nani needs a break. I'm taking off a few weeks to finish wedding preparations anyway."

"I'll stop by and take you all to dinner later. How's Jesse dealing with the prewedding frenzy?"

Kaia laughed softly. "He seems to be taking it in stride."

They chatted a few more minutes; then a police car pulled up behind his car, and an officer got out. The man's gaze met his, and recognition flooded his face. Mano's smile faded. Sam Briscoe. He said good-bye to Kaia.

Sam stopped. "Oana. I didn't know you were here."

Mano gave a curt nod. "I heard you'd moved back here after your stint in the navy. I had no idea you'd joined the force though." Stupid to get his hackles raised like this. He and Sam had been friends once—before Leilani Tagama had come between them.

"Yeah, once action gets in your blood, it's hard to settle for a normal job." Sam turned toward the house. "I'd better get inside. You coming?"

Sam obviously thought he knew all about why Mano was here. Surely Annie hadn't called to have him escorted off the property. Sam knocked on the door, and Annie opened it almost immediately. Her full lips tightened when her gaze flickered over Mano's face. She was petite, only about five-two. He remembered a time when her face got as red as a hibiscus when he appeared. She'd adored her "big brother" Mano once upon a time. So much for hoping a small part of her former admiration still existed.

He carried the boxes into the living room. A part of him wanted to leave the boxes and not speak to the Tagama family any more, but he knew he had to stay. Besides, he wondered what was going on with the detective's arrival. The tension and fear in the room left him uneasy.

Sam took out a notepad from his shirt pocket and uncapped his pen. "You say Leilani is missing?"

Mano was kneeling by the boxes, but he jerked up his head and looked at Annie. "Leilani is missing?"

Sam raised his brows. "You didn't know? I figured that's why you were here."

Mano shook his head. "I brought Tomi's belongings."

Sam's face clouded as he looked back at the Tagama family, and he tapped the pen against the paper.

Annie ran her hand over her hair with a distracted air. "You have to find Leilani, Sam. She didn't come home last night. I thought maybe she spent the night with friends, but they haven't seen her, and she didn't show up for work this morning. I found her necklace out at the volcano. She never goes there. She's terrified of it."

Mano leaned against the wall. He'd just listen. Maybe he could help at some point. A part of him wished he could play the hero and maybe salvage his relationship with the Tagama family. It was probably a pipe dream. He watched Annie. She had always been a steady, albeit invisible, sergeant who kept the family running smoothly. The bright polish on her toenails was the only color she ever wore, and her toe ring the only ornamentation. Even that bright spot was missing today and work boots covered her feet. He'd noticed her limp. Maybe she'd twisted her ankle.

"You've called all her friends?" Sam asked.

Annie nodded. "Her closest. No one has seen her since Thursday afternoon around five."

Sam glanced at his watch. "It's just now twenty-four hours. Not that it matters as far as we're concerned. There's no time period to wait. I'll put in a report, and we'll see what we can track down. Could I take a look at her room to see if there's a note or any clues there?"

"How stupid of me! I didn't think of that. I just checked to see if any of her clothes were missing. Everything seems to be accounted for." She and her father went down the hall. The officer followed.

After a slight hesitation, Mano went after them. Annie lowered her thick, long lashes, then glanced away without raising an objection. Mano's gaze swept the room. Leilani appeared to be just as careless and haphazard as always. Shorts and tops hung over the rice-paper screen in one corner, a pile of books had fallen over on the left side of the bed, and Leilani's makeup lay in a jumble on the gleaming black-lacquer dresser. His gaze locked on the bright blue tip of a notebook that peeked from the tumbled covers at the foot of the bed.

No one else seemed to have seen it. Sam was rifling through the closet, and Annie was on her knees peering under the bed. Mano stepped into the room and plucked the notebook from its hiding place. He flipped it open and frowned when he recognized it as some kind of religious manual. Chicken skin rose on his arms. "What about this?"

Annie's head came out from under the bed. Her gaze zeroed in on the notebook. "That's the handbook for the new group she's so interested in." She scrambled to her feet as Sam joined Mano. She held out her hand. "Let me see."

Mano handed the notebook to Annie. "What group?" Her frosty expression thawed. The gratitude in her eyes made him try a tentative smile. The warmth in her eyes cooled immediately, and he looked away and clenched his teeth. She had every right to blame him.

She flipped open the notebook. "I'd call it a cult. They claim to be a Hawaiian cultural group, but worship of Ku is at the heart of it."

Ku was an ancient Hawaiian god of war, a bloody god who demanded human sacrifice. Mano grimaced. Some natives were bringing about a resurgence of Hawaiian culture, including religion, though in this case it would have been better left in the past. He'd read the old stories and stood at the sites of some of those sacrifices. The evil in the air had been a palpable presence.

Annie sat on the edge of the bed and began to leaf through the pages. Sam peered over one shoulder and her father over the other. Mano wished to do the same, but he knew better than to get too close to Annie. She was uncomfortable enough with him just being here.

"I can't believe she'd belong to something like this," Annie said. She tossed the book onto the bed. "It's a bunch of bunk about having power with Ku. Leilani knows better than this." Her dark eyes burned with an inner fire.

Sam picked it up. "I'll take it to headquarters and look it over." He went back to the closet and began to sort through the jumble of shoes on the floor. "You're sure nothing is missing?"

"Not that I can tell." Annie joined him. "I'll go through it. Leilani wouldn't want you looking at her personal things." She stood and went to the dresser, where she began to put the cosmetics in order.

Mano had to hide his grin at the emergence of her old bossiness. The real Annie was still in there somewhere. He took the opportunity to study her again. Her short, dark hair flipped up in a carefree way that was kind of cute. The cut skirted her shoulders and suited her long, graceful neck and slim frame. She had the longest eyelashes he'd ever seen. Thick and lush, they framed large expressive eyes that always told exactly what she was thinking. Her hands had always fascinated him. The fingers were long, like a pianist's, and he'd often teased her for having "monkey hands," because they were never still. They almost seemed to have a mind of their own. When she was sitting idle, they would roam around whatever was close by, picking up an ornament on a table or playing with the fringe on her cutoff jeans.

Those busy fingers quickly set the dressing table to rights. She wore an expression of intense concentration, and Mano wondered what she was thinking. He couldn't believe the Tagama family would have to endure another tragic loss. He hoped Leilani was off somewhere with a new friend. She never met a stranger, and she was always on the lookout for fun. She'd turn up in a day or two laughing about all the fuss. Or else . . . Another idea surfaced, and he turned it over in his mind.

Annie turned, and Mano caught a glimpse of fear in her eyes. His hope about Leilani vanished. Before he could stop himself, he touched Annie's shoulder as she started to walk by.

She stopped, and her eyes widened. Her lips trembled, and she pressed them together and jerked her body away. She stalked past him and hurried through the door and down the hall. Mano drew in a deep breath. His gaze met Edega's, and the older man looked away. His expression turned vague, and he vanished down the hall after his daughter.

Sam raised his brows. "Am I picking up some tension here?"

"What was your first clue? They blame me for Tomi's death."

Sam grunted. "You do leave a trail of damage behind wherever you go."

Mano turned and went down the hall. Sam brushed past him to enter the living room first. Mano listened as Sam offered reassurance to the Tagamas and then departed. Once Annie closed the door behind the officer, Mano glanced at the boxes he'd hauled in from the car. Could his flash of inspiration be right? "I went through the apartment and boxed up everything of Tomi's." He laid his hand on the top box. "This one is his clothing, and the other two boxes have stuff like electronics and his personal things." His voice faltered when he saw Annie's eyes tear up. He dropped his gaze.

"*Mahalo* for bringing them." Annie's voice was a stilted whisper. Her gaze locked on the boxes. She reached out her right hand and then drew it back.

Mano wanted to bolt for the car, but he had to finish. "I'd like to talk to you both for a few minutes. Can we sit down?" He didn't wait for an answer but moved to the sofa and perched on the edge of the cushion.

Edega frowned as he went to his recliner by the window. "Annie will listen. Then I would ask you to leave us."

Even Annie winced at her father's attitude. Wilson came out from under the chair, and she picked him up and began to stroke his head. Mano eyed the mongoose and wondered about Annie's purpose in keeping it. Most people on Hawai'i hated the animals for destroying the bird population, and Annie had never been one to go against the grain. She cared too much about what other people thought of her. The animal must mean a lot to her for some reason.

Mano forced the muscles in his jaw to relax. *Just get it over with.* Annie moved to the chair opposite him. She was staring at a spot just past his right shoulder. A cramp lodged in the calf of his leg, and he began to jiggle his knee up and down.

He wasn't sure how to start. The silence between them seemed to have a life of its own. Mano heard a mynah squawk from the trees behind the house. A breeze brought the scent of white ginger through the open windows. He tried to gather his thoughts, but they remained a jumble of regret, fear, and anticipation. He cleared his throat.

Annie finally lifted her gaze to his face. "This isn't a good time. What do you want with us?"

"I thought you might have questions about what happened." Mano held her gaze.

She swallowed but continued to stare at him steadily. "I have all kinds of questions. Most importantly, why?"

He wanted to pretend he didn't know what she meant, but he couldn't play that kind of game with them. But oh, how he didn't want to explain. "I wish I could make sense of how it happened, but it's still confused in my head."

Annie leaned forward. "You let go of him, Mano. He trusted you, and you let him down. And us as well. He would have drowned before he let go of you." Tears magnified her eyes. "Explain it then." Wilson squeaked in her grip.

He found himself caught in the depths of her pain-filled eyes. "The mission had been meticulously planned. Four of us were to parachute down with two Zodiac rubber boats. Tomi and I had our scuba gear, and it was our job to extract the kidnapped prisoners from that Iranian hellhole. The drop went just like we'd planned. The boats inflated, and Tomi and I went overboard and swam along the bottom of the bay to shore." He swallowed hard. He wished he could leave without telling them the full story.

Edega moved toward the door. "I'll be in my office." He slammed the door to the garage behind him.

Annie put out her hand as though to stop her father, but Edega didn't see. What had happened to the caring man Mano used to admire? Mano hadn't expected a red-carpet welcome, but he had assumed the family dynamics would be the same. Instead, Edega had turned into a petulant child who depended on his daughter for everything. And Annie let him. He wished someone else would help her deal with what he had to tell her.

"Go on," Annie said.

The cramp in Mano's leg grew, and he stood and went to stare out the window. He couldn't watch her face. "When we got to shore, they were waiting for us." He curled his fingers into the palms of his hands. "Bullets flew around us. Tomi was hit right off. He yelled at me to get out of there. I remember grabbing him and dragging him into the water with me. We left our dive gear behind so we could move faster. We were swimming for the boat." *Tell her.* He resisted the impulse. No amount of explanation about his illness would erase what he'd done. Revealing his weakness would make it worse, not better. "I don't remember anything after that until I woke up on the ship, and they were asking about Tomi."

"That's it? You don't remember? You *have* to remember what happened."

He wheeled. Her eyes were dark pools in a face as pale as jasmine rice. "It's the truth. I can't change it."

"I've heard enough of this tall tale." She stood. "Get out."

"There's more, Annie."

"I won't listen to another word." She grabbed his arm and tried to tug him away from the window. Surprisingly strong for such a tiny woman, she pulled him toward the door.

He didn't try to fight her. At the door, her grip slackened, and he pulled his arm from her grasp. "I found a bank account book in Tomi's things. There's two million dollars in it." He plunged his hand into his pocket and withdrew the slim booklet.

Annie swayed as she stared at the account book in his hand. "You're lying," she whispered. She reached out to take the book, then snatched her hand back.

"I wish I were."

"Where did it come from?"

"I don't know," he said simply. "Tomi was my best friend. I thought I knew everything about him. I want to figure out what happened to him, Annie. And where he got this money. When we were doing reconnaissance for the rescue mission, Tomi got involved with the consul's daughter. But I can't believe . . ." The questions had eaten at him the whole time he was recuperating. *Had his best friend betrayed them all for money?*

"You're despicable," Annie said. "Now you're accusing him of espionage? I'm not going to listen to another word of this." She tried to close the door, even though he stood in the way.

"Wait," he said. "I don't think he's dead. And I'm wondering if maybe Leilani is with him."

Three

nnie's legs wouldn't support her, and she leaned against the doorjamb. Wilson made a noise and nibbled on her cheek. She rubbed the mongoose's head. "What are you saying?" A sudden spurt of hope shot through her. Could Tomi be alive? Fear warred hope. What did the money mean? And why would Tomi let them think he'd died?

"I know this is a shock," Mano said, his tone suddenly gentle. He took her elbow and guided her to the couch.

She sank onto the sofa. "How could he still be alive? The navy said he was dead."

"He was assumed lost at sea. I thought I let go somehow. But I'm telling you the truth: I just don't know what happened."

When Annie was five, she got lost in the rain forest. She wandered in the brush for eight hours before her parents found her. The same panic rushed at her now, the sense of losing the landmarks, of wandering in a strange land where what was once familiar became distorted and menacing. If what Mano said was true, their lives were about to be turned upside down. Again. Hadn't they suffered enough?

She reminded herself that Mano let go of her brother. Maybe this false hope was his way of dealing with the guilt. If Tomi were alive, he would have contacted her by now. "Have you told the navy about the money?"

He shook his head. He hesitated. "If Tomi is alive, he'll be in big trouble with the navy. He's AWOL, and if the money—" He shook his head. "I don't want to tip them off yet."

"How do you know he's alive?" Just saying the word *alive* made her heart race. *Alive, alive.* Tomi might walk through the door any minute. Was it possible? She warned herself not to get her hopes up.

"He called me two nights ago."

She wanted to believe him. But why would Tomi call Mano but not her? "You're sure it was Tomi?"

His gaze dropped. "I think so. He said it was, and it sounded like him."

Annie allowed the smallest hope to flicker a little stronger in spite of the trace of doubt in Mano's voice. "What did he say?"

"He told me to bring the bankbook to you, that he'd get in touch with you to get it back." Mano pursed his mouth, and a line of worry crept between his eyes. "I would rather not involve you in this, but I didn't know what else to do. I had no idea Leilani was missing."

"What makes you think she's with Tomi?" Annie could only hope that was true. Her brother doted on Leilani. He wouldn't let anything bad happen to her.

"It makes sense that maybe he got in touch with her."

"Then what about this necklace?" She held out the delicate pendant.

"Tell me exactly where you found it." His expression sharpened.

Mano had a way of focusing on a problem so intently that he gave her confidence. Almost against her will, she stepped closer to him and began to tell him about her afternoon. His dark eyes never wavered from her face. Maybe he could figure this out. Though she still wasn't ready to believe everything he was saying, she allowed herself to lower her guard and hope he might get to the bottom of this.

"So no one else was on the lava shelf? Had you been there long?"

"I was taking readings. We were there maybe an hour."

"Annie Tagama, volcano cowboy." He grinned. "Or I guess I should say cow*girl*."

If he only knew how ridiculous that was these days. She was a volcano *coward* now. He hadn't said anything about her limp. Maybe he hadn't noticed. "Do you suppose Tomi could have dropped it there on purpose so I'd find it? Maybe it was supposed to be a message."

"What kind of message? Why wouldn't he have just told me?"

"I don't know. But it might explain the necklace's presence."

Mano nodded. "She'd never go out there, would she? She avoided the volcano like swimmers avoid jellyfish."

"I know, that's what worries me. I should have looked around a little more." She glanced out the window. "It's still light enough to see. Maybe I'll run back over there." Her gut clenched at the thought of going near that shelf again.

"I'll go with you."

He was always one to step into the gap, but she couldn't let him. Not this time. "I'll handle it. It's my problem."

"It's mine too. Tomi is my best friend. And you and Leilani are like—like sisters to me. I've got a month's leave coming. I'm staying until we get to the bottom of this."

He might think of her as a sister, but he'd wanted more from Leilani. The problem was Annie always wanted to be more than a sister to Mano. She thought she'd pulled that yearning out by its roots when they got word of how Tomi died. She must have missed a piece, because it came surging back with one glance into his eyes.

The sun bathed the lava fields with a pink glaze. Mano was glad he was wearing his shoes instead of his flip-flops. The *a'a* lava would cut his slippers to ribbons and then start on the soles of his feet. He and Annie skirted a hissing steam vent that belched sulfur and gases in a nauseating stench. Every time he came out here, he wondered how Annie could stand working in such a hellish place.

"It was right in here someplace." Annie walked slowly and carefully along the lava bench.

Was that fear on her face? He didn't think she was ever afraid out here. And what caused her limp? From the expression on her set face, he knew now was not the time to ask. He stepped to the edge, where the ground fell away. Steam hissed from fumaroles around the caldera.

"Not there!" she said sharply. "Step away from there."

Mano glanced over the edge. This area hadn't had any landslides in decades. Lava no longer encroached here, and the only heat that rolled out was from the underground steam. Still, Leilani would have run screaming in the other direction at the sight. She wouldn't come right up to the edge. He backed away and returned to the path. "The necklace was found right here?"

She nodded.

He stepped off the path again and headed toward a group of rocks that had been belched from the volcano at some point in the past. The formation reminded him of a pile of cannonballs left over from the Civil War, round and black as though they were waiting to be loaded into the big gun.

The ground was a little smoother here. He'd always been fascinated by volcanoes. It was one reason he'd spent so much time at the Tagama house. The talk around the dinner table between Annie and her father was always interesting. There was a curious chemistry among them all—Annie's mother, Adele, was so quiet and attuned to all their needs, while her three grown kids and her husband filled the house with noise and excitement. At least two of the kids were noisy. Annie was a carbon copy of her mother, directing everything with a firm yet quiet hand. Adele treated Mano like one of her own, and because his own mother abandoned him when he was a kid, Mano reveled in her attention.

Now, with only Edega and Annie at the house, everything was different. Mano didn't think he could remember a time when the house wasn't full with good-natured teasing and laughter. What had

Tomi been thinking to risk ruining his family this way? When Mano found him, he'd demand some answers.

He rounded the rock formation and stopped. His heart slammed against his ribs. "Annie, come here," he called. Maybe she could explain this, though he didn't see how. She joined him immediately, and he heard her gasp. She reached out and grabbed his forearm. He winced as her nails dug into his skin, but he didn't pull away.

"A *heiau*," she breathed. "What is it doing here?"

In the old days, Hawaiians built massive temples, or *heiau*, to worship their gods. Many of the ancient temples ranged from the size of a basketball court to bigger than a football field. This one was much smaller than average. Only about eight feet square, the customary stone base was crudely composed of lava rock. But all the basics were there, including a wooden structure atop the stone base.

Mano stepped up to the *heiau* and entered it. A stone altar had been erected under the roof of ti leaves. An idol of lava stone, wood, and feathers sat at the head of the altar. The idol's gaping mouth was lined with some animal's teeth.

A drone of flies caught his ear, and he looked down to see the insects buzzing around a sticky mess at the base of the altar. Annie put her hands over her eyes and moaned. She backed away. Mano wanted to turn tail and run. The air thickened with sinister intent. He forced himself to examine the blood. A hiss of relief escaped his lips when he realized the mess held traces of animal fur.

He needed air. Turning, he bolted after Annie. She was trembling. "It's not Leilani," he assured her. "It's an animal."

"Who would build a *heiau* out here?" she whispered. "Could you tell what god that was?"

He shook his head. "I'd guess it's Pele, but it's hard to say."

"What about Ku?"

He stared at her. "You think Leilani could have been part of this?"

"I hope not, but with her necklace here . . ."

"I'd better call Sam. Maybe he can figure it out." He dialed his cell phone and told Sam what he'd found. Annie was staring at the temple. She blinked rapidly, and a shimmer of moisture clung to her lashes. He wanted to pull her into his arms, but he curled his fingers into his palms instead. She wouldn't welcome such a forward gesture.

Annie moved toward the *heiau* again. Her hand shook as she extended it and pointed toward a wisp of fabric that decorated the idol. "That's from Leilani's favorite top."

We'll see what we can find out," Sam said. He slipped his notebook back into his pocket. "I might check out Aloha Shores."

The Aloha Shores area was home to a different sort of residents. With no running water and no electricity, the people who called the subdivision home still lived the hippie life. It was rumored that the greatest contingent of witness protection–plan people lived there.

"What makes you think they could have anything to do with this?" Mano asked.

Sam shrugged. "A few groups there engage in some pretty wacky things. This qualifies, don't you think? Last I heard, one group was meeting to build a *heiau* to Ku. Maybe that's what this is." He swept his hand toward the remains on the altar.

Mano shook his head. "But why here if they're worshiping Ku? Pele is the volcano goddess." He had never been to Aloha Shores, but he might poke around out there himself.

"Who knows what people like that think? Tomorrow is Saturday, so maybe I can find some residents at home."

"Mind if I tag along?" Mano asked.

"This is my turf. I'll handle it." Sam's gaze held a trace of hostility. He followed Mano and Annie toward the SUV.

Sam had always been territorial, but Mano wasn't going to take no for an answer. "I'll stay out of your way."

"Please, Sam?" Annie put her hand on the detective's arm. "Let us come."

Sam's face softened. "Okay, if it means that much to you, Annie." He glanced toward Mano. "Let's see if Leilani comes home tonight. If not, we'll head out tomorrow morning."

Annie had little to say as they returned to the Tagama house. Mano didn't know how to comfort her. He'd never been good with words. She drove methodically, her gaze never leaving the road. She still hadn't regained her color.

She parked behind his rental car. "Still think Leilani is with Tomi?" she asked.

"That's hardly a unique top," he said.

"True." She sighed and rubbed her forehead. "I'm just not going to worry about it until we hear from Tomi. Maybe you're right."

"You didn't say anything to Sam about the call from Tomi or the money?"

"No, and you're not to say anything either," she ordered. "Once we hear from Tomi, I'll figure out how to handle this."

He grinned. "Whatever you say, boss. Though Sam might have an idea of where to look for your brother."

She nodded and looked out the window. He got out and went to his car. He needed to talk this through with someone. Good thing his sister was on the island. He drove along the road to Jillian's house, where Kaia was staying. The topography changed from bare lava fields to rain forest, then to tropical greenery. He followed the coast for five miles.

He turned into the driveway and honked to alert Jillian. Since she'd been separated from her husband, Jillian had been easily spooked out here, Kaia said. No one answered the door, so he wandered down to the water and found the two women sitting on a lava rock outcropping. This inlet had little sand, though the snorkeling was good.

Kaia waved to Heidi, Jillian's eight-year-old daughter, who was romping in the water with Nani, the wild dolphin who had begun "talking" to Kaia. "Don't go too far out," she called. She turned, and her gaze met Mano's. "You're later than I expected."

"Yeah." His sister's gaze scrutinized his face. He stared at her, willing her to realize he needed to talk to her alone.

"What is it?" she asked.

So much for women's intuition. "Later," he muttered.

"Watch me, Kaia!" Heidi grabbed Nani's dorsal fin and let the dolphin pull her through the water.

Kaia's face registered awareness that something was wrong. Before Mano could decide how to get her alone without arousing Jillian's curiosity, a figure shadowed them. Mano looked up to see a stocky man with a neatly trimmed beard. He was staring at Jillian as though he'd like to gobble her up. The man had a neck as thick as a sumo wrestler and broad shoulders to match. His dark auburn hair was shaggy and fell over his broad forehead. He blinked, and his sea green eyes met Mano's gaze.

Jillian turned. Her gaze traveled up to rest on the man's face. She gasped. "Noah?"

Noah Sommers? Mano had heard all about how the man had deserted his wife and child and published Jillian's research under his own name. Mano's hackles rose.

Noah jammed his hands into his pocket. His smile seemed anxious. "Hi, Jillian," he said.

The color left Jillian's face. Her lips parted, but no words came out. Scrambling to her feet, Jillian brushed the sand from her legs, then grabbed her coverup. "Noah. To say I'm surprised to see you would be an understatement."

Mano exchanged a glance with Kaia. He gave a slight shake of his head at the protectiveness he saw in her face. This wasn't her battle to fight.

Noah nodded. "I can imagine."

Jillian's jaw clenched. "Can you? I was devastated when you disappeared and the article with my research came out with your name attached to it. And you changed it too, published lies. *Betrayed* doesn't begin to describe how your treachery affected me."

His face contorted, and he dropped his gaze to the ground. "I want to see Heidi."

"I assumed as much. That's why you're here, isn't it? It certainly wouldn't be to *apologize*." Jillian jerked her coverup closed.

"I understand why you haven't taken my calls, but we have to talk, Jillian. We have our daughter to consider."

"Oh yeah, you considered her when you stole my research and took off, didn't you?" she shot back. "Don't try to put this on me."

Her nose was red, and Mano could tell she was struggling not to cry. Mano wished they were anywhere but here. This was too private to witness. He took Kaia's hand and started to leave, but Jillian held out her hand.

"Please don't go," she said. "Noah isn't staying."

Noah began to scowl. "You can't hide your head in the sand this time, Jillian." He nodded toward Heidi and Nani. "What's with the dolphin?"

"That's none of your business. Except you might be interested to know Nani saved Heidi's life while you were off gallivanting around."

"What are you talking about?" For the first time Noah seemed to be showing real emotion.

"Your daughter was kidnapped by some maniac who planned to use her to get to Jesse. But my brother saved her. Kaia and the dolphin too. You should have been here, Noah. She's asked and asked for you."

"I'm here now," he said. "But I'd rather you didn't tell anyone I'm on the island. Not yet."

Mano exchanged another glance with Kaia. What was that all about? And Noah kept glancing around as if he was worried someone might see them.

Jillian put her fists on her hips. "Are you running from something? I don't want Heidi in danger. She's been through too much already."

His blue green eyes swept her figure. "You look good, Jillian. I've missed you."

Mano saw the way Jillian's body language changed. The rigidity left her shoulders. She must still love the creep.

She stiffened again and stepped back. "Heidi, come here," she called.

Heidi's blond head turned to look. Her jaw dropped. "Dad? Dad!" She stood in the waves and began to slosh through the water toward them. Her pink bathing suit had a dolphin on the stomach. Behind her, Nani leaped out of the water and did a flip. Heidi reached the sand and ran to her father. He knelt and she catapulted into his arms. He didn't seem to mind being soaked with seawater. He stood with her in his arms, and she wrapped her legs around him and held on.

Watching them, Mano wondered how a man who seemed to love his daughter so much could do what Noah had done.

four

nnie turned off the rice cooker. The serene kitchen decorated in shades of taupe, soothed her. Here, she was most at
home, most in control. Cherry-blossom rice-paper blinds over the
window above the sink added a splash of color. "Dinner, Father,"
she called. Miso soup bubbled on the stove, and the aroma of teri
stir-fry filled the kitchen. She lifted Japanese puff rolls, called shu
cream puffs, from the oven and prepared to fill them with custard.

The aroma whetted her appetite—as long as she kept her mind
from straying to the sacrifice she'd seen. The phone rang, and looking at the caller ID, she saw it was her friend Fawn. "I should have
called you," she said when she answered. "I'm sorry."

"Was Leilani at home?" Fawn sounded worried.

"No." She told Fawn about the *heiau* she and Mano found, and
the remains of Leilani's shirt.

"Did you call the police?"

"Yes, but Sam doesn't seem too worried. He thinks Leilani has
gone off on a lark with a new boyfriend."

"I guess that's possible."

"Yes, knowing Leilani, I guess it is." Annie hesitated. Mano had
said not to tell anyone about Tomi, but this was Fawn. She was as
closemouthed as it was possible to be. Annie opened her mouth to
tell her friend, then closed it again. No, Mano had asked her to stay
quiet. She would honor her promise.

They chatted a few more minutes. Fawn hung up after promising
to pray for them all. Edega had still not appeared for dinner, so

Annie called him again. While she waited, she glanced through the
mail. Her hand hovered over an envelope from the mortgage company. Not another one. She didn't want to open it but knew she had
to. Tearing the back flap, she pulled out the sheet of paper inside
and scanned it. If they didn't get the back payments caught up in
one week, the bank would begin foreclosure.

Foreclosure. Her appetite left her. There was no way they could
catch up. Where would they go? Her father wandered into the
kitchen, and she stuffed the letter into the pocket of her jeans. She'd
figure out something. She'd tried to talk to her father about it several times over the past couple of months, but he always brushed
her off. She was on her own with this one.

Her father stared at the scientific calculator in his hand but
hardly seemed to see it. "I think our research will bring in a flood
of publicity," he announced. "We should be invited to every volcano study in the world with what we know now."

Annie tried not to smile. His research would hardly change the
world, but since her mother died, he had become preoccupied with
this study exhausted by other scientists years ago. "I need to talk to
you," she said, putting the food on the table. Wilson stood nearby
on hind legs, making small leaps into the air like a circus animal.
Annie laughed and dropped some food on the floor. Wilson
pounced on it.

Her father's lips tightened. "One day you will come home and
discover I have gotten rid of that animal myself." Her father sat at
the table and made a note on a scratch pad. "Is there anything to
drink?"

"I made jasmine tea." She grabbed the teapot and poured him
a cup. He was still jotting down notes when she brought the steaming mug back to the table. Often she was as invisible to her father
as the tide that rolled the waves to shore. As long as the house ran
smoothly, her father and Leilani looked past her. Let one thing happen, and they would howl for her to fix it. Maybe Fawn was right:

she mothered them all too much, trying to make up for their loss.

But the thought of stepping back, of not being needed, made her stomach clench. If she'd watched over her sister better, Leilani might not be missing now. "I need to talk to you," she told her father again. She perched on a rattan stool at the granite counter and locked her heels on the lowest rung.

He finally looked up from his notes. "I heard the phone ring. Did Leilani call?"

Her mother had always said Edega Tagama had the peculiar ability to ignore anything he didn't want to think about, though Annie never noticed while her mother was alive. She wanted to shake him, to tell him that his family was unraveling right under his nose. Staring at him, however, her anger melted away. He'd become almost childlike—he needed her so badly.

She picked up Tomi's bankbook and held it out to her father. "Mano gave me this," she said.

The vertical lines between his eyes deepened. He took it and opened it. His eyes widened, and she heard his soft exhalation. "This has Tomi's name on it. Where did Mano get it?"

"He found it in Tomi's things." She told him about the phone call from Tomi, and his frown changed to an astonished smile.

He jumped to his feet. "You're saying your brother is alive?"

"And Mano thinks Leilani might be with him." Maybe she shouldn't have said that. Neither she nor Mano was convinced of the possibility now that they'd found the altar.

"My son is alive." His eyes began to glisten.

"We don't know for sure yet."

Her father watched her like a *keiki* seeking a parent's reassurance, so she gave him a confident smile. "Tomi is supposed to get in touch with me. I'm sure he'll answer all our questions then. Until then, I'm assuming Leilani is with him and is fine. Either that or she's with friends."

"Good. I want to show him how the last piece of my research

has fallen together. It should be ready for publication in a few more weeks. My son is alive," he said again in a tone of marvel.

If he could find someone to publish it. Annie wanted to encourage him, but he didn't seem to realize his research wasn't fresh. Her gaze dropped to the bankbook on the table. What if that money really existed? Could they use some to get caught up on the mortgage? She scooped up the bankbook and stuffed it into her pocket with the bank's letter. She sat beside her father at the table, but all she could do was pick at her food. She put her plate down for Wilson. He crouched like he was about to pounce on a chicken, and then growled ferociously as he began to tear at the meat. When her father finished, she cleaned the kitchen, then decided she had to do something.

She found her father engrossed in a TV comedy. He had his feet on the Maru table in front of the sofa. Mother would have had a fit, but Annie didn't have the heart to scold him. "I'm going to go see Jillian," she told him.

He grunted and she went out to her SUV. She carried Wilson with her. The mongoose snuggled against her, then looked up as though they were having the most pleasurable evening. Annie laughed and scratched his head. She'd leave him home, but Heidi loved the mongoose. Of course the *keiki* loved anything that flew, swam, or crawled. Annie ran her window down and let the fragrant scent of plumeria waft over her. The natural aromatherapy eased the knots in her shoulders.

She dug out her cell phone and made sure it was on. There was no sign of any missed calls. Leilani might call any minute. Or Tomi. But why hadn't they called already? They knew how Annie worried. Driving down the dark, narrow road, she tried not to think of the *heiau.* She shivered in spite of the warm air.

Lights blazed from Jillian's house. Annie pulled in and gathered up Wilson, who squeaked, then wriggled with excitement as Annie approached the house. She heard the sound of women's voices through the screen door. Maybe it was the TV. She didn't see any extra cars in the driveway, only Jillian's red Neon.

Heidi came to the door moments after Annie knocked. "You brought Wilson," she squealed, swinging open the screen door. She clicked her tongue. "Hi, Wilson. Want to come see me?" She held out her arms and the mongoose moved toward her, then fell into her arms like a rag doll. He was so spoiled.

Almost immediately, Heidi's cat came out from behind the sofa. Wilson and Checkers had formed an uneasy truce, though Annie often caught the cat licking her chops when she watched the mongoose. Checkers meowed and leaped at Wilson, but the mongoose uttered a warning noise, letting her know he was king of the roost now, and she'd better beware. The cat dashed back to her hiding place.

"Keep an eye on them," Annie told Heidi. "Is your mom in the kitchen?"

"Uh-huh," Heidi said from where she sprawled on her stomach in front of the mongoose. She glanced up at Annie. "I thought maybe you were my dad. He came to see me today."

"He did?" Annie examined the *keiki's* expression. Was she serious?

Heidi rolled over on her back. "I tried to make a paper mongoose like you showed me. It didn't come out very well."

"We'll have another origami lesson soon," Annie promised. One of the low voices that emanated from the kitchen belonged to Jillian, and from the tension in it, Annie thought maybe Heidi was telling the truth about her father's reappearance. She touched the top of the little girl's head and went to the kitchen. Annie hesitated in the doorway.

"I don't trust him," Jillian said to the other woman.

"I hope I'm not interrupting," Annie said in the sudden lull of conversation.

Jillian's head jerked around, her tight mouth relaxing when her gaze met Annie's. "Annie. I wasn't expecting you." Her eyes went to the cow clock on the wall. "You're out late."

Annie glanced at the clock too and was shocked to realize that it was nearly nine. "I'm sorry to barge in so late." The other woman turned her head, and Annie recognized her. Annie offered a tentative smile.

The woman stood and held out her hand. "So you're Annie. I'm Mano's sister, Kaia."

"I recognized you from your pictures. Mano talks about you all the time."

"What's wrong?" Jillian pulled out a chair beside her. "I just fixed some chamomile tea. Would you like some?"

"Sure." Annie sat between the two women and waited until her coworker poured a cup of tea from the blue teapot. "Gorgeous teapot," she said.

"Kaia brought it to me. Isn't it beautiful? It's the plumeria pattern from Banana Patch Studio. I think it's a hint that Kaia wants some for her wedding." In spite of the light way Jillian chattered, an underlying strain tightened her mouth and left lines around her eyes.

Kaia's happiness was the last thing Annie wanted to talk about right now. Especially since her eternal crush on Mano had passed from the ridiculous to the impossible. She put some sugar in her tea and took a sip. "*Mahalo.*"

"What's up?" Jillian asked.

"Did you happen to see my sister out at the volcano yesterday or today? Did she stop by the observatory looking for me or anything?"

Jillian raised her eyebrows. "No, and I was in the building most of the day. She's terrified of the volcano, isn't she? Is something wrong?" She frowned. "I did see her in Volcano yesterday, though."

"She's missing." Annie's voice broke. She cleared her throat and told them about the necklace. "What was she doing when you saw her?"

"Just walking to the general store. I asked her if she needed a ride to work. She smiled and waved and kept on going."

"Did you notice what she was wearing?"

Jillian thought a minute. "A turquoise and yellow shirt with white shorts."

The same shirt Annie and Mano had found on the *heiau.* "That's what she had on the last time I saw her too." She told them about the altar and the bloody shirt.

"You're sure that shirt is what she was wearing the last time you saw her?" Kaia asked.

"Positive. It had a low neckline, and I prodded her about changing it."

"Maybe she thought your advice was good," Jillian suggested.

Annie shook her head. "Not Leilani. I don't know why I even bothered to voice my opinion. It just makes her more obstinate."

The silence in the room spoke more loudly than a phreatic eruption. She hadn't planned to tell them about Mano's theory, but it rushed out into the silence. "Mano thinks she might be with Tomi." She realized she'd broken her promise to Mano and pressed her fingers to the bridge of her nose. At least this was his sister. She dropped her hand.

Jillian blinked then frowned. "Who did you mean? You said— Tomi." Her tone was hushed as though she were afraid to say Tomi's name.

"Mano doesn't think Tomi is dead."

Jillian's eyes widened, and Kaia looked at Annie with compassion in her eyes. "He never said anything about it to me. Did he actually see Tomi?"

Annie shook her head. "He said Tomi called him. Mano recognized his voice."

A flicker of doubt darkened Kaia's eyes. "I hope someone isn't playing a trick on Mano. I know losing his best friend was hard on him. Maybe he believes what he wants to believe."

Annie hadn't considered how her brother's death affected Mano. "He seems very certain about it." In spite of her confident words, she wondered if she'd so easily swallowed Mano's claim because she wanted to believe it too. Could Mano be deluding himself—and her? What if it was someone playing a prank for some reason? She touched the bankbook in her pocket. There was still the money to consider. She didn't know what to think, but remembering the passion in Mano's eyes, she knew he was convinced of it.

"I don't know," she said slowly.

"I'll talk to him, see what it's all about," Kaia said. "He wanted to talk to me earlier today, I think, but we were interrupted." She glanced at Jillian.

Annie glanced at her friend too. "Heidi said something about her father coming to see her. Has Noah shown up?"

"Yeah, like the proverbial bad penny." Jillian glanced down at the table and fiddled with the handle on her teacup. "I think he's running from someone. He wouldn't talk about it. He's different— thinner and more serious. I don't know what to think."

"Maybe the two of you can get together and talk," Annie suggested. "I'm glad he's finally facing the music. This limbo you've been in is no good for you or Heidi."

"I know. I'm just not ready to listen to him spout some 'reason' for what he's done. There is no excuse for his actions." Jillian's expression hardened, and she took a sip of her tea.

"He's still Heidi's father," Kaia pointed out.

"I know that," Jillian said sharply. "I would never keep her from him. But he'd better not expect me to kiss and make up as if nothing happened."

Annie wanted to suggest counseling, but she kept her mouth shut. The couple's problems weren't any of her business, and from Jillian's tone, she knew her friend wasn't ready to hear it. "I'd better get home. Maybe Leilani has called."

"Wouldn't your dad let you know?" Jillian rose with her.

"Not necessarily. You know how scatterbrained he is."

"He'll be back to himself one of these days. It's been a hard year." Jillian trailed behind her to the living room. Kaia followed as well.

"I'm not so sure. He's so obsessed with the old research. It's as if he's forgotten the curiosity he used to have for new facts."

"Give it time. Hey, I hear the earthquake swarms at the seamount have been increasing."

Annie had been tracking the myriad small quakes for several weeks now. Swarms were a series of earthquakes of the same size that occurred in a short time. "There were more than two thousand last week. We might be seeing some action soon." Earthquake swarms were a good indicator of a pending eruption, and the topic was one of Annie's pet projects. Excitement pushed away her fear about Leilani, at least temporarily. "With a major eruption, we might have another island forming from Loihi. Word's getting out. I wouldn't be surprised if geologists from all over the world start dropping in."

"If you're up to it, maybe we could take a look on Monday while we're down replacing the pressure recorders. Try to beat the rush." Jillian stooped and scooped up Wilson. "Don't forget your rat." She wrinkled her nose and handed the mongoose to Annie.

"I'll be praying there's good news waiting at home for you," Kaia said, touching her lightly on the arm.

Annie wished she could absorb some of Kaia's optimism. Something was very wrong. Leilani might be thoughtless, but this kind of antic was unlike her.

five

Leilani Tagama lay huddled on the hard cot. She wasn't sure how she got here or where she was. Had she consumed that much liquor last night? She groaned and pressed her throbbing forehead into the blanket. She was hungry and hurting. The top she'd worn was gone, and in its place was a man's aloha shirt that reached clear to her knees. She couldn't remember what happened to her own clothes.

Struggling to sit up, she winced at a stabbing pain in her arms and realized her arms were bound behind her. Red hot needles of sensation poked her where her arm had fallen asleep. She managed to prop herself against the wall. It was too dark to see much. Just shadows. Dim light shone from around the edge of the blind that covered a tiny window.

She gasped and fought to free her hands. "No," she moaned. After several futile moments of struggle, she realized the bonds wouldn't budge. She forced back the panic and looked around. She was alone. Scooting across the hard cot, she swung her legs over the side and tried to stand. A rope tied her feet together and then tethered her to the steel post of the cot. She gave it an experimental tug. Maybe she could work the rope loose.

Fifteen minutes later she gave up. The only way she'd leave here was if someone let her go. Panic fluttered in her chest. What if she'd been dumped here to die and no one ever came back? She opened her mouth to scream, but the door opened and a huge shadow moved toward her. A suffocating cloth that stank of a chemical smothered her voice. She fell into the waiting darkness.

The black cinder road that led to Aloha Shores was full of potholes. Mano swerved to avoid one that looked hungry enough to chomp on the undercarriage of his small rental car. The action threw Annie against him. She yanked her shoulder away and righted herself.

"Sorry," he told her.

"No problem." Her cheeks were red, and she looked out the window.

There was something different about her this morning. Mano couldn't put his finger on it. Her glossy black hair lay tucked behind her ears and just touched her chin. She seemed older, more mature than the young girl he had remembered. Surely the tragedies of the last year had changed her.

She also seemed annoyed.

"Where are we supposed to meet Sam?" she asked without looking at him.

"At the entrance." Mano focused on the road and narrowly missed a wild mongoose that dashed under the wheels of the car. "Look, let's clear the air. What's your beef with me this morning?"

She finally looked at him. "You mean other than the fact you show up here accusing my brother of some kind of espionage? Then you tell me he's still alive, even though you have no proof."

He flinched. "Are you questioning my truthfulness?"

"Maybe more your sanity. Maybe your guilt made you think the man who called was Tomi."

"I know his voice." Mano supposed he shouldn't have been surprised at her attitude. After all, he hadn't believed it himself at first. But didn't she know him well enough to believe him? "He said he was coming to Hawai'i and would call you when he got here."

"I hope you're right. If he's alive, then I can quit worrying about Leilani, since she's probably with him. But until he calls me, let's drop it. I don't know what to believe."

"Fine," he said tightly. With a supreme effort, he relaxed his jaw and nodded toward the bleak landscape. "Have you ever been out here?"

"A coworker, Monica Rogers, lives out here. She loves it. Of course, she put in a generator for electricity."

"What about water?" Mano slowed the car to a crawl as the road degraded even more.

"Most everyone out here uses catchment systems to collect rain water. It seems to work out okay."

They stopped at the NO TRESPASSING sign, which warned of dire consequences to uninvited visitors. "I don't see Sam," Mano said. Hardly anything moved here. He'd expected to see children playing on this Saturday morning, but the harsh land-scape, devoid of any life, stretched in all directions. Houses stairstepped up the steep lava rock hillside and seemed to peer down suspiciously at them.

"You'd better call him."

Mano nodded and dialed Sam's number. The detective answered and told him he'd been called to a break in. "I'll see what I can find out," Mano told him.

"Let me handle it." Sam's voice was impatient. "Look, I have to go. Don't make any waves. Leilani will turn up."

Mano hung up the phone without answering.

Annie raised an eyebrow. "No Sam?"

"We're on our own," he told her. He put the car in gear and let it roll forward. The tires clunked into ruts in the lane, and he winced. "If we get stopped, we'll say we're visiting your friend. You think she'll mind?"

She hesitated. "No, I'm sure that will be fine, though I'm not her favorite person."

"I can't imagine anyone not liking you." He cut his glance toward her.

She flushed but didn't meet his gaze. "We've just had some professional differences." She nodded. "Let's stop to see her first. She might have seen something."

Most of the houses were rustic with scrubby yards where a few chickens scrabbled in the black, sandy dirt. Some were beautiful homes that wouldn't be out of place in the nicest of neighborhoods. The owners of those houses had made an effort to soften the rocky landscape with flowers and shrubs.

"There's the address." Annie pointed to a neat bungalow that perched on a hillside.

A woman was sweeping the front steps. Blond hair framed her pudgy cheeks and nose. He guessed her to be in her midforties. She stopped at their approach. Her guarded expression didn't lighten when her gaze went to Annie. "Is something wrong at the observatory?" she asked in a high, squeaky voice.

"No, everything is fine," Annie assured her. "Did you hear my sister is missing?"

"Leilani?" The woman shrugged. "Hasn't she done this before? I'm sure she'll turn up."

Mano studied her detached expression. She seemed almost hostile. "We found a *heiau* at the park. Do you know of anyone here in the estates who might have built it?"

Her strained smile faded. She crossed her arms over her chest. "I'm not into religion. I can't help you. Besides, you shouldn't be here. Only residents and invited guests are allowed on the property."

"We really need to talk to some people involved with the Ku cult," Annie said. "Have you seen anyone new in the area?"

"No. Look, I have work to do. If you're not here on business, I don't have time to blather." The woman went into her house.

Annie pressed her lips together when the door banged. "That was a bust."

"Let's take a stroll and see what we can find," Mano said. He took her arm and started toward the next house.

Annie tugged out of his grasp. "Maybe we should wait until Sam can come with us. Someone might call the cops on us for trespassing." Annie sounded worried. "It was a stupid idea anyway. These people out here may be strange, but that's no reason to assume they are part of that cult."

The whole atmosphere felt odd. Mano wanted to lift the rock that covered the secrets and see what slugs dwelt underneath these seemingly serene homes. "Did Leilani ever tell you about who she met at the meetings?"

Annie shook her head. "She was secretive. I wasn't even aware until I saw that notebook about a month ago that it was a Ku cult."

Mano wasn't sure what to do. Someone had to know about this cult. "Let's drive around a little. No one will know that we weren't invited." He escorted her to the car. Annie fastened her seat belt and ran her window down. Mano drove slowly along the gravel roads, crisscrossing the mountain in silence for an hour or so.

Annie nodded toward a particularly nice house. "You'd think they'd be afraid of another lava flow through here. The last one was in 1984."

"It could happen where you live too." He braked at a stop sign. "We're not accomplishing anything. No one seems to be out this morning, which strikes me as odd. Saturday is prime time for yard work."

Annie didn't seem to be listening. "You know, my boss lives near here. Not right in Aloha Shores, but close enough she might know something. Let's go to her house."

Mano followed Annie's directions. The house was within sight of Aloha Shores's gates. He parked by the picket fence. "Wow, look at her garden." The anemic soil had been replaced with rich, dark dirt, and lush plants filled the ten-foot square area in sharp contrast to the scrubby vegetation in the rest of the yard.

Annie went ahead of him to the door and knocked. Mano glanced around as they waited. He thought he heard slack-key guitar music drifting from the back of the house. Whoever was playing was a master. The chords had been tuned to a major seventh note, a "wahine" tuning that was Mano's favorite.

When no one came to the door, he touched Annie on the elbow and jerked his head. "Around back." She followed him. The difference between the front and back yards was jarring. Back here, the ground had been left in its native condition. Hard bits of lava-rock gravel crunched under his boots. He saw a group of people seated in a circle on yard chairs. The two men and one woman all had guitars, though only the woman was playing.

His attention focused on the woman. She was nearly as tiny as Annie. Though gray streaked her sleek black hair, her skin was smooth and unlined. He judged her to be about fifty. Dressed in shorts and a sleeveless top, her small hands plucked delicately at the guitar keys. "Who is that?" he whispered to Annie.

"My boss, Gina." Annie stepped around him and took the lead. She walked to the edge of the group.

The men looked up, and Mano noticed them eyeing Annie. He scowled at the one with the most appreciative stare, but the guy only had eyes for her. Mano stepped into the man's line of vision, and his movement caught Gina's attention. Her fingers stilled and the guitar's twang faded. She raised her eyebrows.

"Annie, what are you doing here?" She rose and laid the guitar across her seat. "Is everything all right?"

"Not really. My sister is missing. I wondered if you'd seen her." Annie's voice sounded strained and tired.

Gina's gaze searched Annie's face. "Leilani? Perhaps she's gone off with her friends again."

"Maybe. But she's never gone off without at least calling the next morning. It's been two days since anyone saw her. She can be a little airheaded, but she knows how I worry."

Gina touched Annie's shoulder. "You take on your whole family's problems. Leilani is an adult. She'll be all right."

"We found an altar out at the park," Mano said.

A slight smile tugged the corners of Gina's lips. "Offerings to Pele aren't unusual. What does that have to do with Leilani?"

"This wasn't just a food offering. It was an actual *heiau*, and an animal had been sacrificed. Leilani was going to meetings of some kind of Ku cult. Have you seen anything like that going on at Aloha Shores, or anywhere else?"

Gina frowned. "One always hears rumors of radical cultural activities. Maybe this is nothing more serious than that. Just because some natives are exploring their ancient heritage doesn't mean Leilani is in danger."

"A bloodstained shirt like hers was by the altar."

Gina inhaled sharply at the revelation. "You're sure it was hers?"

"Well, no, not really. But with her missing and then finding the necklace . . ."

Gina patted her hand. "A coincidence about the shirt then."

Mano could tell the woman was fond of Annie, and that raised his estimation of her. "Have you ever met Annie's brother, Tomi?"

Gina's dark eyes widened. "Tomi? No, he was away when I moved here, then later . . ." She looked away.

He nodded toward Annie. "We wondered if Tomi might be hiding out here."

One of the men snickered. Gina gave him a warning glance. "I must apologize for my son, Jason. His manners aren't the best." The young man's nostrils flared, and he looked away. "I don't understand. Are you saying Tomi is alive?"

"Yes, it looks that way."

She nodded to the other man. "This is Evan Chun. He's teaching us to play slack-key guitar, though I confess I don't have much aptitude for it."

The man nodded. Chun was close to Gina's age. His sleek

black hair fell over one eye, and he had a gold dragon earring in one ear. His bony knees poked from below his shorts, and he reminded Mano of an oriental Ichabod Crane. The guitar he held in his long fingers was a Gibson, an expensive one.

Gina turned her gaze back to him again. "So explain this about Tomi and what you're doing here."

"I got a call from Tomi last week."

She didn't show any surprise but just nodded. "I see. And what makes you think he'd be in Aloha Shores?"

"It's a good place to disappear."

"Maybe."

"Have you seen anything?" Annie put in eagerly.

Gina shook her head; then her eyes widened. "I've seen signs of occupancy at the cottage at the end of Pali Road." She turned to Evan. "Have you sold or rented that place to anyone?"

Evan nodded. "A John Smith rented it from me last week."

Mano straightened. With a generic name like that, it could be Tomi. "What did he look like?"

"Never met him. We conducted the transaction over the phone," Chun said.

"We'd like to go out there." Annie took a step away from the circle.

"Let me check it out for you," Gina said. "Only residents are allowed to wander the grounds, but no one ever stops me. I think they believe I live there."

"I want to come," Annie said firmly. "You've only seen pictures of Tomi. If he's disguised, you might not recognize him."

"Okay. But we'll take my Jeep. Everyone knows it." Gina turned to Jason. "I'll be back in half an hour. Don't go anywhere. I have some things for you to do today."

Jason rolled his eyes, but he said nothing. He picked up her guitar and carried it toward the house. Gina led the way to her Jeep, an army green Cherokee that had been recently waxed. Mano took

the front passenger seat. Gina pulled out of the driveway and barreled over the rough potholes. They went airborne several times.

Mano glanced back to make sure Annie was surviving the
rough ride. She'd been staring at the back of his head. She flushed
and looked away. He turned back around and resolved to have a
talk with her at some opportune moment. He couldn't tell what she
was thinking, but the strain between them was getting to him.

Gina jerked the Jeep to a halt at a path that led through scrubby
shrubs. It wound around a hill and disappeared. "This is as far as we
can go. The rest is on foot." She got out and slammed the door.

Mano jumped out and moved the seat for Annie to exit the
Jeep. "Does she always drive like that?" he whispered. A dimple
appeared in Annie's cheek, and he realized he'd been watching for
her smile.

She nodded. "She likes to live dangerously. She thinks it keeps
her young."

"She'll be lucky to hit sixty." He held out his hand, but she
ignored it and moved past him. He stifled a sigh and followed her.
Gina walked nimbly along the narrow path. She led them around
several piles of boulders and up a steep hill. At the top of another
hill, he saw a small cottage.

"That's it," Gina said.

She increased her pace. Annie and Mano jogged behind her. As
they neared the cottage, Mano's optimism faded. Some of the window panes were missing, and the door looked like a stiff wind
would detach it from the structure. The place hadn't seen a paint-
brush in twenty years. Surely Chun was wrong. No one would rent
this derelict place.

Gina stepped briskly up to the flimsy door and rapped. To
Mano's astonishment, he heard footsteps from inside, and the door
swung open. He didn't expect the familiar face that peered out.
Noah Sommers.

Noah's eyes widened. "Mano, what are you doing here?"

"John Smith, I presume," Mano said dryly.

Noah flushed. He pushed open the screen door and stepped onto the step. "Is Jillian all right?"

Interesting that his first thought was of Jillian and not Heidi, Mano thought. "She and Heidi are fine. I'm actually looking for someone else. Are you staying here alone?"

Noah hesitated, then nodded. His eyes flickered away from Mano. He was lying; Mano was sure of it. "Sorry to disturb you then," Mano said. As they walked back to the Jeep, he wondered what Noah was trying to hide.

Gina returned them to Mano's rental car and then drove off. "What now?" Mano said, more to himself than to Annie. They wouldn't find any information here about the cult. If Tomi would only call, they might be able to let go of their worry. "Any other ideas where your brother might be hiding if he was on the island now?"

A line crinkled between her eyes as she thought. She finally nodded. "There's an old man up the mountainside from our home. He doesn't generally let anyone up there, but he liked Tomi and let him build a clubhouse on his property when we were kids. I think it's still there. I've been meaning to go see him anyway. Jillian and I have been trying to talk him into letting us put GPS receivers on his lot. Want to try there?"

"Sounds like a possibility. Tell me more about him." Mano drove toward the Tagama property.

"His name is Orson Kauhi. I think he's as old as the lava fields he lives on." She smiled and turned the radio down. "GPS helps us figure out where the ground is heaving and sinking. That data could help pinpoint new magma chambers. Jillian's convinced the area holds real potential for one, but Kauhi has refused to let us do any research on his property."

Mano knew the fields in her area were formed by the 1926 flow. If she was serious about Kauhi's age, that would make the man nearly eighty or more. "Family?"

She shook her head. "His wife died before I was born, and they didn't have any kids. I was scared of him when we were little. Maybe I still am. Tomi used to tell me he was Pii, the dragon in man form."

Mano knew the legend. Pii lived on a steep precipice and could rush incredibly fast to fight his adversaries. "Is this guy big?"

"Huge. That's one reason I believed Tomi. He never leaves his place."

"How does he live?"

"He grows everything he needs on his mountain. I imagine he orders clothing by mail or phone."

"Sounds like we're stepping into the mouth of the barracuda."

"He's probably harmless. I was young and impressionable the last time I saw him." She pointed. "Go to the road past our house and turn."

He followed her directions until they could go no farther. The road ended in a field of lava rock. Black boulders lay strewn up the hillside as though a giant had tossed them there. "Do you know where his house is?"

"There was a narrow trail here that Tomi always used to take. I'll see if I can find it." She got out and stood by the car. "Here it is." She set off up the steep slope. Mano followed her. Her boots loosened small stones, and they skittered down past him. He struggled to navigate the many boulders. They were both huffing by the time they reached the crest.

Pausing at the top, he gazed at the bleak landscape. "Is that a house?" He pointed to a dark structure camouflaged by the black lava rocks.

"That's it!" Annie started off toward the cabin.

Mano hurried after her. "Should we shout or something? Warn him that we're coming?

Before Annie could answer, a shot reverberated in the air. He pulled her down behind a boulder. "He's seen us, but I don't think he's trying to hit us."

"Let me talk to him." She struggled to get up.

"Wait, let me see if I can spot him." He lifted his head and looked toward a pile of black boulders. "I think he's over there. Call to him and tell him who you are."

She peered over the top of the boulder. "Mr. Kauhi, it's Annie Tagama, your neighbor. I need to talk to you."

The call of a hawk overhead filled the silence. Then a voice boomed out. "Show yourself, Miss Tagama, you and your friend."

Mano and Annie stared at one another. "We don't have much choice," he whispered.

She nodded and stood slowly with her hands in the air. Mano did the same. A man stepped out from behind a rockfall. He was nearly seven feet tall. His shaggy black hair held only a few traces of white.

"I've never seen such a tall Hawaiian."

Annie barely nodded. She stepped out. "Can we put our hands down now?"

Orson Kauhi lowered his rifle. "Make it fast. I don't have all day." His glower deepened.

As they came within three feet of the man, Mano realized he was older than he appeared from a distance. His face was lined with wrinkles, and his muscles were atrophied. In his prime, he must have been terrifying to a child. Annie smiled, but Mano could sense her fear and wondered if Kauhi could as well. Mano put his hand on her back.

"I was wondering if you'd seen my brother, Tomi, lately, Mr. Kauhi."

He stared at her from under bushy eyebrows. "I heard he died."

"That's what we thought, but there's talk he might be alive. Leilani might be with him. Did you ever see my younger sister?"

"She's the nosy one, always coming here and peeking in my windows. Not like you. You were too scared." Kauhi continued to glower, but amusement seemed to lurk in his dark eyes.

"Have you seen her lately?"

He reached out and Annie flinched, but he just touched her shoulder. "Go home, little girl. Forget about your sister. Live your own life. You worry too much about your family."

She glanced at Mano, and he read the desperation in her face. He cleared his throat. "Have you seen either Tomi or Leilani in the last week, Mr. Kauhi?"

The big man shook his head. "No. Now leave me."

Annie bit her lip. "One other thing. The GPS receivers. It's critical we place some here to gauge the earth's movement. You'd have final say on exactly where we put them. You turned down my coworker's request, but would you please reconsider?"

"No. Like I've said, I don't let anyone on my land. Not now, not ever. Study your volcano somewhere else. Ku protects me here as long as I keep the outsiders away." He turned and moved swiftly away.

Ku. Mano gave a start. Maybe this guy was part of the cult. "Mr. Kauhi, I've got some more questions."

The big man ignored him and went into the cabin. The door slammed. Annie started to follow, but Mano grabbed her arm. "Forget it. He won't change his mind. I'll check out the mountain after dark."

Six

nnie rinsed the sink and hung up the dishcloth to dry. After Mano dropped her off, she had called Sam, but he didn't have any new leads on Leilani. Then she'd cleaned the house from one end to the other, trying to maintain as normal a state as possible. Leilani would call when she was ready. She always did.

Wilson lay curled under her feet, and she nearly tripped over him several times. She gently pushed him away with her foot, and he growled softly. "Cool your jets," she told him. The doorbell rang, and she went to answer it. Glancing out the living-room window as she passed, she saw Fawn's car. Good, she needed someone to talk to. She swung the door open and saw her friend standing there with a baggie full of goodies. "Yum, what is it?"

"Wheatless carrot cake." Fawn wore a hot pink beach coverup and reef shoes.

"Um, *onolicious,*" Annie said, paying the highest compliment she could. She was being only half-sarcastic. Though Fawn's concoctions sounded horrible, they were generally tasty. "As long as it doesn't have grass in it."

Fawn stepped inside. "No grass, just natural vanilla, maple syrup, rice flour, and organic eggs. No sugar or wheat."

"It smells good," Annie said cautiously. She followed Fawn to the kitchen. Her friend put the cake on the counter. "How about a swim? You need to do something fun today."

"I should clean the bathrooms." Annie's protest was half-hearted. She could use a diversion.

Fawn put her hands on her hips. "You need some exercise, an outlet for the stress. Go get your swimsuit."

When Fawn had that stubborn expression on her face, there was no getting around her. "You win." Annie hurried to her room and grabbed her suit and equipment from a box labeled "swim gear." She changed and pulled on her swimsuit. The scars on her foot were still an angry red, and she rubbed them with some pure lanolin Fawn had given her. At least her reef shoes covered half of the scars.

Being around Fawn always lifted Annie's spirits. She joined Fawn in the living room. "I can't stay out long," she told her friend. "I'll need to get dinner started in another hour or so."

"What are we having? And I'm up for Scrabble afterward." Fawn's expression was innocent.

Annie grinned. "More therapy? I'll take it. Scrabble sounds good. I've got to be sharp for the tournament next month."

"You and your Scrabble." Fawn shook her head and followed Annie out the back door. Annie whistled for Wilson, and he came running toward them full speed ahead. He loved to swim. She grabbed the surfboard propped against the back wall of the house. They trod the path made of crushed lava rock down to the water. The property ended in a small black-sand beach. Annie shed her coverup, put on her mask, and walked toward the water carrying her fins. She waded into the waves and slipped them on. Wilson plunged in behind her.

Fawn donned her fins and dove into the waves. She came up sputtering. "Hey, there's a bunch of honu out here today!" she shouted, referring to the Hawaiian green sea turtles.

Annie joined her, and her tension began to dissipate as she watched Wilson chase the schools of brightly colored tang, butterfly fish, and unicorn fish. She slowly swam alongside a huge honu that turned to stare at her before rolling over and diving deeper. The waves were good today. She called Wilson, and he swam to her. Tossing her fins and mask to Fawn, she helped him onto the surfboard, then paddled out to the break. A perfect wave came, and she caught it. With her toes hanging off the end of the board and Wilson between her feet, it was a perfect ride.

Breathless and elated, Annie flopped onto her back on the board. The warmth of the late-afternoon sun touched her face. Out here there were no worries, no problems. As she turned, she caught sight of a figure on shore. Mano. She glanced around for Fawn, but her friend had already seen him.

"Let's go talk to him. I haven't seen the yummy Mano Oana in ages." The two swam to shore.

"Is anything wrong?" Annie called. She stayed in the water as Fawn hurried to the shore and grabbed her beach coverup.

Mano shook his head, then stepped to the water with Annie's coverup in his hand. He held it out, and she had no choice but to rise from the water and go toward him. She slipped her arms in and buttoned it up. If only she could cover her feet too. But maybe he wouldn't notice.

She tried not to limp as she walked, but thinking about it made her limp more pronounced. Mano's gaze sank to her feet. She saw his eyes widen as he spotted the angry red scars. "What happened to your foot?" Wilson came out of the water, shook himself, and draped his body around her ankle.

Annie's gaze connected with Fawn. Fawn nodded slightly as if to encourage her. "Just an accident on the job," Annie said.

"Let me see." Mano knelt at her feet and took hold of her ankle. Wilson growled a warning but didn't try to snap at him.

She didn't want him to see, but the warmth of his fingers paralyzed her. She heard him whistle low.

"That must have been some accident. It looks like burn scars."

"A lava bench gave way, and she stepped in hot lava," Fawn said. She shut up when Annie frowned at her.

Mano got to his feet and stared into her face. "It takes guts to keep working after something like that."

She wanted to confess that she'd been a pretty poor employee since the accident, but she clamped her mouth shut. She couldn't bear to spoil the admiration in his face. "It was pretty painful," was all she could say.

"No wonder you're so worried about Leilani. First your mother and then your accident . . ." His voice trailed away, and he glanced down at her foot. "I missed seeing that bright nail polish." His voice was amused.

She didn't want to talk about her mother or anything else, least of all her shame at the scars on her feet. She turned and found her reef shoes where Fawn had tossed them, then hastily bent and slipped them back on. "What are you doing back already? Did you find out something?"

"You left your purse in my car." He pointed to her purse where he'd left it by a rock. "I thought you might need it."

"*Mahalo.*" She wanted to hold onto her anger with him. Lack of conflict made her vulnerable.

Fawn jumped into the conversation. "It's good to see you, Mano. We're just about to go fix dinner. You might as well join us."

Annie caught her breath at her friend's brazen invitation. Fawn winked at Annie, and Annie scowled back. Her matchmaking wasn't welcome. Fawn was studiously avoiding her ferocious scowl.

"Sounds great! I'm starved." Mano picked up Annie's purse, tucked it under his arm like a football, then followed them to the house.

Annie scooped up the wet mongoose and hurried on ahead. Let Fawn talk to him if she was so eager to invite him to stay for dinner. The two chattered like old friends, and Annie remembered how well the pair had gotten along before Tomi's death shattered their lives. Jealousy welled in her, and she shoved it away, appalled at the unwelcome emotion. She loved Fawn and wanted her to be happy, but the thought of that happiness involving Mano made her claws come out. She told herself she should be ashamed, but her gloom persisted.

She fixed seared Spam with Hawaiian slaw and macaroni salad. Fawn's carrot cake would do for dessert.

"You remembered how much I like Spam," Mano said.

"It's generally a safe bet for everyone," she said. "The islands have the highest per capita consumption of Spam in the country."

Fawn's cell phone rang. She glanced at the caller ID and made a face. "My brother. I'll be right back." She flipped her phone open and walked with it to the living room.

Annie's father finished his meal. "I don't wish to be rude, but I have much work to do this evening."

"Go ahead," Mano said. "I understand work issues."

Edega nodded courteously and went to his office.

Annie kept her eyes on her plate. She didn't have the energy to make small talk with Mano.

Mano cleared his throat. "Are you ever going to get over being mad at me?" he asked softly.

Annie knew she was being childish. "I still have no proof that anything you've said is true," she said. "We wasted half the day looking for Tomi, and there's no guarantee he's even alive. Besides, you've accused my brother of treason. How do you think I should feel?"

"I think you should trust me."

"That's pretty hard to do, considering you left Tomi to die in foreign waters." Her gaze lingered on his face. "I never took you for a coward. What really happened that day?"

He looked away and didn't answer her question. "I've told you all I know, Annie. I care about your *'ohana*. That's why I'm here."

She just wished he could care about her with the same passion his voice showed for her family.

*M*ano left after dinner, begging off when Fawn threw down the Scrabble challenge. Annie knew he intended to scope out Orson Kauhi's land. She was so distracted that Fawn beat her in three games of Scrabble.

"Your mind is obviously not on the game," Fawn said. "I'm done for the night. Will you be at work Monday?"

"I have to be." She wanted to keep searching for her sister, but she had no idea where to look. Besides, she was already in enough trouble at work. Gina liked her, but she'd made it clear Annie wasn't to shirk any more duties.

Fawn hugged her. "It will work out. I've been praying."

"*Mahalo.*"

Fawn smiled and patted her shoulder. "Try to make it to church tomorrow."

"I'll try." Annie shut the door behind her friend, then went to find her father in the garage. Her father had turned it into an office years ago. A top-of-the-line computer sat in one corner, and papers overflowed the battered desk. Seismic equipment was scattered around the room.

"How's your paper coming?"

"Working on the final touches," her father said. He gave her a sly glance. "Once my work is published, we'll have more research money than we know what to do with. I know you've been worried about money, but this will fix everything."

It was always going to fix everything. Annie didn't know how to tell her father that the research paper was hardly earthshaking. He hypothesized that there had been violent explosive eruptions on Hawai'i in the not-so-distant past, even though the prevailing scientific opinion was that Hawai'i was created by gentle lava flows. Don Swanson's research had already documented explosive events, but her father had conveniently ignored the other man's research.

She didn't have the heart to burst his bubble, not when his face glowed like this. "I'm going to lock my car." She went to the outside door. The knob jiggled loosely in her hand. She stepped out and angled the door so it caught the light from the garage. She stooped to look at the lock. She'd installed it just last month, but the shiny brass surface was marred with scratches, and deep gouges had been dug into the wood around the hardware. Though the dead bolt and knob lock had foiled the intruder, an uneasy feeling settled in her stomach like a lump of hard lava. Why would someone try to get into the garage? The cars were parked outside.

She showed her father the damage. He just shrugged and went back to his desk. "Probably kids," he said.

She doubted that. If someone broke into the garage, they could easily gain access to the house. "I'm going to check the windows," she told her father. She grabbed a flashlight, then went around the corner of the house, stepping over the profuse bougainvillea in the planting beds. Her foot ached from so much walking today, and her limp was more pronounced than usual.

She didn't expect to see anything. The barred windows should discourage even a persistent intruder. The flashlight's beam illuminated the first window. It looked undisturbed. She went to the window that was screened from the road by silversword. Two of the bars no longer blocked access, and a third bar barely clung to its position. Fangs of broken glass protruded from the window frame. One more bar and the intruder would have gained access.

Something must have frightened him off. "Father, come here," she called.

He grumbled under his breath as he exited the garage and came to join her. "I'm busy, Annie. I don't have time for your nonsense."

She pointed to the window. "This has to have been done in the past week. I washed all the windows last Saturday."

He studied it carefully. "We're home at night. Why didn't we hear it break? I didn't notice it either."

"You wouldn't notice anything other than your computer missing." She smiled. "He must have done this in broad daylight while we were gone. That took guts. I wonder if any of the neighbors saw anything."

Her father had a worried frown. "We should call the police."

"I'll call Sam again," she said. They went back inside, and she pushed the phone's redial button. She was dumped into voice mail, so she left a message asking Sam to call her. "I'll call Mano and ask him to come back." He'd given her his cell number, and she dug it out of her purse and dialed it. His deep voice washed her fear away. "I hope you're not in the middle of something," she told him.

"Not yet."

"Someone has tried to break into the garage. I can't reach Sam. Could you come help me check it out?" She hated to ask him for anything, but she didn't know who else to call.

"I'm just down the road. I'll be right there."

He must be at Kauhi's place. She put the phone down and went to tell her father Mano was on his way. He'd quickly lost interest in the vandalism and was back at his desk.

"Fine, fine," he muttered. His gaze was on the computer screen.

Annie sighed and went back inside to wait.

Mano clicked his phone off. The stress in Annie's voice worried him. The problems never seemed to stop for them. Could the break-in attempt be related to Tomi? He still hoped Leilani was with her brother. Until Tomi made contact again, they were in limbo though. If he could get his hands on Tomi, he'd strangle him.

Could Tomi have really been involved in espionage? It seemed hard to equate his good-natured friend with something so treacherous. But there didn't seem to be any other explanation for the money. Two million dollars. It was hard to take in.

His cell phone rang again, and he answered it. "Mano, here."

"Hey, buddy."

Mano's gut tightened. "Tomi? Where are you?"

"Here on the Big Island. I told you I'd be heading this way."

It sounded like Tomi. Mano grew even more confident that he wasn't mistaken about that. "Where? I'll come get you."

"No!" He hesitated. "I—I'm in some trouble, Mano. I need your help."

"What can I do?"

"Do you have the bankbook?"

"Yeah, I gave it to Annie like you said." He heard Tomi's exhalation of relief. "Tomi? What's wrong?"

"I'll tell you when I see you. Tell Annie I'll call her when I decide what to do."

Tomi's usual confidence was missing. He sounded almost despondent. And desperate. "I'll tell her," Mano said. "Tell me what's wrong. Maybe I can help."

"I'm not sure anyone can help," Tomi muttered. "I've been so stupid." He cleared his throat, and his voice became stronger. "I'll be in touch."

"What about Leilani?" Mano blurted out.

"Leilani? What—out—er?" Tomi's voice was breaking up.

"I didn't catch what you said, Tomi. Leilani's missing. Annie found the necklace she always wears. It was by some fumeroles. We were hoping she was with you."

"I have—seen—home . . ." The connection died.

"Tomi? I didn't get that. Tomi?" He tossed the phone in his pocket and flattened the accelerator. He wanted to be with Annie when Tomi called.

Wilson crawled into Annie's lap and nuzzled her neck. She stroked his soft fur. It took Mano longer to arrive than she'd expected. When she finally saw his bulky form through the rice-paper screen, her relief surprised her. She held the door open for him.

"Sorry it took me so long." He stepped inside. "I had another call from Tomi. He asked if I gave you the bankbook."

Her emotions surged like the tide after a storm. "Did you ask him about Leilani?" She couldn't help the hope that softened her voice.

Mano's eyes softened. "Yeah. He started breaking up so I couldn't tell what he said. My bet is that she's with him."

Annie let herself hope. A persistent voice inside asked why Leilani hadn't called, but she ignored it. Tomi hadn't called either. There was likely some good explanation.

"He said he'd be in touch soon." He touched her chin with his fingers and tilted her head up so her gaze connected with his. She could smell the soap he'd used this morning, something sharp and sporty. She knew she shouldn't welcome his touch, but the warmth of his fingers held her immobile.

He was too close. She jerked her chin out of his hands and stepped back. "Come to the living room. Father had better hear all of this." Wilson squeaked in her ear, and she clutched him for comfort as she led the way. Her father had emerged from the office and now sat in his chair opposite the Mizuya cabinet, whose simple lines held the TV. He held a notebook and pen. His expression grew wary when his gaze rested on Mano. They had both thought Mano the villain too long to easily let go of their distrust, but she suddenly realized that if Tomi was alive, everything else Mano had told them must be true too.

She had to listen to him now, had to work with him on this. If Tomi was in trouble and had dragged Leilani into it, she had to do what she could to help them both. Irritation flashed through her. She was a scientist trained to investigate lava flows, not missing persons. She wasn't equipped for a job like this. But so long as Sam continued to sit on his thumbs, she had no choice.

She sat on the couch with one leg curled under her and Wilson on her lap. The phone rang. She looked at Mano. "That might be Sam. I left a message for him to call about the smashed window."

"Don't tell him anything about your brother. Not until you talk to Tomi."

She nodded and grabbed the phone. "Tagama residence."

"Annie, you called?" Sam's voice sounded distracted and a trifle irritated.

"Um, yeah, I found a smashed window in the garage. It looks like someone was trying to get in. And there were scratches on the lock at the door."

"We've had a rash of vandalism out your way. Those rotten kids." Sam sighed heavily. "I'll send someone out to take a report, but I doubt we'll find out who did it."

"I—I wondered if it had anything to do with Leilani's disappearance."

"What do you mean?"

"I'm not sure. We've never had anyone try to break in before. I just thought it might be connected. Since the garage is attached, someone could gain access to the house more easily." Saying it like that, it sounded inane and childish. Sam was likely to be suspicious and wonder why she'd called. The disinterest in his voice replaced her embarrassment with annoyance.

"Ask your neighbors. Someone broke into their garage and then into the house just last week. It happens, even here. Look, I've got to go. I'll call you the minute I hear anything about Leilani. I'm swamped right now. I'm sure Leilani will show up. She probably found a new boyfriend who turned her head." He was sounding more and more impatient.

He hung up before she could say anything else. It was probably just as well, if Leilani was with Tomi. If Annie only knew for sure, she could relax. "He's not going to do anything." She put down the phone and looked at Mano. "Tell Father what Tomi said," she told him.

Mano sat in the armchair and began to tell her father about Tomi's call. Wilson cautiously approached his leg and sniffed him. She smiled as the mongoose crept into his lap. Wilson didn't like many people. She turned her gaze to her father and watched hope spring to life on his face. It matched that in her heart. For months it seemed their family would never recover from the blows they'd been dealt. Now things were topsy-turvy again, but in a way that made her think they could roll back the clock.

"Now, what about this break-in?" Mano asked, his gaze bouncing from her to her father and back again.

Annie rose. "It would be better to show you."

Mano lifted Wilson off his lap and stood. Annie led Mano to the garage. She went to the broken back window. Some of the glass had fallen inside as well, but it didn't appear the intruder had touched anything inside.

"He almost made it in," Mano said. "Is there anything valuable here?"

"My father's research." She lowered her voice. "And that's nothing groundbreaking."

"Could it be someone looking for Tomi?"

"I don't think he'd lead anyone back to us," she said slowly. "I don't want to believe that."

"Jillian didn't want to believe Noah would steal her research either," Mano pointed out. "The Bible says a man's heart is desperately wicked, and who can know it? We're all capable of more evil than we realize."

She'd always known Mano was religious. Though she attended church, it seemed to have less and less relevance to her life. "Let's keep to the facts," she said. "My brother is not evil." But she wasn't as sure as her voice sounded. How did he get all that money? And why would he let them think he was dead?

"Whoever it is, you need protection. Since there's nothing of value in the garage, it's likely someone was trying to gain access to the house. We need to tighten security out here." He glanced around the garage. "I'll add some locks. Do you have any big chests we can move in front of the windows?"

"There's an antique shelving system over here." She led him to a monster unit that used to be a sort of post office.

He groaned. "I'll get a hernia moving it."

"I'll help you." She flexed her arm to show her muscle, and then grinned at his amused expression.

Mano's grin faded. He looked around. "There's an appliance dolly. That will help." He went to the dolly and wheeled it back to the shelf unit. "Stand back."

She stood her ground. "I'll help. I'm no hothouse orchid—I'm the hardy Hawaiian type." She got on one side without waiting for him to answer. She found a fingerhold and heaved it an inch off the floor, though her muscles protested. Together they managed to get the unit onto the dolly and moved it in front of the broken window.

Mano was sweating by the time they finished, and a sheen of perspiration dampened Annie's face as well. "What about the other window?" she asked.

"The bars are intact there. But I could nail some boards across it." Mano rummaged through a lumber pile left from when Tomi built the back deck. He emerged with several boards, which he nailed in a crosshatch pattern across the window.

"That should hold them," he said in satisfaction. "I need to call a locksmith."

They went inside, where she gave him the phone book. While he made his call, she went to the back deck and sat in the moonlight. Inhaling the fragrance of the flowers, she realized her brother could walk through the door any minute. Leilani too. Their family would be complete again. At least as complete as it was ever going to be with Mother gone.

Seven

Mano was wide awake and on edge when he left the Tagama house. Too keyed up to go back to his hotel room, he decided to finish scouting out the adjoining land that belonged to Kauhi. He kept his headlights off and crept along the dark road illuminated only by the moon. Parking in the black gravel, he pulled out his key and got out.

Rocks loomed like dragons in the dark, unfamiliar landscape. His sneakers crunched on the rough rock underfoot even though he tried to be quiet. The night air held a scent of flowers. There was no wind, so every noise seemed loud. If Kauhi was alert, he'd be shooting that rifle with no warning. It was probably stupid to be out here.

A light shone in the shack where the old man lived. Mano could see a shadow moving inside. Good. At least Kauhi wasn't prowling around out here in the dark. The windows were open, and Mano could hear the old guy singing a tuneless song in Hawaiian. He skirted the cabin and wandered through a moonscape land of barren lava fields softened by the occasional ohia tree and tree fern. He nearly fell into several holes. What was wrong with him? His head felt strange—fuzzy. Realization dawned. He was having a diabetic reaction. He needed to get back to the car and take care of it.

He stumbled back the way he came, crashing into boulders and stumbling over shrubs. His confusion and befuddlement deepened, and it wasn't until he was back to his car that he realized something was running down his face. He opened his car door and touched the sticky mess on his head. His hand came away bloody. Did the old man shoot at him? Mano couldn't remember. He fell into the car and fumbled in the glove box. His lips were numb as he managed to unwrap a Hershey's Kiss. He popped it in his mouth and chomped it down quickly. Leaning his head back against the headrest, he waited for the hypoglycemic symptoms to subside.

His body was betraying him. Rage and frustration bubbled behind his foggy state. He didn't want this—didn't want to be less than whole and strong. The exertion at Annie's must have tapped his blood sugars and led to this sinking spell. The helplessness of the diagnosis made the future seem as murky as his thoughts. His mind began to clear as the carbs kicked up his blood-sugar level. He opened his eyes and held out his hand. It shook, and he realized he was still too shaky to explore Kauhi's tonight.

He dug a notebook out of his pocket and jotted down the time he'd taken the candy. His mealtimes were spaced properly. It must have been the extra exertion. The doctor said it would take time to figure out how to regulate his illness, but he needed to be as alert as possible if he was going to help the Tagama family.

As soon as his head and vision cleared, he started the car and drove back to his motel. He parked outside and found his room key. He noticed a figure standing outside his door and then recognized the man. Noah Sommers. Mano got out and quietly closed his car door. Noah was on his cell phone with his back to the road. Mano approached as silently as he could, hopeful he might overhear something that would illuminate Noah's purpose in returning to the island. Gravel crunched under his feet, and Noah looked up.

"Gotta go," he said, clicking off his cell phone and pocketing it. "Hey, Mano." He frowned. "You look like crap. Is that blood on your face?"

"I don't know. You don't look any better than I feel." Noah's wrinkled aloha shirt appeared to have been slept in, and his hair stood up on end. The dark circles under his eyes added to the malaise on his face. "Were you looking for me?"

"Yeah." Noah shoved his hands into the pockets of his shorts.

Mano unlocked the door to his room. "Come on in."

"*Mahalo*," Noah said. He followed Mano inside.

The maid had cleaned the room, and it still smelled faintly of pine cleaning products. Mano tossed his key on the desk. "Let me wash my face." He went to the bathroom and winced when he looked in the mirror. His face was scraped and bloody. No bullet holes though. He must have fallen against lava rock. At least Kauhi hadn't heard him. After scrubbing his face with soap and water, he went back to the bedroom.

Noah sat in the desk chair doodling on a pad. Mano sat on the edge of the double bed. "So what's up?"

Noah looked up and dropped the pen on the pad. He laced his fingers together and stared at the faded carpet. "I need your help. I know you don't really know me, but I don't know where else to turn. Jillian says you're with the navy. I can't go to the cops, so you're the next best thing."

Mano was supposed to be on vacation. Apparently there would be no rest on this leave. Mano got up and rummaged in the small refrigerator. "Want a bottle of water?" He missed the old days when he could drink half a dozen cans of Pepsi a day. Now all he drank was water. Just another way his life had changed.

"No thanks." Noah shifted in the chair and began to jiggle his knee.

Might as well get it over with. Mano went back to the bed. "I'm not sure I can help you. I'm on leave right now."

"I know, Kaia told me. But I'm desperate. I did something stupid."

Mano straightened. He'd assumed Noah wanted to talk about Jillian's research. "Go on."

Noah looked up finally. "I know it looks bad what I did to my family."

"Yeah, it does." *Bad* wasn't the word for it. More like *disgust-*

ing.

"My reasoning seemed sound at the time. Now I'm not so sure. I think I've gone from the lava bench into the caldera." He stood. "Maybe I'll take that water after all." He helped himself, unscrewed the cap, and took a swig. He set the bottle down on the desk. "I guess I'd better give you some background."

Mano wished he would get to the point. "Okay."

"You ever play craps, Mano?"

Mano blinked. Where was Noah going with this? "Not really. I put a quarter in a one-armed bandit once."

"Good for you. Don't ever get started." He lifted his head and stared at Mano. "We're a lot alike, I think. You live for the thrill of a new adventure. I can see it in your eyes. So did I once. I gambled and lost my family, my reputation, my career. Take a tip from me and learn to temper that adventurous spirit. The thrill of the chase doesn't last. An empty house is pretty lonely."

Mano moved restlessly. Noah's observations hit a little too close to the mark. "You'd better get on with what you have to say."

"Our type is always in a hurry." Noah stared into space. "Sometimes all we're left with is time." He blinked, and his eyes came back into focus. "Are you aware there's going to be a casino on the island? And more than just a casino. A bunch of hotels and homes."

Mano frowned. "No, but I guess it shouldn't surprise me. Casinos are a blight everywhere else."

"They promised me a great job if I could make sure Jillian's research wasn't published. So I changed it, made it suit their purposes. I thought I could make her understand. But I don't even have the words to try to explain it to her."

Noah's babbles made no sense to Mano. "Why are you telling me this? What's this have to do with me being in the navy?"

"I want my family back, and the only way for that to happen is for me to tell the truth. But that might get me killed. If you poke around on your own and uncover the story, I'll be free to tell what

I know."

"Seems a convoluted way to go about it. Just tell the truth and ask for police protection. Talk to a reporter for added protection."

"I don't have any proof. It would be just my word against theirs. If you find out what's going on, there would be something to go on."

"You're not making any sense. How could having a casino on the island lead you to steal your wife's research?"

Noah hesitated. "Jillian's research—the research that didn't get published—concluded that a new magma chamber was growing under the area they want to develop."

"Weren't they concerned all their money would be thrown away if an eruption occurred?"

"At this stage, they'd lose more if word got out. They're neck-deep in contracts. Besides, I told them what they wanted to hear—that it was likely flawed data."

"Is it?"

Noah shrugged. "Maybe. It's hard to say. Jillian is a good vol-canologist, but even if she's right, it wouldn't happen for years."

"I didn't think these things could be predicted so easily."

"They can't. I doubted that anything would happen in the next twenty years. They'd rake in millions before it happened—if it ever did. And money was tight. My company was downsizing; my job was on the chopping block. I had to do something. So I took their money and published the research as my own. I hadn't counted on Jillian throwing such a tantrum."

"You're an idiot," Mano said. "You trashed Jillian's professional reputation, then expected her to forget it?"

"I miscalculated." A muscle in Noah's jaw flexed.

"What about publishing a retraction? That should be simple enough. You don't need me for that."

Noah shook his head. "They'd make sure I never got it to print."

Mano blinked slowly as he thought. "What's the area in

question?"

"They're buying up Aloha Shores and several private tracts. The Tagama's land and the mountain just behind it."

Mano hadn't heard of any offers to buy the Tagama land. Then he thought of the money in Tomi's bankbook. Had he secretly sold the family's land to the casino? Alarm should be setting his nerves on edge, but a strange lethargy played havoc with his thoughts. He realized his blood sugar was still too low. He just had to hold on until it climbed a bit more. He popped a hard candy from the bedside table into his mouth.

"Want one?" he offered to Noah. Before Noah could answer, he heard glass shatter. Something stung the side of his face. He put up his hand and touched something wet on his temple. His fingers were red when he lowered them. He stared at them. Blood.

Something pinged on the wall, and what was happening finally penetrated his foggy brain. "Get down!" He dove for the floor. Another bullet plowed into the carpet by his head. He heard a series of soft thuds and saw Noah running for the door. "Wait!" Mano called. He got to his hands and knees as Noah threw open the door and rushed out into the shadows.

Mano staggered to his feet. His head was spinning, and the heat on his cheek told him he was still bleeding. The shooting had stopped. He stepped to the doorway and looked outside. Taillights winked in the darkness as Noah's vehicle pulled onto the street.

He heard the sound of running feet and instinctively stepped back and slammed his door shut. A thump came from the other side of the door. "You okay in there?"

Relief as sweet as guava nectar flooded him. It was the motel proprietor, Aaron. Mano opened the door. "Someone shot at us. Call the police." His head spun, and he stumbled back toward the bed. Lights danced in his vision like *menehunes* with tiny lamps. He sank to the edge of the bed and put his head between his legs, then fumbled for another piece of candy. He sucked on the sweetness, hoping his confusion would soon lift.

"I'll call an ambulance too." Aaron stepped inside and grabbed the phone.

Mano dimly heard him speak to the police in an excited tone. Gradually the sugar began to make a difference, and his thinking cleared. Aaron handed him a tissue from the bathroom. He took it and blotted the blood from his cheek.

"You'd better not touch anything," he told Aaron. "The police will need to sweep the room." Most likely they wouldn't find anything but bullet fragments. But there might be something outside. In the distance he could hear sirens. They grew louder, and he stood to go meet the police, then swayed.

"I think you'd better sit down before you fall." Aaron caught him by the elbow.

"I'm fine." He tried to tug his arm from Aaron's grip, and the movement made the room spin. He sat back on the bed. The sirens grew louder, and he smelled the scent of something he couldn't identify—something sweet yet cloying that filled his head and sinuses. He shook his head to clear it, then put his head between his legs again.

Dimly, he heard the sirens stop. He lifted his head when Sam came running through the door. The officer had his pistol out. His face changed when he saw Mano.

"Oana, I should have known you'd be mixed up in this somehow."

Mano's head was clearing. "You can put your gun away, Rambo. The guy's gone."

Sam scowled but holstered his gun. "What happened here?"

"You tell me." Mano gestured toward the window. "Someone decided to use me for target practice."

Sam drew near the bed and glanced at Mano's temple. "Looks like he didn't miss."

"I think he was aiming about four inches closer in." Mano

dabbed at his temple again. He looked at the wadded tissue, but it was nearly clean of blood now. The wound was beginning to stop bleeding.

Sam's lips tightened. "Check him out," he barked to the paramedics. He glanced around the room.

Mano looked around, trying to see the scene through Sam's eyes. The funky walls were an aqua-on-steroids color. The bedspread was just as gaudy, a mess of garish oranges and greens. This place must not have been updated since the sixties. "A bullet hit the floor there." Mano pointed. "And one went into the wall there." He showed Sam the hole by the desk, a blond piece of furniture marred by numerous nicks and cuts. The place was clean and that was all he'd cared about.

"Any idea why you'd be a target?"

Mano hesitated. His gut told him Noah had been the target, not him. But Sam was liable to scare Noah off, and Mano wanted to find out more about the casino deal and whether it might be linked to Tomi. "I have no idea."

"There were quite a few shots, so whoever it was meant business." Sam stooped and peered at the bullet fragment on the floor. "Looks like .357."

Mano didn't reply. If he had to confess to Noah's presence later, he would. Right now, he needed to find Noah. He flinched when the paramedic dabbed a stinging liquid on his wound.

"That's going to need stitches," the man told him. "It wouldn't hurt to get an X-ray."

"Slap a butterfly bandage on it, and let me out of here," Mano said. He glanced at Sam, but the detective was intent on gathering the evidence. Maybe he wouldn't notice if Mano stepped around outside to the window where the bullets came in. Mano's head was clearer now.

The paramedic turned him loose, and he went to the door. Another car with flashing lights on top pulled into the lot. Sam had called for backup. Mano needed to act fast. He grabbed a flashlight from his car and rounded the corner of the building.

"Don't touch anything," Sam called after him.

Mano flipped on the flashlight and shone it on the ground. The light touched crumpled candy and gum wrappers, soda tabs, and a shave ice cup. He could barely see the imprint of where someone had stood in the grass, but it didn't tell him anything.

He swept the light back and forth across the area one more time and then caught a glint of metal. Probably another soda tab. He knelt and parted the grass carefully. A ring winked up at him. He started to pick it up, then realized he'd be in trouble for tampering with the evidence. He dug a pen out of his pocket and lifted it so he could see it more clearly.

It was a man's ring. The onyx stone was topped with a gold "A." A bit from one of the prongs was missing. Mano dropped it back into the grass and put away his pen. "Sam, out here," he called through the broken window. Once the detective joined him, he pointed out the ring. "It could have been here for a while, but it might be evidence."

"I told you to leave this to me," Sam growled. "We'll handle the investigation." He picked up the ring, his hand clad in latex gloves, and stared at it. "Are you sure it isn't yours?"

"Positive," Mano said. He took a step back.

"You're hiding something, Oana," Sam said. "I'm going to find out what it is. You might as well tell me now."

"Is that your usual manner—to harass the victim?" Mano was ready to get out of there. He'd had all of Sam's attitude he could take. "Look, let's put our history behind us and focus on the problems." He stalked off toward his car. Noah knew better than to go to his rental. Maybe Jillian would know where he might be.

*A*nnie's covers were in a tangle. Wilson growled as she thrashed once again and rolled over in the bed. "Sorry, sweetie." She wiggled her fingers, and he nibbled on them. She stroked his head, deriving some comfort from his warm little body. She fluffed her pillow and propped it against the headboard. She flipped on the light. Sleep wasn't coming so she might as well do something useful.

She glanced at her Bible on the stand beside her bed and reached for it, then changed her mind and picked up a thick research paper she'd been wanting to read. Flipping open the cover, she pulled her knees into a tent position and propped the manual on her legs. Wilson poked his head between the pages and closed his eyes.

She laughed and eased him onto her chest. The article was just getting interesting when the phone rang. Wilson sprang to his feet and began to bark. Annie brought her hand to her throat. Who would call at this hour? The luminous numbers on her alarm clock said twelve twenty. She almost let it ring, then realized it might be Tomi.

She picked it up and clicked it on. "Hello?" she said softly.

"Annie?"

The voice was like nothing she'd ever heard. Some kind of weird electronic sound altered the person's voice. Her pulse kicked into high gear. Maybe it was Leilani—or someone who had her. "This is Annie." Her knuckles hurt where she gripped the phone.

"This is just the beginning," the voice whispered. "Are you enjoying the ride, Annie? Better fasten your seat belt, it's going to get rough. Your family ruined my life. Now it's your turn. And it's all Tomi's fault."

"Who are you?" Annie heard the panic in her voice, but she didn't care. "What do you want? Is this about Leilani?"

The laugh that followed raised the hair on the back of her neck. "She'll join her mother in hell. You ever wonder how she *really* died?"

Annie heard a click. "Hello? Hello?" She shook the phone, then threw it across the room and burst into tears. What had the caller meant about her mother? She'd committed suicide. Annie kicked off the covers and practically fell out of bed in her scramble to retrieve the phone. She had to call the police. She got through to the station and told the officer on duty about the call. He took down all the information.

"So you weren't specifically threatened? Maybe it was someone who knows your sister is missing and is trying to rattle you."

Annie hadn't thought of that. "You think so?" She wished she could believe it. "The voice seemed so—so—*evil*." She clung to the hope that Leilani was with Tomi. If she only knew for sure.

"Those electronic voice synthesizers can really be upsetting," the officer said. "We'll check it out. I'll talk to Sam about putting a tap on your phone."

She didn't mention what the caller said about her mother. No sense in putting the call into even more dispute by passing along that lie. Annie hung up the phone not at all comforted.

Eight

The fresh, clean scent of the sea washed over Annie's face. Nani did a backward flip and splashed her, and Annie laughed. Nani had such personality. Annie slipped her mask over her head and let it dangle around her neck. Yesterday after church, the day had dragged by while she waited for the phone to ring. It never did. Her work today would keep her mind off the silence in the house.

Fawn sat on the edge of the boat and pulled on her fins. "You're sure Nani knows what she's supposed to do?" she asked Jillian, who was steering. Wilson stood on his hind legs on the dash. His nose quivered as he sniffed the wind.

Jillian nodded. "Kaia showed her and said she was ready." Her voice was hoarse, and she fished a tissue out of her pocket and wiped her red nose. "We're always hearing stories of wild dolphins helping people who are shipwrecked or drowning. This is my first up-close-and-personal experience with a wild dolphin though, and I'm disappointed I don't get to go out with you."

"Where is Kaia?" Annie asked. She pulled on her own fins. The brilliant turquoise of the bay washed away the last traces of the weekend's stress. There was no sense in worrying right now anyway. She couldn't do anything until she heard from Tomi and Leilani.

"She went back to Kaua'i. She's in the middle of wedding plans." Jillian cut the engine, and the boat sloughed sideways. "It's a little rough out here. I should be going down with you." She wiped her nose again.

"We'll be fine." Annie slipped into the water, and it wrapped her in a warm caress. Wilson leaned over the edge of the boat and barked at the dolphin. Nani rose out of the water, twirling several times before splashing back down. She swam to the boat and chattered at Wilson.

"I think she likes Wilson," Annie said. She hit the water with the palm of her hand, and the dolphin swam to her. Nani thrust her nostrum into Annie's hand. She smiled and patted Nani. The wet inner-tube feel of the dolphin's skin brought a sense of comfort that surprised her. "Ready to help us, Nani?"

Underwater volcanic studies were something of a rarity. It was more difficult to collect data, especially when there was plenty of live flow accessible on ground. But the lava and sea interacted in fascinating ways that had yet to be fully understood. For example, the lava helped maintain the ocean's salt levels. The prospect of new discoveries thrilled Annie.

The dolphin chattered and zipped away, then rose in her dolphin dance and splashed Annie. She pulled her mask into position and brought the regulator up to her mouth. Fawn joined her in the water, and they both struck out for deeper water with strong strokes. "Give us an hour," Annie shouted to Jillian.

Jillian nodded, and the boat pulled away. It wasn't safe to anchor the boat here. The water was too hot to properly cool the engines, and the ash suspended in the water could ruin the engines as well. Jillian would come back and look for their buoy.

Nani came close again, and Annie reached out and grabbed the dolphin's dorsal fin. Nani pulled her to the edge of the cliff, then dove along the underwater slope. Schools of brightly colored fish darted across her vision: butterfly fish and yellow tangs. A bright blue parrot fish peered into her mask, and she paused to enjoy the experience. A sea turtle did a lazy turn just below her. The visibility was better than usual, so the vent must not be spouting off too badly today.

Fawn touched her shoulder and pointed down. Annie saw a

mound of pillow lava. Underwater, the lava cooled so quickly that it formed a crust over the molten stone and resembled a pillow. A small crack showed the hot glow within. The noises of hissing and popping filled her ears. They'd have to watch out for explosions.

They could go closer to examine the pillow lava, but they needed to train Nani so they could take her to Loihi. The dolphin zipped past them and swam down to the oozing sore. The instruments strapped around her would gather the information they needed. They would take water-temperature readings, test for gases and salt content, and collect numerous water samples to evaluate the processes that control the earth's chemistry. This use of the dolphin had been a brilliant stroke of genius on Jillian's part.

Annie took temperature readings and checked oxygen content. She found it hard to concentrate on the work at hand amid so much beauty. Sharp lava cliffs rose to her right, and the mystery of lava tubes and caves beckoned. She'd explored some of them over the years, but every time she came down here, things changed. It was always new and exciting.

Her light passed over something brightly colored on the seabed. She peered at it through her mask. What could it be? It was fluorescent green and didn't look like coral or anything natural. Maybe a diver had left an article of clothing behind, though it had to be wedged under a rock to be down here instead of washed ashore with the tide.

She could go get it herself, but she might as well use the opportunity to direct Nani. She pushed on the clicker in her hand to call Nani. The dolphin swam to her. Annie wondered if she could get the dolphin to understand she wanted her to fetch the item on the ocean floor. She pointed, and Nani swam around her for a few moments. She pointed again and this time made the clicking sound with the device in her hand. The dolphin zipped down again and nosed along the seabed. Maybe she'd realize Annie wasn't interested in anything natural like rocks and fish.

Nani's nostrum touched the fabric, or whatever it was. Annie couldn't see exactly what the dolphin was doing, but she seemed to be trying to grab it in her teeth. Nani finally turned, and Annie saw she had it in her mouth.

The dolphin swam close to Annie and nudged her with her nostrum again as if to tell her to take it. Annie saw it was a slipper. Just one. Surfah brand, bright green. She took it from Nani's teeth. Leilani had slippers like this, and so did a zillion other residents and tourists. But Leilani's were missing from her room, so she must have been wearing them the day she disappeared.

Annie turned the thong over to check the size. Seven, just like Leilani wore. Fawn was looking over her shoulder at the slipper as well, but Annie knew her coworker would have no idea what it could mean. Maybe she was jumping to conclusions. These slippers were a dime a dozen, and this shade of green was popular. But the lump in her throat refused to be swallowed down.

The hissing and popping noises grew a notch. Annie looked at the slope and realized the terrain was sliding. An avalanche of black volcanic rock and ash moved quickly down the slope. She struggled to maintain her position. A roar filled her ears, and she wasn't sure if she was swimming up or down. Nani bumped her, and she grabbed hold of the dolphin's dorsal fin as space and distance seemed to rush past her. Was she rising to the surface? Shaking her head to clear it, she glanced at her depth gauge and realized she must have swum down when the rockfall started. Nani had helped her level out. Annie had forgotten all her training about underwater avalanches. If not for Nani, she would have found herself three hundred feet down and having to spend some time in a hyperbaric chamber.

She pointed up, and Fawn nodded. They swam toward the surface into water that got hotter near the top. The dolphin swam in circles around them. Pausing occasionally to decompress, all Annie's fears returned. Was this her sister's slipper? She didn't see how it could be. Leilani would never come out here.

Her head broke the surface, and she spit out her regulator and turned to her friend. "Leilani has a pair just like this," she gasped.

Fawn pulled her mask down around her neck as she treaded water. She took out her regulator. "So do I," she said. "Don't assume they belong to Leilani."

Annie nodded. "I know, I know. But it's the same size and everything. I'm scared, Fawn." A wave struck her, and she swallowed a mouthful of salty water. She choked and sputtered, then caught her breath again.

"Let's call it a day." Fawn's gaze was sympathetic. They swam away from the volcano to cooler water, and Fawn released the buoy so Jillian could find them.

Her mind on the slipper, Annie could hardly think about the data they'd just collected. She'd hoped working would get her mind off her brother and sister, but instead everything had come crashing in again. If only Tomi would call and tell her Leilani was with him. She depended on him, on his good-natured take on things, his strong will and nature. She was used to being the strong one, but she was tired, at the end of her strength. She couldn't go on like this much longer.

She heard the sound of the approaching boat. Fawn stuck up her hand, and Jillian stopped to pick them up. As they rode to shore, Annie showed Jillian what they'd found.

"I've seen half a dozen women wearing those," Jillian said. "I'm sure it's nothing to worry about."

Annie wanted to believe her. As they approached the shore, she recognized Mano's stocky form walking on the dock. Something constricted in her chest: that old, unwelcome feeling for the man who loved her sister. She saw it in his face every time Leilani's name was mentioned.

Her eyes burned, and she tried to tell herself it was the salt water. There had to be some way to uproot these feelings. She'd walked in the shadow of Leilani's beauty too many years to ever think a man who followed her sister with starry eyes could see past her own plain exterior to her heart and prefer her. It wasn't going to happen.

*M*ano watched Annie step off the boat. The black wet suit she wore made her appear even tinier. Her mask hung around her neck, but she'd already dropped her air tanks off her back. Her black hair clung to her head, and she trailed seawater as she stepped onto the dock. She came toward him with a guarded expression, and he wondered if she was ever going to be her old self around him again.

She tugged her mask off over her hair. "We got some good readings," she told him.

Mano looked at the slipper in her hand. "What's that? A souvenir?"

"It was lodged under a rock on the seabed. Nani got it for me." She nibbled on her lower lip. "Leilani has a pair just like it."

"Ah." No wonder the color had leaked from her face, and she wouldn't meet his gaze. "And you think it might be hers? What would it be doing clear out here? Did she swim here much?"

"She never swam much, and certainly not out by a live lava flow. Her favorite pastime in a bikini was to lie on a beach somewhere and accept the admiration that came her way."

"Sometimes you sound like you didn't like your sister," he blurted before he could bite back the words. He regretted it when he saw the way her face changed.

She blinked rapidly. "I love my sister, but I see her for who she is. Which is more than I can say for most men." She bit her lip and looked away.

It was a jab, and the barb pricked him. Maybe he deserved it. He'd joined Leilani's legion of admirers without resistance. It had taken him awhile to get over her, but he'd finally accomplished it.

He decided to ignore her comment. "Has Tomi called you?" he asked her.

Her face clouded even more. "I haven't heard a word from Tomi or Leilani. I thought you said he promised to call soon."

"He did. Does he have your cell phone number?"

She nodded. "I should check it." She angled a glance up at him. "I had a weird phone call Saturday night from someone using a voice synthesizer. Whoever it was said our family was going to pay for something. And the person insinuated Mother didn't kill herself."

He straightened. "Did the person mention Tomi's money?"

She shook her head. "But they said they were sending Leilani to hell." She shuddered.

A fierce wave of protectiveness washed over him, and he wished he could embrace her. He thrust his hands into the pockets of his denim shorts. "You called the cops?"

She nodded. "They said they'd consider putting a tap on the phone." She left him and Jillian and moved toward her Nissan, which was parked along the road. Fawn trailed her.

Mano turned to Jillian. "Any call from Noah since the shooting at the motel?"

She shook her head. "I told you I'd call if he contacted me. What makes you so sure he was the target? You deal with dangerous types all the time. What if someone followed you here?"

He shrugged. "It was just the way he took off, like he knew the danger was more than I even realized. Tell me about the research he published. Do you have any idea why he released it in his own name?" He didn't want to tell her what Noah had said about it until he heard her version.

Jillian shook her head. "I'd been working with GPS receivers out along the southwest rift zone. I had a model I was pretty sure was accurate. It suggested the area was overdue for a lava flow. The GPS showed expansion, and I postulated that there was a new magma chamber growing." She wiped at her nose. "As to why he would publish it under his own name, I have no idea. Only Noah could tell you that. He quoted my stuff but changed the data to hide any likelihood of a lava flow. He trashed everything I'd been working on."

"This is near the Tagama property, right?"

She nodded. "Annie knows about the danger out there. But there should be plenty of forewarning. Earthquake swarms and the like."

How did Tomi and Leilani fit into all of this? Maybe they didn't. Maybe what they were involved in had nothing to do with the volcanoes. Though that was the likely scenario, it didn't feel right to Mano. There was some link he was missing.

Annie came back toward them with rapid steps, nearly running. "There's an unidentified missed call on my cell phone," she said, out of breath. "Maybe it was Tomi. Do you think he's on the island?"

"He said he was. He'll call back."

"I'm going to strangle him when I get my hands on him!" she burst out. Her eyes reddened, and she bit her lip. "I'm going to call Sam and tell him to get that tap on the phone done."

"I'll try calling him," Mano promised. He walked away from the women and went toward the pier. No reason to let them watch him crash and burn with Sam.

The detective was in. "Detective Briscoe," he barked.

"Sam, it's Mano. The Tagama family has still heard nothing from Leilani. Annie wants that phone tap done."

"We're working on it," Sam said.

"What about the phone call Annie got on Saturday? Any idea what that was about?"

"That might have been a prank," Sam said. "If it happens again, the tap will give us more information."

"When will it be ready?"

"Get off my back, Oana! I've got more problems than you know. A stabbing in Pahala, two break-ins in Volcano." He let out his breath in an impatient sigh. "Look, I've got to get back to work."

"But—" Sam was gone before Mano could finish his question.

"Nothing," he told Annie when she joined him by the rolling surf.

She pressed her fingers against the bridge of her nose. "I want to talk to Tomi, but since he's not calling, I can't sit idly by. I'm going to talk to Leilani's friends. Maybe one of them has seen her."

"Good idea. Sam will howl about it though," he reminded her.

"At this point, I don't care. I'm not sleeping and neither is my father." She stood. "Do you have any ideas about the money in Tomi's account? Other than espionage, of course."

"Not a clue." He didn't like admitting it. He would have sworn Tomi held nothing back from him. Not ever. He didn't know his best friend like he thought he did. "What shall we do first?"

She glanced at her waterproof watch. "I have some number crunching to do with this data we just got. Can you meet me after work? I'd like to talk to Leilani's best friend, CeCe Dillon. I have no idea if Sam has even talked to her, and I'm going nuts waiting."

"I'll go with you. I have something to do first. I'll meet you at your house."

"Fine." She walked away to join the other women.

His gut told him Noah's problem with the casino developer might be tied up with Leilani and Tomi. Mano needed to find Noah. He'd have to sneak onto the Aloha Shores, but it was the middle of the day and maybe the residents would be at work. He probably should tell someone where he was going in case they caught him and threw him to the sharks. He grinned at such a melodramatic thought.

Nine

"What do you want with me?" Leilani Tagama huddled against the wall. The meager light from the lamp cast her in a sickly yellow glow. A dirty handkerchief hid her eyes.

The big man felt a stab of regret that surprised him. He didn't want her to identify him. He didn't like his orders anymore than Leilani did. But it had to be done. She'd seen too much. The boss wasn't taking any chances. "You hungry?"

"Starved."

Her arms appeared thinner, and there were hollows under her eyes. She'd probably lost weight in the three days she'd been here. Most of the time he kept her drugged, so she was easier to handle. Once she ate, she'd be sleepy again from the sedative mixed in the rice. He wrapped her hands around a bowl of rice and Spam.

She took it eagerly and began to cram it into her mouth. He gave her a cup of water as well. "Can I have another blanket? I'm freezing."

This deep in the rain forest, the temperature was hovering around fifty-five, and the cabin had no heat. The cold and damp pierced deeply. "I'll get you an extra blanket once I tie you up again."

Tears spilled down her dirty cheeks. "Please, just let me go. I won't tell anyone I was kidnapped."

He knew her better than that. She spilled her guts to anyone who would listen. She would have to die sooner or later. But not yet. The boss had plans for her.

*A*nnie clicked *save* and leaned back in her chair. She rubbed the aching muscles at her neck, then glanced at the palm-tree clock on her desk. Nearly three. She'd skipped lunch so she should be able to go in another half hour. CeCe would still be at work, but by the time Annie hooked up with Mano and got to Kapa Technologies, she would just be getting off. Anxiety gnawed at her stomach. Where was Leilani? Surely she was okay. Annie had to keep believing that. She shut down her computer and went down the hall to tell Gina she was leaving at three thirty.

Her boss was kneeling on the floor with a watering pail in her hand. She saw Annie. "All done?"

"Yep. It's saved on the server for you to look at." She stepped forward and held out her hand to help Gina to her feet.

The older woman took her hand and struggled up. "I need to lose about ten pounds," she muttered.

"You look great," Annie said.

Gina smiled. "You're nothing if not loyal, Annie. The last time I looked great was when I was your age. See these wrinkles?" She pointed to her eyes and smiled. "They show my age rather effectively." She nodded toward the picture hanging on her wall. "On the day I was married, my husband said I looked like Aphrodite. I'm afraid I'm more like Medusa these days."

"You're beautiful still." Annie turned to look at the picture, thinking it was Gina's wedding picture, but it was an artist's rendition of Greek gods and goddesses. On a shelf below the picture were several figurines of the same deities. "Who's this one?" she asked, picking up a marble figurine.

"That's Athena. Isn't she beautiful? This is Apollo." She picked up another figurine made from jade. "This is Nemesis. I picked her up in Athens last year. Isn't she exquisitely made? I collect Greek mythology figurines to remember my heritage. She's my favorite."

Annie put it back and nodded. That answered the speculation in the office about Gina's background and accent. "I was just leaving." Gina could talk all day about her passion for Greek mythology, and Annie didn't have time to listen. It was kind of cute though. The scientist enamored with myths.

Gina's smile faded, and her expression grew more businesslike. "Jillian needs some help with her data. It's not coming out right, and I suspect she has an Excel formula wrong. Can you give her a hand before you go?"

"I really don't have time today. Can it wait? Leilani still isn't home, and I wanted to talk to her best friend."

Gina studied her face. "Aren't the police working on it? What do you hope to accomplish?"

"The detective in charge still thinks she's just off with friends."

"That's happened before, hasn't it? I remember about a year ago when she left for a couple of weeks."

"But she called then. We've heard nothing from her." She told Gina about the weird phone call.

"I think you're making a mountain out of a molehill. Kids play with those machines all the time. Even Jason used to have one. I confiscated it when he played a practical joke on his grandmother. I need you to get your head together. The results of this project need to be ready for publication next month. I hate to play hardball, Annie, but some of our grant money is riding on this."

"I know, I know." Annie went toward the door. "I'll give her a hand for a few minutes. I skipped lunch though, so I could leave early."

Gina sighed. "Okay, you can leave at three thirty today, but I need you to start focusing. I'd find Leilani for you if I could, but sometimes we have to leave it to the professionals."

Annie just nodded and went down the hall toward Jillian's office. Jillian wore a frown and chewed on a pencil as she stared at her computer screen.

"I got the data entered," Annie told her. "It's on the server."

Jillian's face cleared. "You're too efficient. Think you can do anything with this computer model?"

"Let me take a look." Annie sat in the chair Jillian vacated and pulled up the database. She began to go through the lines of data. She was so tired that the numbers began to run together. Her head throbbed, and she pressed her temple as she looked at the screen.

"I don't see anything," she said finally.

"Me neither. But it's not working right."

Annie glanced at her watch. It was time for her to go. "I'll look at it in the morning when I'm fresh."

"I hope to have it figured out by then." Jillian sighed. "Gosh, can you believe the tension here lately? Monica has been biting everyone's heads off."

"She's mad at me."

"I know. Watch your back. I think she's out for your job."

"I suspected as much. The way I feel today, she could have it." Annie smiled to show she was joking. She went toward the door. "Good luck with the model. If you don't have it back up by tomorrow, I'll look at it again."

She stopped at Gina's door. "I'm gone. See you tomorrow."

Gina looked up and nodded. "Try to get some rest tonight. You look terrible."

"I'll try." Annie stepped into the hall. Her cell phone rang, and she grabbed at it. "Hello."

"Are you alone?" The whispered voice sounded like Tomi. Her chest tightened, and she caught her breath.

"I'm just heading to the car." She continued on toward the door.

"I need to see you."

It had to be Tomi, though he seemed hoarse. Maybe he was just trying to disguise his voice. She clung to her hope. "Tomi?"

"Who else?" He chuckled.

The laugh convinced her, and joy surged through her heart. Her brother was alive. She couldn't quite take it in. "Where do you want to meet?" She peered at her watch. Mano would be at the house in fifteen minutes.

"How about the Place of Refuge? Seems appropriate somehow."

"Are you that far away?"

There was a long pause on the other end of the line. "I can't tell you where I am. But meet me there in three hours. And bring the bankbook."

"Tomi, let me talk to Leilani," she ordered. The phone clicked. "Tomi? Tomi?" She shut the phone with a snap. She would see them both soon enough. She raced for her SUV. Mano would be furious if she left without him. Tomi didn't say to come alone, and he'd been in contact with Mano, so surely it was all right to bring him along. What would she say to her father? It might be best if he didn't know anything about this until she actually saw Tomi with her own eyes.

She rolled down the window and inhaled the salty air. The sunshine seemed brighter, and the air even more fragrant. Tomi had called her. She had to believe it was really her brother. Surely no one else could sound that much like him. And she was going to see him and Leilani in just a few hours. She wanted to laugh, to sing, maybe jump out of the vehicle and do cartwheels. Her smile broadened. Things were looking up at last.

Mano glanced at his watch. He was going to be late to meet Annie. He'd wandered all over the compound without seeing Noah. The ramshackle house Noah had rented was deserted, so Mano traipsed from the edge of the cliff that looked out over the water to the inner jungle area on the north side of the subdivision. A few people had eyed him strangely, but no one challenged his right to be here.

He turned to walk back to his car and found a figure standing in the path. Evan Chun, dressed in a tropical linen suit, was smiling as he blocked Mano's way to the road where his vehicle was parked.

"Lieutenant Oana, I didn't expect to find you here."

Busted. The smirk on the developer's face told him Chun was enjoying Mano's discomfiture. "I was just walking around," he muttered.

"Looking for real estate? I have a couple of properties for sale."

Mano decided to play along. "Maybe. I've thought of moving to the Big Island. The remoteness of this area is nice, but I'm not sure I could get along with having to catch rainwater."

Chun blinked as though he hadn't expected that response. He swept his hand over the area. "I'll give you a hint, Lieutenant. This is all going to change soon." He dropped his voice. "There will be every modern convenience and luxury houses that will rival those in Kohala."

Mano lifted his brows. "You've managed to get utilities out here?" Developers had tried for years to take advantage of this area. It held a wild beauty that called to the soul, but the lack of water and electricity put most people off.

"It's coming, it's coming." Chun managed to look modest and triumphant at the same time.

Mano had heard that one before. The Hawaiian Ocean View Estate project, known on the island as HOVE, was supposed to have accomplished something similar. It fell through, and the property values in that area were still in the few-thousand-dollars-an-acre range, though residents didn't seem to mind.

Evan continued to smile. "Better grab some acreage while you can."

"What all do you own?"

"About half of Aloha Shores's properties. But I'm working on picking up a few more properties. I have a particularly nice lot that overlooks the shore break. Want to take a look?"

It might not hurt to cultivate the connection to Chun. "I'd love to, but I have an engagement I'm late for. Can I have a rain check?"

"How about tomorrow? I have another client interested in that property, and he's looking at it on Wednesday."

"I'm free at ten tomorrow." He might get another chance to look around for Noah. The man had to be around here somewhere.

"Nine would be better."

"Fine. I'll meet you at the front gate at nine." Mano began to walk back toward his car. It was probably a waste of time, but he was curious what Chun had up his sleeve and whether he and his development plans were associated with Noah's casino people. From what Chun had said, he must know about the casino project. He wondered how many people the man had milked of their property for a song. But maybe he was judging Chun too harshly. The sellers were probably all too glad to unload their property and get back to civilization.

He drove along the black macadam road toward the Tagama house. It wasn't far from the Aloha Shores estates. He thought again about what Noah had said about the casino project. Maybe today would be a good time to ask Annie if she'd been approached to sell the family property.

Annie was standing in the yard when he pulled up. She was smiling, and he suddenly noticed how white and even her teeth were. Her dark eyes sparkled, and there was a flush to her cheeks. His own lips curved in an answering smile as he ran down the window. "Hey, what's up? Did Leilani call?" Her smile faltered at his question, then came blasting back at a full wattage.

She shook her head, and her silky hair swung against her cheek. "No, but Tomi did. We're supposed to meet him and Leilani at the Place of Refuge."

"Leilani is with him?

She bit her lip. "He didn't say, but I'm sure she is."

He hoped she was right. "We'd better get going. It will be

almost dark by the time we get there. What's he thinking? Couldn't
we have met somewhere closer?"

"I asked him about it, but he didn't say why he wanted to meet
there." She hopped in the car and fastened her seat belt. "I left a
note for Father and told him we'd be gone until late." Her blush
deepened. "I told him I was going to dinner with you."

"I guess I'd better buy you dinner then, to make an honest
woman out of you." He grinned and dropped the gearshift into
drive. From the corner of his eye, he saw her biting her lip and
knew he'd embarrassed her even more. Still, he began to look forward to spending the evening with her.

"You don't have to do that," she said in a low voice.

"I want to. We'll see Tomi, then stop for dinner at the Kilauea
Restaurant." The restaurant at Volcano was renowned for its
unusual dishes like antelope and rabbit. The thought made his
mouth water, and he realized he hadn't eaten since breakfast.

"That's too expensive," she protested.

"You're worth it," he told her with a grin. "Besides, I'm on
vacation."

"Some vacation."

"You don't know the half of it." He told her about the conversation with Evan Chun. "Has he approached you to sell?"

"Not that I know of. If he had, we might be tempted." She
looked away.

"Money troubles?" he asked cautiously.

"You don't know how badly." A long pause stretched between
them before she continued. "Father took out a mortgage on the
property without telling me and spent it on some research equipment. We've never been able to get caught up, and the bank is
threatening to foreclose."

Noah had implied that the Tagama land was part of the casino
project. Was that because Tomi had already negotiated to sell it?
Mano decided to probe. "Who holds the deed to the property?"

She raised her eyebrows but answered him. "My father, of course. Why?"

He shrugged. "I'm still wondering how Tomi got two million dollars."

She inhaled sharply. "You're thinking he might have sold our property?" She was shaking her head as she asked the question. "Even if he had the power, it wouldn't be worth that much. Not so close to the volcano."

He decided to tell her what he knew. "It might be if a casino wanted to build on it."

"What are you talking about?"

He told her what Noah had said.

"But that's crazy! Why would they build a casino there? Another lava flow could happen along at any time. Besides, there are prettier locations."

"But the volcanoes are a huge draw. And there's no other night life around. It would probably be a huge success."

"It doesn't matter anyway. The deed is in my father's name. Tomi couldn't touch it."

"Unless he forged your father's name."

"So now he's guilty of espionage *and* forgery? I thought you were Tomi's friend! I should never have brought you along tonight." She folded her arms and hunched against the door.

He wished she'd trust him. Her window was partway down, and the wind ruffled her shiny dark hair. He could barely keep his eyes on the road and wondered what had come over him. She was like a little sister, so why was being in her presence so exhilarating?

"I'm not an ogre, Annie. I care about your family. Whatever trouble Tomi is in, I want to help get him—and you—out of it. I've got some savings. Let me loan you the money to get the mortgage caught up."

She shook her head violently. "I wouldn't think of it. We'll figure a way out of it." The laugh that escaped her lips held no real mirth. "With the two million dollars in that bankbook of Tomi's, our money troubles would be over."

"Don't go spending any of that. I'm afraid whoever gave it to him is going to come looking for it. You could be in a world of hurt if they can't get it."

"I was joking." She turned the radio down.

He nodded and fell silent. The time flew by as they drove north. He took Highway 160 toward *Puuhonua o Honaunau*. Place of Refuge. He stopped the car in the parking lot and got out. It had been years since he'd been here, and he glanced around at the site as if seeing it for the first time.

In ancient times, *kapu* law ruled the lives of the commoners. If a commoner broke one of the laws—like if a man ate with a woman, or a person allowed his shadow to fall on a chief—the penalty was death by club, strangulation, spear, or fire. In severe cases, the offender's entire family would be put under a death sentence. The communities had great incentive to make sure the laws were obeyed, because the Hawaiians believed the gods retaliated against lawbreakers by sending tsunamis, volcanic flows, and earthquakes.

A condemned man's only chance of survival was to flee to a place of refuge and perform the rituals mandated by the *kahuna pule*, the priest. Only then could he return home with no repercussions. This site had also been the location for the *Ali'i's*, or the chieftain's, palace. Standing on this site, he imagined what it must have been like to run for one's life to this place. Coconut trees dotted the landscape, and he could see the Great Wall, a structure a thousand feet long, ten feet high, and seventeen feet thick. It originally separated the Place of Refuge from the palace grounds.

The noticeable stillness made him think no one was here. He turned as Annie joined him. "Did he say where he'd be?"

She shook her head and cupped her hands around her mouth. "Tomi!"

Mano hid his grin. Her tone said, *Don't mess around.* She was like one of the Hawaiian hens calling to her chick. "It doesn't feel like anyone is here."

"He said he'd be here." She advanced across the fine golden sand toward the water. "You check out the open-air buildings. I'll look around the *hale*."

"Okay, Mom," he said.

Her eyes widened. "Sorry, I'm being bossy, aren't I? Tomi hates it too."

"I didn't say I hated it. I like your spunk."

A smile tugged at her lips. "Nothing usually gets done unless I do it. You have a better idea?"

"Nope. Lead on, *kahuna*."

She chuckled. "I'm not wise. But I want to find my brother and sister, though I might wring both their necks when I do."

Examining her face in the last rays of the fading sunshine, Mano saw only love and commitment. Annie was one of those people who gave her whole heart to her family. He wondered what it would be like to be the center of her world.

Ten

The soft sand underfoot muffled their steps. It was almost sunset, and the coconut trees had a golden glow as they swayed over the beach. Sea turtles munched near the canoe landing. Though the surroundings should have soothed her, Annie's nerves were on full alert.

Only birds called from the trees. The deserted beach took her aback. This time of day, people usually hung around to watch the sunset, but Mano's car was the only vehicle in the lot. They passed the reconstructed *Hale-o-Keawe*, a kind of mausoleum that originally contained the bones of twelve chiefs. Bones were considered to have *manu*, or supernatural power. The thatched structure was surrounded by a stick fence, and several *ki'i* stood guard. The fierce faces on the wooden statues added to Annie's sense of unease. A few full-scale models of ancient houses and temples surrounded the mausoleum. Tomi could be in any one of them.

"Tomi!" Annie shouted again. The loudness of her voice felt out of place on the sacred grounds.

Mano seemed at ease. "Have you ever seen the lava tube just past the caves with the bones?"

She shook her head. "I haven't come here often."

"Me, Bane, and Kaia used to run through the lava tube and jump off into the water below. That's how I got this." He pointed to a faint scar on his forehead. "The ceiling in the lava tube is shorter than you think. I'll have to show you sometime."

He almost acted like he was enjoying being with her, but she

knew better than to let herself hope. The glamorous type like
Leilani was more his style. But how she wished it were different.
She limped toward the water.

Mano turned back to the mausoleum. "Maybe he walked here.
Let's check inside."

Annie didn't want to go in there. She knew she was being silly,
but chicken skin prickled her back. She forced her feet to move forward, to follow Mano. He must have sensed her trepidation,
because he stopped and took her hand. His warm fingers closed
around hers, and the shock stiffened her backbone and strength-
ened her courage. She squeezed his hand. "*Mahalo,*" she whispered.

He smiled. They walked toward the mausoleum again. "I don't
like this," she muttered.

"Me neither. It feels wrong. Probably nerves. I've never been
here when there weren't half a dozen tourists gawking." He gave her
fingers another gentle squeeze. They reached the door to the *Hale-
o-Keawe.* Mano tried the door, but it was locked. "He must not be
in there." He looked behind him toward the canoe landing and
frowned. "Someone is paddling ashore. Maybe it's Tomi."

Annie jerked around. The sun was in her eyes, and all she could
see was golden light bathing the water. She squinted and shaded her
eyes with her hand. "I can't tell." She pulled her hand from his and
ran toward the landing.

"Annie, wait!"

She ignored Mano's call and flew across the sand. Her feet sank,
and the sand sucked at her boots. In her hurry, she stepped in the
water rather than balancing on the rocks that thrust up out of the
sand. Waves surged over the tops of her boots and washed sand
inside. She reached the rocky landing just seconds before Mano
grabbed her arm. She shook him off and turned eagerly into the
fading sun. The sound of the kayak's paddles swished through the
water and mingled with the static of the surf.

The boat scraped bottom. Mano sprinted forward to grab hold

of the kayak while Annie stared into the face of the man in the boat. Her brother, Tomi. He had their father's build—slim with long thin muscles. He'd evidently given up trying to grow the sparse mustache, because his face was smooth now. She noted his black hair needed a trim. Dressed in khaki shorts and a T-shirt, he really was there in the flesh.

Her lips parted, but no words emerged. Her gaze locked with Tomi's. His impish grin seemed tentative, as though he was waiting for her to chew him out, but all she wanted to do was run her fingers over his face and touch him to assure herself he was really alive.

She ran forward, her feet slipping on the volcanic rock under the water. "Tomi?" she croaked before her throat closed, and she couldn't utter another word. The brother she thought dead was standing there in the twilight. He was thinner than she remembered, probably by twenty pounds at least. He wriggled out of the kayak and stepped into her arms. She buried her face against his chest. He smelled faintly of perspiration and sea salt. But he was real, oh so real. No figment of her imagination, no dream, no spirit. Though her communion with God had been nonexistent lately, thankfulness welled up inside her.

Tomi held her tightly. Mano stepped away to give them privacy. His chin rested on the top of her head. His chest rumbled under her ear, and she realized he was laughing. She lifted her head and stared up at him. "What's so funny?"

"I never thought I'd see my levelheaded little sister show such emotion. I'm usually just told what to do." His dark eyes were amused but held a trace of tenderness that softened his words.

"Is that how you see me—a colorless, emotionless drill sergeant?" Funny how it was impossible to gauge how someone else viewed a person. If someone had asked her, she would have said her family thought of her as the strong one who made sure things got done. They should have realized she loved them more than life itself. Hadn't she devoted herself completely to her family? She'd chosen the career her father wanted, let Leilani outshine her at every turn, and catered to Tomi's whims without a murmur.

"Sorry, sis. I didn't mean it that way." He dropped his arms and stepped around her out of the water that lapped at their ankles.

She glanced into his face. "Leilani didn't come with you?"

He went still. "I haven't seen Leilani in more than a year, Annie. I told Mano she wasn't with me."

A weight descended onto Annie's chest, and she couldn't speak. Her fingers clutched at Tomi's shirt. She'd pinned her hopes on finding both her siblings tonight. "Your cell phone cut out, and he didn't understand what you said."

"I had no idea what he was talking about."

"Where could she be?" she whispered. "She hasn't been seen since Thursday." Her gaze searched her brother's face.

Tomi's eyes narrowed. "I don't know, but she'll have to answer to me when we find her. She knows better than to worry everyone."

"What if something's happened to her?"

"You know how thoughtless she is. She'll turn up."

"We have to find her."

"We will. I've got problems too, though." He went toward the buildings, where Mano waited.

She followed him as he approached Mano. Her steps slowed when she saw the two men facing one another. Mano's fists were clenched at his side, and his jaw was so tight she expected a growl to emanate from his teeth.

Annie joined them. She put her hand on Mano's arm and found it hard and tense.

Mano didn't seem to realize she was there. "I think we're due an explanation," he said tightly.

"Leilani isn't with him," Annie murmured. Mano cast a quick glance her way, and she felt his tension ease.

"I'm sorry. I know you were hoping to find her too." He focused his gaze on Tomi again. "We're still waiting on your explanation. Where have you been all this time? Why did you let us think you were dead?"

Tomi's smile faltered. "I'd rather explain it to all of you at once. Let's wait until we get home and have Father there too. Did you bring the bankbook?"

"I have it in the car," Annie said. "In my handbag." She bit her lip at the quick glance Mano threw her way. She hadn't told him Tomi told her to bring it. "I'll go get it."

"We'll all go." Tomi held her hand, and they walked in step toward the parking lot with Mano trailing behind.

"You're limping," Tomi said. "Are you okay?"

"Just a little accident." She'd tell him later. She could sense Mano seething, and her own emotions boiled with a mixture of elation, despair, and puzzlement. Tomi didn't seem eager to explain what was going on. But the pain in his eyes tugged at her heart. Though he was older, she'd always taken care of his every need. She wanted to soothe away the little-boy-lost look in his face. She itched to get him home and fix him something to eat. He needed fattening up. She'd worry about Leilani later.

They reached the parking lot. "I'll get my handbag." She went to the passenger side. The window was shattered, and tiny bits of glass lay on her seat. "Mano," she said in a faltering voice. "My handbag is gone."

He joined her. "We should have locked it in the trunk." He stooped and peered inside. "Doesn't look like anything else is missing. All my CDs are here."

Tomi pounded on the trunk lid. "No! Why did you leave it in the car?" The color had drained from his face. "I was counting on you, Annie."

Annie had never seen her brother scared, but she saw fear in the perspiration on his forehead and in the way his Adam's apple bobbed. His fear terrified her as well. "What's wrong, Tomi? What kind of trouble have you gotten into?"

Tomi managed a smile that held a trace of his usual bravado. "We have to get that bankbook back. Then things will be fine."

"Can't you just call the bank and freeze the account?" Mano put in. "You're making this harder than it has to be."

Tomi sighed. "You don't get it, do you, buddy? I can't just waltz into the bank. I'll be shot before I get to the front of the line."

Shot. What was Tomi into? Annie was almost afraid to know. "I'll call Sam. We need help."

"No!" Tomi shook his head. "No cops. You're going to have to help me."

There was so much he wasn't saying. "You're scaring me," she whispered. "What about that money, Tomi? How did you get it?"

He glanced around. "We have to get out of here. We're too exposed."

Annie began to panic. "What can we do?"

Tomi rubbed his forehead. "I don't know, I don't know." He stared at her. "Help me, Annie. I don't know what to do."

Annie pressed her fingers to her throbbing head. "Let me think." His expression paled as he watched her anxiously. "They won't be looking for a woman," Annie said. "Mother has an old wig in the garage. You could dress like a woman."

"They'll be looking for disguises." Tomi's eyes narrowed. "But not two women. You have to go with me."

"Don't involve Annie in your messes," Mano interrupted. His dark eyes held deep worry.

"He needs my help," Annie said.

Tomi nodded. "Right, and it's her fault the bankbook is missing. Besides, no one will recognize us. It's a perfect plan." He frowned. "But we have to move fast before the thief gets my money. The bank is closed tonight, but I need to be there when it opens in the morning."

"Your money? It sounds like it belongs to someone else—and they want it back," Mano put in.

"Not exactly." Tomi chewed on his lip. "Come on, let's go." He reached through the broken window and unlocked the back door. He opened it and got in.

Annie opened the passenger door and started to sweep the glass bits from the seat.

"Don't do that," Mano said. "You'll get cut." He gently moved her out of the way and grabbed a CD holder from the floor and used it to scrape at the glass. "Why don't you sit in the back with your brother? I'm sure you want to touch him and make sure he's real."

"How did you know?"

"I know sisters. That's what Kaia would want to do." He grinned down at her, then opened the back door and let her slip in beside Tomi.

Annie laced her fingers through her brother's as they drove back toward Pahala. "Some of our mother's clothes might fit you," Annie said. "There are some in the garage with that wig."

"I always knew your practicality would come in handy," Tomi said, squeezing her hand.

Annie closed her eyes. Bossy, levelheaded, practical. She was learning more and more about herself all the time, and she wasn't liking what she was discovering. Did everyone see her the same way? No wonder men weren't interested. Her gaze went to Mano. She'd never attract someone like him.

"You're quiet," Tomi said. "Are you mad at me?"

"Just trying to take it all in," she said. "Why did you let us think you were dead?"

"Ah, Annie, I'm sorry. I was stupid. I'll explain when we get home." He sounded unutterably sad and weary.

"And about Leilani? Where is she? Tell me the truth, Tomi," she said. "Where is our sister? Has something happened to her? Did you get her involved in something?"

"I swear I don't know. I haven't seen her since I left here." He fell silent, then shifted. "You haven't gotten a call demanding money for her release, right? So it's not about a ransom."

"No call. Is that good or bad, Tomi? Does this involve you and the money?"

"I don't think so. I hope not." He wasn't meeting her gaze. "Have you talked to her friends?"

"Not yet. We thought the police could handle it, and then we thought she might be with you. We were going to go see CeCe and then you phoned."

Mano's voice spoke out of the darkness. "Annie got a call that said you'd brought this on your family."

She heard Tomi gasp. He lurched away from her. "Dear God, help us all," he whispered. "What have I done?"

Annie wanted to huddle in the corner and let someone else take care of this. She wanted her mother to come back and save them all. But she would have to find the strength to protect her family on her own. The force of circumstances had begun to grind away the old shell around her, the mask she'd worn all her life, like lava pounded into sand by the force of the waves. She might never be the same again.

Eleven

A thousand thoughts ran through Mano's head. Tomi had always been a free spirit, ready for an adventure. That was part of his infectious charm. And Mano was always right there beside him. Until now. Mano's mistake, which he believed had cost a friend his life, dampened Mano's adventurous spirit. Finding out that Tomi was alive and well had relieved his guilt but deepened his sense that life wasn't only about fun and adventure.

He glanced in the rearview mirror to see Annie with her forehead pressed against Tomi's arm. She was going to think she had to fix this, even if it was more than she was capable of doing. He dragged his attention back to his driving and pulled into the Tagama's driveway. Light spilled from the garage windows, but the house was dark.

"Good, looks like Pop is hard at work. How's his research coming?" Tomi sounded distracted.

"Fine. He says it's ready to publish." Annie turned in the seat. "What is going *on*? My head is in a whirl. I want to know what you've done, Tomi. I can't make it right if I don't know what it is."

Tomi shifted in the darkness of the backseat. "I don't think you can fix it anyway, sis."

Mano didn't like the sound of that. Tomi had returned for a reason, but he didn't seem eager to give them any answers. If Mano had to ferret out the truth without Tomi's help, then that's what he'd do. He had to know for his own peace of mind. Living with the images of Tomi's white face in the water had haunted his dreams for months.

He turned off the car and then glanced at the clock on the dash. It was time for him to eat something. He leaned over and extracted a protein bar from the glove box. "Anyone want one?" he asked.

Tomi and Annie shook their heads. "Let me tell Father you're here," Annie said. She opened her door.

"Wait, I want to surprise him." Tomi hopped out with her.

Annie hesitated, then smiled. "He'll be glad to see you. We were both afraid to hope what Mano had said was really true."

Her brother slung his arm around her, and they walked toward the house. Mano swallowed the snack in two bites and followed. He had to hear this, even if he might not like what Tomi was about to reveal. Annie reached the outside door and stopped. She was staring at the door, which hung on only one hinge. A large hole had been busted through by the doorknob.

Mano shouldered past her and stepped inside. "Edega?" he called. The chair at the table had a broken leg and lay upside down, but the rest of the office didn't seem to be disturbed. The door to the house stood open.

"Father?" Annie ran past him. Her head whipped from side to side as she tried to spot her father.

"Go with her," Mano told Tomi. Tomi nodded and followed. Mano began to search behind filing cabinets and under tables, but there was no sign of Edega Tagama.

Tomi came back out a few minutes later. "The house has been ransacked. I bet they were looking for the bankbook. Or for me. No sign of Pop, though."

Annie clutched her hands together. "Maybe he wasn't here when they broke in."

"Why is the chair knocked over?" Tomi's gaze shifted uneasily.

Annie's dark eyes focused on her brother's face. "You'd better tell us what's going on, Tomi. This is related to you somehow, isn't it?"

Tomi looked away. He lifted the chair from the floor and put it back in place.

"Answer me!" Annie moved to block his path.

He rubbed his eyes. "Probably."

"You've got to tell us what's going on." Annie pushed her hair out of her face. "Do you know where our father is?"

Mano watched Tomi. He avoided Annie's gaze and busied himself with tidying up the garage. To Mano, he seemed a man plagued with guilt.

Annie's cell phone rang, and they all jumped. Her gaze locked with Mano's, and he read her panic. "Just answer it," he said softly. "Stay calm and if someone has him, try to arrange to get him back."

"I'm scared," she whispered.

"You can do it."

She exchanged gazes with her brother. "You answer it, Tomi."

He shook his head. "No one knows I'm here. I can't tip them off. You've always been strong, Annie. You can handle it."

The insistent chirp came again. She glanced at the phone, and relief flooded her face. "It's Fawn," she whispered. She flipped open the phone. "Hi, Fawn. Yes, I'm fine." She listened a few more moments. "Okay. I'll see you when you get back then." She hung up and turned to Mano. "Now what?" she asked Mano.

"Now we call the police."

"No!" Tomi's eyes were hollow. "You can't do that."

"This is out of your hands, Tomi. Your father's life is at stake."

"I know," Tomi muttered. He sank onto a chair and put his head in his hands. "I've been so stupid. You're both going to hate me."

Annie knelt by his chair and pulled one of his hands down. "I could never hate you, Tomi. You're my brother. I still can't believe you're alive."

"Maybe not for long." He raised his head and stared at her, then glanced up at Mano. "Even you can't help me with this one, buddy."

Things were beginning to click for Mano. "It's about that girl, isn't it? The Iranian girl—what was her name?"

"Afsoon." He gave a slight smile. "Her name means *spell* or *bewitchment*. It seems pretty appropriate right now."

"Wasn't her father some kind of diplomat?"

"Yeah. He was part of the Iranian consulate." He gave a rueful smile. "I was such a chump. First time in my life I ever felt like that about a girl. Once she had me hooked, she told me she'd been ordered to get close to me to find out when the navy was moving in to rescue the two prisoners. If she failed to deliver, she was going to be killed. I swallowed it."

"You told her when we were coming. That's why there was so much enemy fire. Were you really hit, or was it all part of the plan?"

"I gave her a different time, but she figured it out from something I said." He shook his head. "I can't believe I was so stupid. I remember being hit by a bullet and you dragging me to the water. I woke up in their custody. They wanted more information from me. When I refused, they told me they'd planted that bankbook with the two million dollars, and they'd expose me as a spy if I didn't give them what they wanted."

"I remember trying to tow you to the boat. You were unconscious. I don't remember letting you go, but I must have."

"You were acting strange that day. Kind of forgetful. Were you okay?"

Mano didn't answer. He wasn't ready to go there. When he'd awoken on the boat, he was sure he'd saved his friend. The censure in his commanding officer's eyes nearly killed him. He told Mano Tomi was presumed dead. At the time, no one knew what had happened, but Mano soon learned he'd suffered from his first diabetic reaction. The guilt plaguing him had almost done him in. All over a girl.

"A spy," Annie whispered. "You didn't give them more information, did you?"

"No, I got out of there with Afsoon's help. She had some feelings for me even if she used me." He squeezed his eyes shut. "She was killed helping me get away."

"Oh no, Tomi, I'm so sorry." Annie pressed his hand to her cheek.

"So they're still after information from you?" Mano asked. "What information?"

Tomi looked away. "I need to get that bankbook and give them back their money. Then maybe I can go to the navy and see if I can get out of this mess. But if I go with that threat of blackmail hanging over my head, I'll be court-martialed."

"They'd lock you up and throw away the key," Mano said.

Tomi nodded. "We have to get that money."

Annie looked out the window. "There's a car parked in front of the house. A big Lincoln." Glass shattered in the window, and she sprang back.

"Get down!" Mano grabbed her arm and pulled her to the floor. Peering over the windowsill, he saw the black car speed away. He glanced at the shattered glass and saw a rock with a paper attached by a rubber band. "What's this?" He grabbed the rock and pulled the paper loose.

Letters cut from magazines had been glued to make a collage of words. YOU KNOW WHAT WE WANT. The words gave him a chill. He heard Tomi groan.

"This is my fault—I'm putting you all in danger!" Tomi backed away, then turned and dashed out the door.

"Wait!" Mano ran after him but stumbled over a chair leg lying in the way.

Annie jumped up as if to run after him, but Mano grabbed her arm and pulled her back. "Let me handle this." He ran into the yard, but Tomi had disappeared. He went back inside the garage to join Annie. "He's gone."

"I'm scared." She hugged her arms around herself. "Leilani is gone, and now Father is missing as well."

"He might have gotten away. Let's look around before we call Sam. Maybe there's a clue to who did this."

He took her hand, and instead of pulling away like he expected, her fingers curled around his. A warm feeling settled under his ribs. He squeezed her fingers, and she still didn't let go. They walked around the side of the house to the backyard. The sound of the surf had a cold, angry tone, ominous as it boomed against the lava rocks. He didn't want to suggest they look for Edega in the water, but Annie led him that direction.

As they neared the shore, he saw a figure sitting on the black sand. Edega had his back against a lava rock and was looking out to sea with a pensive expression.

Annie dropped Mano's hand and ran forward. "Father, what are you doing down here? You scared me."

Edega seemed older, shrunken somehow. He got slowly to his feet. "Some men broke down the door. We're in trouble, Annie."

"I know," she whispered.

"I don't think you do. They say Tomi must give them what they want, or they will kill all of us."

Mano fixed Edega a cup of tea and lit some incense, hoping the familiarity of Edega's favorite things would calm him. He waited until the older man's hands quit shaking before he went to look for Annie. He stepped outside into the backyard and walked slowly down toward the water. Someone needed to be called, but he wasn't sure who. The navy? The FBI? Which would be most likely to help them solve this mystery without putting the family in more danger? Tomi needed to 'fess up and face the consequences of what he'd done. This web was of Tomi's own making.

Mano was still trying to come to grips with the realization that he hadn't harmed his friend. But the fact remained that he could have. His disease had put his friend and the whole mission in jeopardy. He was going to have to make a decision soon about his career, if the navy didn't make it for him. He loved the navy, and the thought of having to walk away from it made him feel he was sinking in black quicksand. Could there even be a future for him outside the navy? His case was under review, and while they might allow him to stay in the service, it wasn't likely. And he'd definitely have to give up his beloved SEALS.

Maybe he could start a dive operation. He rejected the idea almost as soon as it was born. He couldn't do anything where other people's lives depended on him. If he harmed someone, he'd never be able to live with himself. He saw Annie sitting at the edge of the water. She sat clasping her arms around her knees. He felt as lonely and abandoned as she appeared.

Annie looked at the sea rolling into the shore. She was as lost and aimless as the flotsam rolling in with the tide. What had her brother gotten them into? She usually had things under control and in order, and for the first time in her life, she knew she couldn't take care of this, couldn't make everything right for her brother and her father. And Leilani. Her entire family was disintegrating, and there was nothing she could do about it.

Wilson went to the edge of the water and barked. He kept it up for several minutes, and Annie saw a dorsal fin slice through the water. A dolphin. The sea mammal leaped into the air, and she recognized Nani. "So you've figured out how to call Nani, huh, Wilson?"

The bright wash of the moonlight touched the whitecaps as they rolled in to shore. She took off her boots and waded into the water. There was movement behind her, and she heard Mano call her name, but she ignored him and went farther into the waves. Wilson followed her. Nani chattered from deeper out and then swam in to meet them. Still dressed in her shorts and tank top, Annie dove into the water. Wilson clambered onto the dolphin's back. Annie grabbed the dolphin's dorsal fin and let Nani pull her out into the turquoise water.

The soothing warmth always comforted her, and it didn't fail to do that tonight. After swimming for a few minutes, she urged Nani toward the shore. Wilson slid off, and his sleek little body followed Annie to land. Her gaze swept the beach.

Mano sat on a large lava rock. At least he hadn't insisted she come in. She limped as she came across the rough rocks.

"Feel better?" he asked.

"Not really. We have to find out what's going on," she said. "What do we do next?" She sat beside him and pulled her socks on over her scarred feet, then put her boots back on.

Wilson climbed onto Mano's lap and shook himself, flinging water all over Mano. Mano didn't seem to mind. He tucked the mongoose inside his shirt. "I don't have any answers, Annie. Tomi might have some, but until he contacts us again, we're in the dark. We should call the police in on it. Or the navy or the FBI."

She absorbed his recommendation in silence. "What if that gets Tomi into even more trouble? It sounds like these guys mean business. Can we find out who they are? Maybe Tomi would tell you."

"I don't know how to get in touch with him," he pointed out. "His number comes up unknown."

She bit her lip. "Okay. But we can't call in the authorities yet. Not if we have a chance of getting Tomi out of this mess. We're going to have to figure this out on our own. I'm going to go see Leilani's friends first thing in the morning, if Tomi doesn't get in touch about meeting him at the bank. Maybe one of them can shed light on what's happened to her."

"You realize I'm going to be in a lot of trouble if I don't contact the navy, don't you?"

She hadn't considered that. "Why would they blame you?"

"I have a duty to turn in AWOL personnel. And to report anything I know about espionage."

She didn't like the term. "But he didn't really engage in espionage. He gave them nothing useful."

"He gave them enough to figure out the rest. He's got some explaining to do."

"I have to try to help him. And I can't do it alone. I need your help, Mano." What would she do if he refused? She knew nothing about this kind of thing. The silence seemed to last forever, and she realized she was asking him to betray his commitment to the navy. Mano was an honorable man. Maybe she was asking too much.

He finally sighed. "Okay. But only for a few days. If we haven't found your sister and gotten Tomi out of this mess by next weekend, I'm going to have to call in some help." He stood. "I should stay here tonight. I don't think you should be alone. You might be the next target."

She hadn't considered the possibility that she might be in danger. Shivering, she went toward the house. "I could stay with Fawn."

"Good idea."

Mano glanced at her, then quickly averted his eyes. "I can still read you, Mano. You have no intention of leaving us alone. You're planning to camp outside her house, aren't you?"

He grinned, and his teeth shone white in the moonlight. "Maybe."

"We'll be fine. I've got a gun I can take."

"The last thing we need is you with a gun."

"Hey, I know how to shoot," she protested.

"It won't hurt me to sleep in the car."

She didn't protest. Maybe knowing he was out there would keep the fear at bay. She took the cell phone he handed her and called Fawn. She got the answering machine. "I forgot she called to tell me she was leaving tonight. Her brother is getting married Saturday, and she flew to Honolulu to help with last-minute preparations." She punched in another number. "I can try Gina . . ." Her supervisor answered on the first ring and told her to come right over with her father.

"At least no one will think to look for you there," Mano said. "And Gina will make sure nothing happens to you."

Annie nodded. "Her son, Jason, used to be in the military. He's probably got weapons in the house."

"He looks the type."

Annie smiled at the scorn in Mano's voice. "Hey, at least you'll be able check out Aloha Shores. Do you still think Noah has something to do with this?"

"Maybe. I have an appointment there in the morning anyway."

"Evan?"

"Yeah."

She opened the door to the house. "I'll see you tomorrow then. I'll try to get the day off. After your appointment, we can start making the rounds to all Leilani's friends."

"Hey, I'll make sure you get to Gina's." He followed her into the house.

Relief flooded her. "*Mahalo*," she said softly. She went inside and told her father they were going to stay with Gina. He grumbled about it, but she realized he was more frightened than he wanted her to know. They packed an overnight bag, she grabbed Wilson, and they went to her Nissan.

Mano waved at her and started his car. Once his lights came on, she pulled onto the road and drove toward Gina's home. She wasn't totally alone with Mano behind her. If only they were together in the way she dreamed.

Twelve

ano rubbed his burning eyes. He hadn't closed his eyelids more than fifteen minutes at a stretch all night long. Though Annie had insisted she'd be okay, he had parked outside Gina's house just to be sure.

He grabbed the cooler from the backseat, took out his insulin, and prepared his shot. Everything in his life now revolved around this syringe and vials of medicine. It seemed so unfair, and he had begun to question why God had allowed this to happen. Had he not prayed enough, not served enough? He was thirty-two, and he didn't want to have to come up with a new plan for his life.

He got out and stretched the soreness out of his muscles. A movement caught his eye, and he saw Annie wave to him from the window of Gina's house. She motioned him to come to the door. The stubble on his chin was scratchy. He rubbed it with a self-conscious hand as he walked across the yard to the front door. A stranger might think he was a bum.

Annie met him at the door. "Want some breakfast?"

"Yeah, I'd better eat, or I'll be collapsing." He saw her puzzled frown and knew he should explain. He started to tell her but hesitated. He still didn't want her to know. Maybe because she'd always regarded him as strong and heroic. He missed that hero worship in her eyes. She'd never get it back if she knew he was a weakling now, dependent upon the power of insulin to keep him whole.

Wilson sniffed his boots and followed him to the kitchen. He trod terra-cotta tile floors. A faded version of the same color covered the walls, and he paused to admire several paintings of Greece and an arrangement of Greek figurines.

He stepped into the kitchen. The same warm color scheme welcomed the sunshine spilling through the large windows over the sink. The aroma of poi hashbrowns and Spam made his mouth water. When he was away from the islands, it was hard to find Spam on any menu, but it was a favorite here. The protein in it would balance the carbs in the poi.

A tiger cat under the table hissed when it saw Wilson. Wilson barked and started to move toward the cat. "No, you don't." Annie scooped up the mongoose. "You've terrorized poor Baxter enough. Behave yourself." Wilson draped himself over her arm and rested his head on her forearm.

"Have a seat." Her tone cheerful, Gina pointed to the table. She ladled food from the skillet onto three plates.

"Where's your dad?" he asked Annie.

"Still in bed. He and Gina were up late last night talking. Yesterday rattled him more than he wanted to let on, and they really hit it off. You hungry?"

"Starved. It smells good." He pulled out a chair and sat. Annie handed him a plate of food. He bowed his head for a silent prayer and opened his eyes to see Gina wearing a bemused smile.

"I didn't take you for a religious man," Gina said.

"God's been good to me." A stock answer—Mano hadn't been focusing on God's goodness lately.

"You don't seem the type to swallow all that mythology."

"The God I serve is still alive. He's no myth."

Gina lowered herself onto a chair. "So you are waiting for the pie-in-the-sky *someday*. What about enjoying this life today? Good food, friends, a job you enjoy. I think it says somewhere in your Bible to eat, drink, and be merry, for tomorrow you die."

"A proverb based on Ecclesiastes and Isaiah." Mano smiled and picked up his fork. "If you read the whole book, you'll see that it says there is nothing worth having under the sun except a relation-ship with God. That fun, food, and drink don't satisfy. And as for pie in the sky, even if there were no heaven, what God has given me in this life is enough of a reward."

"What's he given you that you couldn't have gotten on your own?" Gina's voice was beginning to get testy. "You seem a very bright man, one who could go far. I'd hate to see you waste your life by not focusing on your career."

Mano was conscious of Annie's interested stare. "Peace, con-tentment, a family I love."

Gina shrugged. "I've got that much. My career, my son. What more could I want?"

Mano thought she sounded a little wistful in spite of her asser-tion. "Inner peace no matter what comes is something you can't get on your own. Only God gives it." He should take his own advice. He'd been railing against God because of his diabetes instead of thanking him for his providence. It could have been worse. He could have died on the beach six months ago. He still had a hope and a future. So what if he had to take insulin? At least his condi-tion could be managed. He should thank the Lord for that.

And maybe God had a plan for his future career. Mano hadn't asked. He'd just been miffed about having to give up his own plans, his own determination. He'd always heard it said that when God closed a door, he opened a window somewhere else. While Mano hadn't seen so much as a glimmer of light under a cracked pane, he knew his God wouldn't fail to provide. He had to be patient.

Annie gave him a glass of orange juice. He hesitated before he took it. It was too much sugar with the poi as well. Maybe they wouldn't remark on it if he just left it on the table.

Jason wandered in. His hair was rumpled, and he was dressed in jersey shorts and a white T-shirt. The unappetizing aroma of sweat and beer rolled off him. Mano saw Annie turn her head, her nose wrinkling.

Gina appeared not to notice. "Your breakfast is on the stove."

He grunted and shuffled to the other side of the kitchen. "I hate poi hashbrowns," he grumbled.

"So don't eat them." His mother's tone was sharp.

Gina saw more than she let on, Mano decided. He finished the last bite of his breakfast. "I've got to go meet Evan Chun."

Gina's head jerked up. "Now?"

He nodded. "At the gate to the Shores. I'm looking at a property with him."

"You don't seem the type to catch rainwater and do without electricity."

"I can always get a generator like you have," he said. Though she wasn't actually in the Aloha Shores subdivision, she was in the same boat with utilities.

She made a face. "It's expensive. Not everyone is happy out here. But once you get used to it, you might like it I guess."

Mano wondered if she knew about Chun's plans. If she did, she didn't act like it. He couldn't imagine she would welcome that kind of change to her world. Though the property values would sky-rocket, all the residents out here would have to give up their privacy and anonymity. It wasn't his place to tell her, though. If Annie wanted to mention it, she could, but he wasn't sticking his nose into that mess. He had enough on his plate without worrying about real estate.

He rose. "*Mahalo* for breakfast. I'd better move along." His gaze lingered on Annie. The sunlight illuminated her face. Her eyes were brilliant this morning. Fringed with thick black lashes, they shone with inner light. He wished he knew what she was thinking, what she really thought of him now.

Annie walked him to the door. "Be careful," she said.

"No one's after me. Keep the door locked. Call me on my cell phone if anything happens. If Tomi calls."

Her brilliant eyes clouded. "I don't know what to think about

Tomi. I'm beginning to wonder if I've ever really known my own brother. I would never have imagined he could get involved with something like this."

"We all mess up," Mano said. He opened the door, stepped outside, and inhaled the scent of plumeria. He jogged to his car then walked down the lane. Chun's sleek black Cadillac was already parked at the gate. The hum of the car's engine was barely discernable over the sound of the flock of spotted doves that took flight and scolded him.

Chun ran his window down. "I was beginning to wonder if you were going to show. Hop in." His gaze went to Mano's car. "Looks like you've got some vandalism."

"Yeah, I'll get it fixed later today." Mano went around to the passenger side and got in the car. The plush leather seat enveloped him. It smelled new and expensive.

A diamond ring winked on Chun's pinkie finger as he wrenched the steering wheel around and turned into the gate. "This first property is a beauty. It's on a cliff overlooking the water." He drove along the rutted lane, through a stand of coconut palms, and past several cabins. "Here we are."

Mano got out and walked to the edge of the cliff. It was a beautiful spot. For a moment, he wished he really was in the market for property. He could envision the house of his dreams sitting on this lot and looking out over the rolling waves.

Chun let him look in silence at first, then joined him at the cliff's edge. "What do you think?"

"Great view." Mano hated to take up the man's time just to gain information and access to the Shores. He pushed the guilt away. He'd come this far, though, so he might as well go through with the plan. "How long have you owned property here?"

"Probably twenty years. I saw the potential when it was still arid and deserted."

"It's still pretty arid. The volcanic rock is hard on the vegetation."

"But it's coming back."

"How much do you want for it?" Mano shocked himself by asking. Maybe he'd buy this after all. He had to settle somewhere eventually, though he wondered what he could do here. The navy was his life.

He could almost see the dollar signs in Chun's eyes. Chun nodded. "There's a full half acre here. You have right of way for a driveway."

"How much?" Mano asked again.

"Three hundred thousand."

He'd been expecting something in the neighborhood of fifteen thousand. "Are you nuts? You probably paid fifteen hundred for it, didn't you?"

Evan shrugged. "It will be worth six hundred thousand in another year."

Mano began to walk back to the car. "Get real. You'll never get that for it. Not out here."

"You'll see I know what I'm talking about when news of the casino and new subdivision breaks."

The mention of the casino was the opportunity Mano had been waiting on. "I've heard something about that. Who's behind it?"

"A company from Vegas called Banos LLC. They're known for their innovative structures. It's going to be a great boon for the island."

Mano had never heard of them. "When do they plan to start building?"

"They've already bought the land for the casino, and the ground breaking should be in about three months. They're still working on the peripheral designs for housing and a theme park. I'm buying up land for them as quickly as I can."

"Have you tried to buy the Tagama land or Gina's land yet?"

"I don't think that's any of your business." He nodded toward the view. "So what do you think?"

"I'll give you ten," Mano said.

Chun laughed. "I don't think so. If that's all you're willing to pay, we might as well go back now."

It was way out of Mano's price range. "Fine by me." He walked toward the car, but before he got in, he saw a man standing in the shade of a stand of trees. Noah. "Go on without me," he told Chun. He didn't wait for a reply and jogged toward Noah. Noah turned and ran. "Noah, wait!" Mano put on a burst of speed.

He was out of breath when he reached the tree where Noah had been standing. He paused and looked around. Where had he gone? He listened. A mynah squawked from the tree over his head. Then he heard the sound of running feet. He took off and followed the sound.

Noah was twenty feet ahead of him. "It's me, Mano," Mano called out.

Noah glanced back. His action caused him to stumble. He fell headlong onto the ground and banged his head against the trunk of a coconut palm tree. Mano reached him as Noah struggled to his knees. Noah's head was bleeding.

"You okay?" Mano knelt beside him.

"Fine." Noah muttered. He dabbed at the trickle of blood running down the side of his face. "I didn't want the other guy to see me."

"I was hoping to find you." Mano helped him to his feet.

Noah swiped his face with the back of his arm and left a red smear across his cheek. "I was wanting to talk to you anyway. You first."

"I was worried about you. Someone shot at us, remember?"

Noah wouldn't meet his gaze. "Kids playing around."

"What did you need to see me about?"

Noah looked away. "I'm going to have to go away again. I want you to watch out for Jillian and Heidi."

"Look, you need to be a man and face the mess you've made.

Quit running away. Tell me more about this casino. Who was your contact? Anyone whose name begins with *A*?"

Noah's eyes widened. "How'd you know that?"

"I found a ring. Whose is it?"

Beads of perspiration dotted Noah's forehead. "I can't tell you anything. Just leave me alone." He tried to shake off Mano's hand that was clamped on his forearm, but Mano hung on. "Look, I can't talk about it. They've made that clear. I don't want anything to happen to Jillian."

"Let's talk to the police. They can protect Jillian."

Noah gave a bitter laugh. "You don't know much, Mano." He jerked his arm away.

No matter how much Mano pleaded, Noah refused to say another word. Mano finally gave up and walked back to his car. Sam needed to know about this.

Thirteen

Gina had obviously made an effort to make her living room comfortable, though it was more cluttered with knickknacks than Annie liked. Figurines and Greek artifacts crowded nearly every flat surface in the room. Annie sat in an overstuffed armchair. She was in no hurry to get going.

"We need to get in to work," Gina said. "You want to let your dad know we're leaving?"

Annie cleared her throat. Did her boss really think she could work with everything that was going on? "I need to talk to Leilani's friends and try to find Tomi."

"Tomi knows how to contact you. It will be better if you keep your mind on your work, and let the police handle Leilani. There's nothing you can do about it. I've found that during times of stress it's best to try to maintain normal habits."

"I don't think I can do that," Annie said softly. "I'd like to take the rest of the week off."

"Fawn's absence leaves us shorthanded. I really need you today."

"I'm not even dressed," Annie said desperately.

"I'll go on ahead. You can come after you get ready. But don't be too late. You and Jillian need to figure out what's wrong with that computer model and get it right." Her tone softened. "This is for your own good, Annie. Believe me, I know it's best to keep busy."

Annie knew Gina was probably right, but she wanted to *do something*. Every day that ticked by without knowing what had happened to Leilani deepened her dread. Wilson curled at her feet, and Annie picked him up.

"I'd like you to go on another underwater excursion with the dolphin when you're done with the computer model," Gina said. She stepped into her slippers and went toward the door.

"I don't have a partner," Annie pointed out. "Jillian still has the head cold, and Fawn is gone."

Gina brightened. "I could go with you, I suppose." She sounded eager.

Her boss took too many chances. Gina thought she was invincible in the water, and Annie would rather dive with anyone other than her. "I have some vacation coming," she reminded Gina. "Can I take off the afternoon at least? By tomorrow maybe Jillian will be ready to dive." She was sure Tomi would try to contact her. He needed her to go to the bank with him and try to get his money.

Gina pursed her lips. "I'm not questioning your right to be off, but I need you. It's best for you to come in." Gina patted her on the shoulder. "Save your vacation for when you can enjoy it. And try not to worry. Your sister will turn up. I'm positive she's okay."

Annie's airways tightened. "How about if I see what I can find out from Leilani's friends this morning? I'll come in and do the dive this afternoon and fix the computer model. Will that be okay?"

Gina sighed. "I suppose. But you need to work the rest of the week. I know it will be hard to concentrate. Sitting in the house and worrying won't accomplish anything."

She obviously wasn't going to budge on this. Annie nodded. "Okay. I'll be in later today."

Her boss walked toward the door. "Call me if you hear anything."

"I will." Annie rubbed Wilson's head as she listened to Gina's car start up and drive away. She glanced at her watch. Nearly ten. She dialed Mano's number and got dumped into voice mail. She left a message asking him to come see her as soon as he was done.

If he didn't get back soon, she'd go see CeCe alone. She couldn't just sit here and do nothing.

Jason entered the room and dropped onto the sofa. He propped his bare feet on the coffee table in front of her. She shrank back into her seat. Though she'd often wished to see admiration for her in a man's eyes, the interest in his gaze wasn't quite what she had in mind.

"I saw a couple of guys hanging around your house," Jason said.

He was just now mentioning this? Though to be fair, he'd come in last night after they went to bed and likely hadn't heard about the men who came to see her father. But he could have mentioned it over breakfast. "Really? When?"

"Night before last."

"Any idea what they looked like?"

He shrugged. "Arabic was all I could tell. Maybe in their forties."

She wondered if he was telling her what he thought she wanted to hear. "What were you doing in the neighborhood?"

He shrugged. "Just driving around."

Though they'd only gone out twice, he'd been smitten with her sister from the first. Could he have been stalking Leilani? "When did you last see Leilani?" she asked abruptly.

His eyes widened. He put his feet on the floor. "So now I'm under suspicion for her disappearance? Figures. For your information, I haven't seen your precious sister in nearly two weeks."

"Where was this?"

He got to his feet with a sullen twist to his mouth. "I have to go to work."

She watched him go and wondered why he was so defensive.

The cavelike structure was nearly fifteen feet high and nearly as wide. It had been formed in the distant past when lava rushed along this way. As the lava cooled from the outside in, it formed the tube. Once the magma chamber was empty of lava, the molten rock slipped out like water from a straw and left the tube behind. Leilani had learned all this from her sister, but knowing about it didn't make the place less foreboding.

Water dripped from somewhere in the cave. They must have drugged her food. At least they'd taken off her blindfold. Not that it helped, as dark as this place was. She shook her head to clear it, then peered around the dim tube. Tree roots hung down from the ceiling, creating a cobweb effect. She shivered at the thought of the huge cane spiders or the lava spiders that might be lurking around here. A thin blanket under her bottom protected her from the cold stone floor, but she was still freezing. She thought about wrapping up in it.

Her gaze traveled toward the mouth of the tube, and she saw a backpack lying near the entrance. The light coming into the cave looked dim, perhaps twilight. Someone would come soon, but maybe she could get out before that. There might be a key to her shackles in the backpack. If her chain reached that far.

Leilani braced herself against the wall and managed to get to her feet, but dizziness assailed her, and she nearly fell back to the hard floor. She waited until the spots in front of her eyes cleared, then began to hop toward the bag. About six feet away from her goal, she ran out of chain. She tumbled to the ground. The hard surface scraped the skin from her knees and chin. She laid her head on the cold lava and began to cry. She wanted to be home in her own warm bed, to hear Annie call her for breakfast. She wanted a hot shower and a toothbrush. But most of all she wanted to feel safe and to be free from these bonds.

A figure came toward her. It was too dark to make out the man's features. "I hate you," she whispered. "Why are you doing this? What do you want from me?"

"You want me to put the gag back in?" The man's voice was harsh. And familiar.

"Do you have any idea where we're going?" Mano turned the wheel and pulled out onto the highway. He'd gotten a replacement rental car before he came to meet her.

"CeCe's office." Annie rubbed the top of Wilson's head and rattled off directions. The mongoose gave a squeak of contentment and poked his nose under her arm, then settled down.

Mano glanced at Annie. She seemed even more subdued than she had earlier in the morning. "Any calls?"

She shook her head. "Nothing. I've been trying to think of where Tomi might be holed up. He and Leilani used to have a clubhouse they loved when we were kids. I want to check there."

"You didn't like the clubhouse?"

"I wasn't invited." She didn't look at him.

There was no self-pity in her voice, just a matter-of-fact statement. Mano realized he had been as bad as her siblings, taking advantage of her reliability. Good old Annie, always at their beck and call. If they wanted a fruit smoothie, she hurried to make it. If Tomi or Mano expressed a desire for pizza or anything else, she provided it. She'd been as invisible as the furniture and just as comfortable. But Mano could see her now, and he was discovering depths to her he'd never suspected.

Why had he thought her so colorless and uninteresting? She had such a strong sense of purpose and a heart as big as Kilauea. It shone from her large eyes, supported the curve of her lips. He'd been blind. Her beauty would last long after Leilani's faded. He was an idiot to have taken her for granted. They all had been.

He cleared his throat. "Where is this clubhouse?"

"Out by Kau. It's a cave really, not a clubhouse. But that's what they called it."

"Want to go there first, or to CeCe's?"

She hesitated. "To CeCe's. We've been trying to do that for

several days. She has a weird shift and goes to work at eleven. The clubhouse can wait."

"You got it." He followed her directions and turned toward Puna. He pulled in the parking lot of Kapa Kandies. A stream of men and women dressed in light blue work shirts were filing into the front and side doors of the brown block building while an enticing aroma of chocolate flowed out.

Annie pointed toward a gold 1987 Ford Escort that sported flower decals on the doors. "There's her car. She's still in it."

Mano pulled up behind the Escort, and Annie jumped out and ran to the driver's door. A young woman got out, and the two embraced. Mano let the car roll forward slowly and stopped it in the parking space beside CeCe's car. He got out to join the women.

CeCe was not what he had expected. She had pink hair twisted up in a roll on the back of her head secured with a pencil. Her bright blue eyeshadow overpowered the pale blue of her eyes.

"I heard about Leilani." CeCe said, releasing Annie from the hug. "I meant to call, but I thought maybe you wouldn't want to talk to me."

"What do you mean? I always want to talk to you."

CeCe's eyes filled. "It was my fault. I shouldn't have let her go with him."

"With who?" Annie's voice filled with fear.

"Tab Watson."

Annie shook her head. "I don't know him."

"Consider yourself lucky. He scares me. But you know Leilani. She was always up for a challenge. We like big guys." She glanced at Mano with a come-hither flutter of her lashes.

Mano wasn't flattered. "How did Leilani know him? Any idea where they went?"

CeCe shrugged. "They've been hanging around together a few weeks. He's part of that religious group Leilani was interested in. I think it was more Tab that intrigued her, and not the religion."

The Ku cult again. There had been no Ku worship on the islands for generations. The thought of it being resurrected made Mano uneasy. "Where does the group meet?"

"I have no idea. Leilani wouldn't tell me." CeCe giggled. "I think she was afraid I was after her precious Tab." She shivered. "Cre-e-e-py. I wouldn't take him if you paid me."

Though her words said otherwise, Mano could hear jealousy in her voice. "You have no idea where this group met?"

CeCe hesitated. "Well, I saw them drive off toward the volcanoes a few times."

"Leilani hated the volcanoes!" Annie's voice quivered. "She wouldn't go there."

"They may not have gone that far," Mano said. "There are other places at the park that are no danger." He took her hand and squeezed her fingers. The gratitude on Annie's face brought a sense of shame when he realized how little she expected from anyone.

"I know," CeCe said hastily. "No way would Leilani go out there. But that's the direction they went."

"Do you know where Watson works?" Mano asked.

"He's a bouncer for Shark Head Bar. That's where me and Leilani met him."

Mano knew of the place. He winced to think that Leilani had been hanging out in a dive like that. "Does he work every night?"

"Most nights. He was there last night. I wanted to ask him about Leilani, but he avoided me."

Annie dropped Mano's hand and embraced CeCe. *"Mahalo,* sweetie. It's not your fault. We'll find her."

She was such a little mother hen. Mano thought she'd take anyone hurt or in pain under her wing. He began to wonder if he could find shelter there himself.

"I've got to go to work." She sounded despondent. "Will you keep looking?"

"You know I will."

"Call me if you hear anything." CeCe waved and followed her coworkers inside.

"I'll see if I can find this Tab Watson." Mano was beginning to think he'd do just about anything for Annie Tagama. "How about dinner tonight?"

"Dinner?"

"Yeah, as in food. You have to eat, and we never got our dinner last night with all the problems. I bet you never even ate at Gina's."

She gave a faint smile. "You're right." She chewed on her bottom lip, then nodded. "Okay. You can bring me up to date on what you find out today."

"I'll pick you up at six." He realized he was going to miss her this afternoon. That wasn't a good sign.

fourteen

Annie drove her Pathfinder into the parking lot by the water and shut off the engine. She was in no mood to dive. Gina was supposed to meet her, a fact that Annie found less than encouraging. She'd dived with her boss one other time and sworn she'd never do it again.

She grabbed her dive gear out of the back and walked down the narrow path to the rocky shore. She saw a woman by the water and recognized Fawn by the bright blue beads in her hair. "I thought you were going to be gone this week."

"The vibes were bad at my brother's. He and his fiancée broke up this morning. I didn't want to hang around for the postmortem. Gina dropped me off so I could ride back with you." Fawn's gaze traveled over Annie's face. "You okay? You look pale. Any word on Leilani?"

"Nothing. I'm really scared." Confessing her terror brought the sting of tears to her eyes. She was so tired of being the strong one.

Fawn enveloped her in a tight hug. "God's in control here, Annie."

Annie sniffled and pulled away. "I wish I could believe that." She was envious of Fawn's calm assurance in the face of any problem. "I—what if she's dead?"

Fawn's comforting pat on Annie's back stilled. "Why would you say that?"

Annie didn't try to stop the tears that began to flow. "I just can't get that phone call out of my mind, that creep saying we're all going to pay for something Tomi did. I think someone has hurt her."

"What does Sam say?"

She shrugged. "He thinks it's just some sick prankster trying to shake us up. He says it happens all the time; someone hears about a missing person or a death and calls and makes claims that aren't true."

"He might be right. You're just tired and scared."

Annie rubbed the moisture from her face. "I hope you're right. But I'm terrified." She hesitated. How would Fawn react to her news? She'd had a crush on Tomi as big as Annie's on Mano. Annie should have told her sooner. "Fawn, I have something to tell you. It's wonderful news, but it's hard to grasp."

"What is it?"

"It's about Tomi. He's alive."

"What?" Fawn's fingers squeezed hers. "Tomi? What are you saying?"

"That's why Mano came. He said Tomi had called him. Tomi called me a few days later, and we met yesterday. He's in some kind of trouble and wanted everyone to think he was dead."

"Why didn't you tell me? You know I—" She broke off, and her face drained of color. "He's alive?" she breathed. Tears filled her eyes. "I can't believe it. What happened?"

Annie didn't want to tell Fawn about the Iranian girl or that her brother was mixed up in espionage. She tried to sugarcoat it. "I don't really know everything. It has something to do with the Iranians. They want him to spy for them." Her lips trembled.

Fawn gasped. "Tomi wouldn't do that!"

Annie was going to have to tell her the whole story. She sighed and launched into the saga about how he'd been shot and taken by the Iranians. "He's trying to get out of the mess, but I don't see how he's going to do it."

"He must have really loved this girl." Fawn's voice was low.

"I think he did. I'm sorry." She laid her hand on Fawn's.

Fawn gave her a sad smile. "It's not your fault, Annie. It's not anyone's fault. Tomi never had eyes for me. I tried my best, but he never gave me a second look, and I learned to live with that. Maybe Mano can help him."

Annie's fingers tightened on hers. "Maybe."

Fawn recovered her composure. "Mano's appearance hasn't helped your state of mind, I bet."

Heat rushed up Annie's neck. "I don't want to talk about Mano."

"You never do. You've loved him for years, Annie. Fight for him this time. Quit standing on the sidelines and make him notice you."

"That approach didn't exactly work for you." The words were out before she could think. She saw the way Fawn recoiled. "I'm sorry, I didn't mean that."

"But at least I tried, Annie. I did everything I could. At least I'll never have to wonder what might have been if I'd given it my all. You have to fight for him."

"I can never compete with Leilani. I wouldn't want to." She was such a liar. Everything in her longed to compete. And win. But she knew better than to try. Leilani always won. Even if Leilani weren't in the running, Annie just wasn't the kind of woman men noticed.

Fawn glanced at Annie's feet. "Your feet are as flashy as a parrot, but the rest of you is as colorless as a mynah. I've wanted to take you in hand for years and dress you in the bright colors your dark hair and eyes beg for. Now is the time. Don't let this opportunity slip away to have what you want."

Annie hated wearing boots all the time. Her feet had been her one vanity. Her mother used to tell her she had pretty feet. They weren't pretty any more. No part of her had beauty now. "I don't want to attract a man by being something I'm not. I want someone to love me for myself, not for the way I dress or the makeup I wear."

Fawn's frown softened. "Don't we all? But men are visual

creatures. You have to get them to look at the exterior first, and then they'll see the interior."

"No thanks." Annie began to pull on her wetsuit. "Let's get this over with. I have to help my brother out of this mess."

"You are so stubborn." Fawn sounded resigned. "Let me know if there's anything I can do to help." She sat on a lava rock beside Annie and began to pull on her wetsuit too. "So what are we doing today?"

"Gina wants some readings from Loihi seamount while we have Nani here. A recent swarm of earthquakes was centered out there. More than any Hawaiian volcano in recorded history." The women put on their reef shoes and went to the dock to wait on Jillian and the boat.

Annie's cell phone rang, and she pulled it out of her bag.

"Annie, it's me." Her brother's voice sounded strained. "I wondered if you found Father last night."

"Tomi. You're okay!" She didn't think she could have stood losing him when they'd just found him. Beside her, Fawn's movements stilled, and she turned her gaze on Annie as she listened. Annie wished she could shake Tomi and wake him up to what he was missing. "Father's fine. He was down by the water."

"Did he say what happened?"

"The men said they would kill all of us if you didn't do what they wanted." There was no answer on the other end. "Tomi, did you hear me?"

"I heard." His voice sounded deadpan. "I don't know what to do, Annie."

"We'll figure it out. Come home. We can talk about it tonight."

"No. I won't bring danger to your doorstep. I'll be in touch."

The phone clicked in her ear, and she put it away as the sound of the boat's engine neared. "That was Tomi."

"So I gathered," Fawn said. "Is he coming home tonight?"

"No." Annie sighed and gathered up her diving gear. "I wish I knew what to do."

"Just ask God. He'll guide you all."

That was Fawn's answer for everything. But surely God expected his children to figure some things out on their own, though in this case, Annie was completely at a loss. She waved at the approaching boat. Jillian nudged the craft close to the dock, and they hopped aboard. Her cold was better, and Annie brought her up to speed on events.

"I still haven't seen Noah," Jillian said, taking them out to sea. "If he comes by, I'll see if he'll tell me more about this casino thing."

The day was cloudy, and the scent of rain hung in the air. They rode rough swells out to Loihi seamount, about twenty miles from shore. No one had ever seen the volcano erupt, because it was so far under water. The USGS had put an undersea observatory called HUGO on the mount, but it hadn't functioned since 1998. Gina and the rest of the team were hopeful that they might collect some data with Nani. The summit was about a thousand feet down, close to the depth limit that Nani could dive.

Annie decided she should try to enjoy the day. So much of their work was spent hunched over a computer analyzing seismographs, GPS receivers, air-quality testers, and gas composition. At least out here she could listen to the birds overhead and inhale the fresh scent of the sea.

"If we had Wilson with us, he'd call Nani," Annie said, smiling at Fawn. Placing Kaia's device into the water, she called the dolphin. Within a few minutes, a dorsal fin appeared. Slicing through the waves, the dolphin stopped a few feet from the boat, poked her nostrum above the water, and chattered to them.

"She seems eager to get to work," Fawn said. She picked up the dolphin's gear and sat on the edge of the boat. She attached it to Nani with an elastic belt that had been designed for the dolphin.

The belt contained tubes that would take samples of the seawater, as well as temperature gauges.

"I'm going to miss her when she goes home." Annie jumped overboard. The water was hot here near the surface. It was like jumping into a hot spa. She knew it would cool as they went down. She pulled on her mask and mouthpiece, then dove beneath the waves. The water was murky with suspended ash. The deeper they swam, the darker it got. The visibility eventually dropped to about five feet.

Nani came close and nudged her, and Annie grabbed the dolphin's dorsal fin. Nani drew her down toward their target. When she was as deep as she dared go, she released the dolphin and fluttered her fingers to tell Nani to go on.

After the first trip to the Kilauea vent, the dolphin knew what to do. She swirled away, and the dark water swallowed her up. The sounds were disorienting—hissing and crashing. The water seemed warmer than she'd expected, and Annie wondered if the flow had increased. She took temperature readings and scooped up some water samples.

Annie glanced at her watch. They'd been down long enough. She signaled Fawn, and her coworker nodded. They began to surface, pausing occasionally to decompress. Annie's head broke the surface of the water, and she spit out her mouthpiece. "That was incredible! I could hardly think with all the noise. I wonder if the swarms were going on while we were down." She called the dolphin to her and removed Nani's belt and equipment, then slung it aboard the boat.

Fawn nodded. "I almost forgot where I was. It was disorienting."

"Let's get back to the observatory and see what the seismograph says."

"I have a feeling it's going to show major activity," Fawn said. "We may be gearing up for something as big as the 1996 event."

Jillian dropped them off at the dock, where they got in Annie's

SUV and drove along Chain of Craters Road. Whether the road stayed open was an ongoing battle with the volcano. Twelve miles of the road were covered by lava from Mauna Ulu between 1969 and 1974, and five miles of the connecting road to the Puna area disappeared under lava from the Kupaianaha vent of the *Pu'u O'o* eruption from 1986 to 1991. Flows crossed the highway near Kamoamoa, closing another mile of road and coursing into the ocean. The park was never static.

They passed dozens of tourists walking the black *pahoehoe* lava. It was smooth and ropey and easier to walk on than the jagged *a'a*. A long line of lava seekers walked in single file along the trail leading to the current lava show. Annie glanced at her watch. It was a three-hour walk, and the tourists usually arrived in time to see the lava in the daylight, then hung around to see the nighttime show.

At the observatory, she pulled into the parking lot and parked beside Fawn's car. "I've got an hour to figure out that computer model before I have to get ready for dinner."

"I'll come help you get ready," Fawn told her.

"It's not a big deal. I'm just going to change into a clean T-shirt and jeans."

"You are not! This is a bona fide date, and you're going to look fabulous."

"You're making too much of it." Annie didn't want to think of this as a "real" date, or she'd be too nervous to go.

Fawn got out of the SUV and slammed the door. "I could shake you. This is your chance, Annie. Take it."

Muttering about pushy friends, Annie got out and hurried to the office. She found Jillian already hunched over the computer in her office. "How's it going?"

Jillian barely glanced up. "This thing still isn't working."

"Scoot out of the way and let me take a look."

Jillian stood and went toward the door. "I'm going to get some coffee. Want some?"

"Sure." Jillian was tall, so Annie's toes barely touched the floor. The results sure looked haywire. She suspected some row or column in the database had been tagged with a wrong label. She launched the spreadsheet program and began to go through it line by line. One row of figures didn't make sense. She needed the original model, and it was in Gina's office.

Annie went to her boss's office and began to go through the filing cabinets. Her thoughts drifted as she flipped through the folders. She didn't want to think about her date with Mano, so she set her mind on her brother. She had to talk to him and try to figure out how to get him out of the mess. She stole a glance at a picture of Gina's family as her mind whirled. Ah, there was the file she sought.

"Find what you needed, or can I help you?"

Annie turned to see Gina standing in the doorway. "I wondered if you were still here." She shut the filing cabinet drawer. "I think I'm making progress."

A relieved smile lit Gina's face. "I hope you can get it done today." She cleared her throat. "Um, I hope you don't mind, but your father called me and invited me to dinner."

Annie's eyes widened, but she smiled. "I admit I'm surprised. He's never shown any interest in anyone since Mother died."

"That's what he told me. I like your father, and we seemed to hit it off. Is it okay with you?"

Was it? Annie didn't want to admit the emotion stirring in her heart was jealousy. "I want him to be happy. You too." It looked like more changes might be coming into her life, and she wasn't sure she was ready to handle them. Gina's flirtation with her father last night had seemed blatant, but then maybe most men liked that. Annie was no expert.

Annie nodded toward the picture of Gina's family. "Your daughter looked familiar, then I realized it's because she looks so much like you. I've never seen her visit. Does she live on the island?"

Gina's smile faded. "She's dead." She looked away. "She and my husband died in the same accident. I should have been there. He never was good at taking care of the children."

Annie ducked her head. "Oh, Gina, I'm so sorry." She'd jumped to conclusions about her boss. Gina hadn't shared much about her family life.

"It was a long time ago." Gina's smile came back. "That's one reason I've felt so close to you, Annie. You're a lot like Michelle." She caught her lower lip in her teeth. "And, um, I really like your dad. More than any man I've met since Alex died."

The softness in her boss's gaze touched Annie. "*Mahalo,* Gina. It means a lot to me."

Gina touched her cheek. "You make me proud, Annie. That's why I push you so hard. I see a lot of potential in you. You're going to accomplish great things in your life." Her gaze strayed to the picture. "Just like Michelle would have."

"What did she do?"

"She was a marine biologist. She died on a dive."

Annie had to wonder if that was why Gina took such chances on dives herself. Maybe subconsciously she wanted to join her daughter. There was no way Annie could tell her boss that, though. "I'd better get that computer model fixed." Annie squeezed Gina's hand, then went back down the hall to Jillian's office.

Jillian was standing over the computer. "I'm all for tossing this thing out the window. How about you?"

"I think I've got the answer here." Annie held up the file folder. "If this doesn't work, we'll go with your plan." She moved past Jillian and looked at the computer. She dropped into the chair. The figures ran together as she looked over the file for the next thirty minutes. She laid it aside. "I still can't figure it out."

"Tomorrow will have to do. I want to spend some time with Heidi tonight," Jillian said. "We'll forget trashing the darn thing until then."

Annie stepped into the hallway to go home. Monica was standing by Gina's door. "If you're wanting to see Gina for some more sucking up, she's left for the day." Monica's lip curled.

Annie forced herself to stand as tall as her five feet two would allow. "Monica, can't we be civil? We've never been friends, but at least we could work together. Have I done something to offend you?"

Monica folded her arms over her chest and glowered. "I'm a better volcanologist than you, but you're the one who gets the cushy projects and all the praise. I've just had it. Ever since you got hurt you act like you're entitled to special consideration. Get over it! So you got hurt—big deal. That's the reality we face every day in our jobs. If you can't stand the heat, get out of the kitchen—or in this case, the lava field."

Annie absorbed Monica's words in silence. Did she have an attitude of entitlement? She was ashamed to admit to herself that maybe she did.

"Oh please, wipe off that expression of shocked hurt." Monica brushed by her abruptly. "You're not a child, Annie. Grow up and do your job."

"You're right," Annie heard herself saying. Monica's eyes widened. Annie turned and bolted for the parking lot. Tears leaked down her cheeks as she ran. Once she reached the safety of her SUV, she leaned her face into the steering wheel and took several deep breaths. She'd been failing everyone lately. She couldn't measure up to everyone's expectations. Not her family's, not her coworkers', not even her own. She didn't know how to fix everything. The burden was too great.

She fumbled with her key and jammed it into the ignition, then drove toward home. How would she get her life in order? Why were things going from bad to worse? She had no answers, only questions. Her thoughts drifted wistfully to Mano and Fawn. They both had such self-confidence. Was it because of their faith? Her own was anemic. Once, she'd had great plans about what she'd do for God, but the last few years her focus had been on her work. But that was okay, wasn't it? She wasn't sure of anything anymore.

Mano stopped to get a shave ice. He ordered the diabetic rainbow flavor with sugar-free macadamia-nut ice cream on the bottom. Oh for the good old days when he could eat the real thing. The shave-ice stand would be a good place to ask for information about Tab Watson. Everyone frequented here, and usually the workers knew the patrons by name.

When the fresh-faced blond girl brought his order, he pulled a napkin out of the holder and then leaned against the counter. There was no one else in line, so he took his time. "You worked here long?"

The girl's eyes brightened, and the smile she sent his way was obviously meant to intrigue him. "Over a year. I haven't seen you here before."

"I'm just visiting. Do you know Leilani Tagama?"

The girl's smile clouded. "Yeah. Sad about her going missing."

"I'm looking for one of her friends. Tab Watson. You know him?"

"Sure, everyone knows Tab." The girl grimaced. "He's a weird one."

"In what way?"

"He's always talking about Pele and Ku and the old religion. Gives me the willies."

"Any idea where he lives?" Mano considered going to the Shark Head Bar tonight, but if Tab was a bouncer, he might not have time—or inclination—to talk.

"You some kind of cop?"

Mano shook his head. "Just a friend of the family's."

The suspicion in her eyes faded. "He lives in a house in the Aloha Shores subdivision. I'm not sure which one. But you can ask." She giggled. "For all the good it will do."

As Mano had discovered, residents of the subdivision were remarkably close-mouthed. Who knew how many of them were in the witness-protection program? In any case, they weren't about to rat out one of their own.

He thanked the girl, took his shave ice, and went to the car. Though it was probably a useless effort, he drove out to the subdivision in search of Watson. The lava fields that stretched up the hillsides were beginning to feel like home to him, as often as he'd been here lately.

A woman was weeding a small herb garden at the first house when he pulled onto the access road. Mano stopped and rolled down his window. "Excuse me," he said, "but I'm looking for Tab Watson. Could you tell me which house is his?"

She didn't even look up. "Sorry, don't know him."

Mano sighed. He'd expected as much. "Thanks anyway," he said. He took his foot off the brake and continued on into the subdivision. He didn't see anyone for several minutes and was about to give up when he saw a familiar figure. His foot went to the brake. The man was massive, the size of a sumo wrestler. Why did he seem so familiar? Mano ran his window down and was about to hail the man when the figure turned and the bright sunlight illuminated a birthmark that ran across his nose. Mano had seen that face many times. Kim Aki. Son of Nahele Aki. The two men had been part of a Hawaiian sovereignty group on Kaua'i. Mano met them when he'd gone undercover for the navy to investigate the group.

Kim didn't see Mano. He was standing in front of the place Noah had rented. Mano turned his head away. He took his foot off the brake and accelerated around the corner. No sense in tipping his hand yet. What was Kim doing here? Mano had gone on to a new mission after the Akis were arrested for trying to detonate munitions on the navy base, and he never learned what happened to them. He'd have to put in a call and find out.

He sped out of the subdivision and drove down the road a

ways, then stopped in a pullout. His brother, Bane, would know the story. He dialed his brother's cell phone number.

"Where are you?" Bane asked.

Bane's terse question startled Mano. "On Hawai'i. I brought Tomi's belongings to his family." He hesitated. Maybe now was the time to tell Bane about his diabetes. He opened his mouth, but the words wouldn't come. Bane was so strong, so wise. As the younger brother, Mano had spent his entire life trying to follow in his older brother's footsteps; it seemed impossible to admit his weakness now. And he had never told his brother that he'd failed Tomi when things got hard. Bane would not have left Tomi in the water.

Mano marshaled his thoughts. "Everything okay at home?"

"*Tûtû kâne* has been a little under the weather. I was going to call you and tell you about it." Bane sounded worried.

"What's wrong with him?"

"I'm not sure. He's been sleeping a lot and complaining of his stomach. Probably just the flu. But you might give him a call. And have you talked to our mother?"

"Oh yeah, I haven't called her lately." Their mother had left them with their grandfather when they and their sister were children. She had only recently reentered their lives. While Mano was glad to reconnect with her, reestablishing the relationship hadn't come naturally.

"You're not calling me just to shoot the breeze. What's wrong?" Bane asked.

"Kim Aki. Whatever happened to him?"

There was silence on the other end of the line. Then: "Funny you should ask. I just checked a few weeks ago. Nahele was convicted when Kim agreed to turn state's evidence. Then he disappeared. Probably off causing trouble somewhere else. Why?"

"He's here."

"On the Big Island? Where?"

"In the Aloha Shores subdivision."

"Did he see you?" Bane's voice grew sharp. "You're not real high on his list of favorite people."

"I know. He didn't see me. Not yet. You have any way of figuring out what name he's using these days?"

"I could try. I think he just scuttled away like a cockroach, though. As overworked as the courts are, I doubt anyone is keeping track."

Mano leaned back against the headrest. He hadn't slept much for three days, and his eyes burned. He closed and massaged them. "I'll follow him and see what I can find out."

"Be careful," Bane said. "He's a dangerous man."

Mano promised to watch his back and hung up. It was almost time to pick up Annie for dinner, and he didn't have much to report. There'd been no sign of Tab Watson. He put the car into drive and headed toward the Shark Head. He'd stop there before going to Annie's house. Another thought struck him. The ring he'd seen after someone shot at him and Noah. It had an *A* on it. Could it stand for Aki?

Annie looked at her reflection in the mirror. Maybe Fawn was right. What could be the harm in trying to look her best? She didn't have any makeup of her own, but Leilani had enough to open her own cosmetic counter. She went down the hall to Leilani's room. The bottom drawer of her sister's dresser contained a jumble of Leilani's discards. She selected some foundation, blush, eyeshadow, and mascara.

Back in her room, she tied back her wet hair, then shook a little foundation onto her fingers and rubbed it onto her face. It was awfully orange. Maybe some pink blush would tone it down. She dotted some cream blush on her cheeks. The garish effect made her gasp. This wasn't working. She rubbed at the too-dark color on her cheeks. Her face looked like a teenage girl's first attempt. She started to smile at the thought.

She either had to forget it or ask for help. Staring at her reflection, she tried to decide. The doorbell rang, and she glanced out the window to see Fawn's car in the driveway. She hurried to the door and flung it open. "Think I'll make a runway model?"

Fawn's smile faltered when she looked into Annie's face. "Um, you decided to try some makeup after all."

Annie covered her mouth with her hand, but she couldn't stop the giggles. "You should see your face. It's that bad, huh? I was thinking about trying out for the part of Cleopatra in the town play."

Fawn's smile broke out. "You'd need more eyeliner for that. But I can fix you right up."

"That's what I'm counting on." Annie went past her toward the bathroom. "I'll go wash this off, and you can start over."

"What are you going to wear?" Fawn went to the closet.

"You've already nixed the idea of clean jeans and T-shirt. How about khakis? But this isn't a real date, you know. He's just going to let me know what he found out today about Tab."

"Uh-huh, whatever you say." Fawn slid open the rice-paper closet doors, which were decorated with a delicate floral pattern. She riffled through the hangers. "Hey, I've never seen you wear this. It would be a great color on you." She pulled out a royal blue silk blouse and carried it past the bathroom. "I'll be right back."

Annie blotted her face with a towel and returned to her room. She heard Fawn rooting through Leilani's closet. She reappeared a few minutes later. "This skirt is perfect with the blouse." It was a black silky skirt with a handkerchief hem.

"That's way too—too something. And the blouse is too loud. I tried to tell Leilani that when she insisted on buying it for my birthday last year."

"You're wearing them."

"Mano will think I'm after him." The thought made her go hot, then cold.

"You are." Fawn propelled her to the seat in front of the dresser and picked up the blow-dryer. "We're going to make Mano gasp with appreciation. Sit still."

Annie watched in the mirror as Fawn put goop on her hair, then scrunched it as she manipulated the dryer. The result was a tousled, carefree look that made her look like a teenager. Maybe she could get into this style stuff. She turned her head this way and that to check out the do. "I like it. I bet I could never duplicate it though."

"It's way easy. I'll show you." Fawn grabbed the bag she'd brought in with her. "I brought my makeup."

"I've got some makeup here. Leilani's rejects."

"I think that stuff was rejected for a reason." Fawn unzipped a hot pink makeup bag and dumped the contents onto the dresser. "Don't worry, it's all natural and won't make you break out."

"I didn't doubt it." Annie giggled and gave Fawn free rein. Her friend began to smooth makeup onto her face. She kept her eyes closed, afraid to see the comic results. Fawn soon moved from her face to her eyes. "I'm going to look like a clown," Annie muttered.

"You're beautiful. Look." Fawn put down the mascara wand.

Fawn's hushed voice scared her. Annie cautiously opened her eyes. She stared at the stranger in the mirror. "What did you do?" Her eyes appeared bigger, brighter somehow. There was just a touch of color on her lips. Nothing was glaring. She didn't even look like she had on makeup. She looked actually—pretty. "You're a genius." She began to reassemble the piles of small makeup pots and stick them back in the bag.

"Quit being such a neatnik." Fawn took the bag away. "I want to show you how to do it. You can keep all this."

"I could never replicate this look." Annie poked a finger in her hair. "How'd you get it to stay back so neatly?" Fawn had drawn one side back in a glittery comb. Every time Annie had tried a similar look, the comb fell out. She shook her head, testing it, but it stayed put.

"Here, watch." Fawn removed the comb and then put it back in, showing Annie how to drag it with the hair, and then push against it.

"Now for the clothes." Fawn tossed her the skirt and blouse. "Put these on."

Annie wasn't going to argue with expertise. She slipped them on and stepped in front of the full-length mirror. The color brightened her skin tone, and the skirt made her legs look longer. "Wow," she said in an awed voice. "I wouldn't say I'm beautiful, but I don't look half-bad."

"You're beautiful. You just didn't know it. You try to fade into the woodwork. I think you were just afraid of the attention." Fawn handed her some silver hoop earrings and a matching necklace. "Your birthday is next month. This is an early birthday present."

"Father hates makeup. Mother never showed me how to wear it, and Leilani delights in upsetting him over it."

"And you always want to be the dutiful daughter." Fawn shook her head. "That's admirable, Annie, but you're an adult. You can make your own decisions."

Annie put on the jewelry, then hugged her friend. "Even if Mano takes one look and runs, I still love you for this. At least I feel more confident."

"You look killer, and he's going to be wowed. It's about time you stepped out from behind your family's shadow and lived your life, Annie. You're thirty. In fact, I'd say it's time you had a place of your own."

"You're going too far now." Annie smiled, but she was serious. "I'll never leave my father alone." If Gina had her way, her father wouldn't need Annie any more. She wanted to feel happy about that. Gina had always treated her like a daughter. She examined her thoughts and found herself strangely calm about the idea. "Father invited Gina to dinner."

Fawn raised her eyebrows. "Wow."

The doorbell rang. "That's Mano!" Panic flared in her chest. "I should change—this is ridiculous. I look like a peacock."

Fawn propelled her toward the door. "You're gorgeous. Go knock him dead."

"More likely I'll die from embarrassment," Annie muttered. Her knees trembled. She scooped up Wilson and hugged him under her chin. He squeaked, then settled down in her arms. "Come with me." She pushed Fawn ahead of her down the hall.

"I'll get the door. Breathe deep." Fawn hurried to the door and flung it open. "Hey, Mano, come on in. Annie is ready."

Mano stepped inside. His gaze went past Fawn and connected with Annie, and his smile faltered. His eyes widened. "Annie?" He cleared his throat. "You, uh, you look nice."

Nice. So much for Fawn's assurance she would wow Mano. Annie forced a smile and dropped Wilson onto the sofa before picking up her handbag. It was going to be a long night. Holding her head high, she went past him toward the car. A feeling as dismal as rain settled in her gut. She wished she could back out of this laughable situation. Only she wasn't laughing. She realized she'd hoped Mano would take one glance at her and look as dazed as if he'd been hit by a tsunami. Instead he was surely laughing at her. He silently held the car door for her, then climbed in on his side.

"Your dad's here." Mano ran his window down as Edega got out of his car and walked toward them. Annie did the same.

"Where are you headed?" Edega asked, stopping beside Annie's open window.

"Out to dinner." Too late she realized she hadn't even thought about what her father was going to eat. Some daughter she was.

Edega frowned. "Did you transcribe those notes for me?"

"I'm sorry, Father, there wasn't time." She reached toward the door handle with the intention of going back inside.

Fawn waved from the door. "I'll do it, Edega." She winked at Annie. "And I'll spring for dinner. How does pizza sound?"

Annie grinned as her father's expression brightened. She rarely let him eat pizza. It was bad for his cholesterol. It was quite a sacrifice on Fawn's part too. She thought pizza was of the devil. "*Mahalo*," she mouthed to Fawn. Fawn's smile broadened, and she looked as satisfied as Wilson after a big meal.

Edega's eyes narrowed. "What did you do to yourself, Annie? You know I hate paint on a woman's face."

Her smile waned. She looked away from her father's accusing stare. "Um, it's nothing," she mumbled. Didn't he realize Gina wore makeup too?

"You go in and wash it off. You can't go out in public looking like that."

Before Annie could slink away to do as her father ordered, Mano put his hand on her wrist. "I think she looks wonderful," he said. "Have a good evening. We need to go if we're going to make our reservations."

Edega's eyes widened. His mouth flopped open like a hungry sea turtle, then he pressed his lips together and seemed to gather his thoughts before he began to speak. Annie couldn't hear what he said, because Mano ran both windows up as he backed out of the driveway. "I've always liked your dad, but he's gotten so autocratic lately. He never used to be like this."

"He's changed since Mother died. I keep thinking he'll get his feet under him and be the father I used to know. Besides, he's right this time. I told Fawn I look like a clown." She willed the words back. Her face burned. The last thing she wanted to do was call attention to the fact that she'd tried to make herself prettier for him. What must he think of her? She turned her head and stared out the window.

"I think you look great." He negotiated the narrow road to the restaurant. It had started to rain.

She'd thought she wanted his attention, but now she wasn't sure. What would he think if he knew the real Annie? She'd disappointed her father and Leilani so many times. She couldn't bear to see disappointment in Mano's eyes. "Did you find Tab Watson?"

"No luck. I thought I'd look more tomorrow. I checked at the bar, but he wasn't due in today." He pulled into the Kilauea Lodge and Restaurant. The place looked a little like a Swiss chalet with stone pillars flanking the wide steps. It sat on a small hillside against a rain forest. The rain was coming down in torrents now. Mano drove past the steps to the parking lot and stopped. He got out and opened Annie's door while she was still fumbling with her seat belt.

"You're getting soaked." She glanced up at him helplessly. "I can't get this stupid thing to turn me loose."

"It's tricky." He leaned past her and fought with the belt buckle.

Rain trickled down his face and dripped on her blue silk blouse. Annie caught a whiff of Hawaiian Surf Cologne, one of her favorite male scents. It made her think of the sun and salt water. The hair at the nape of his neck was thick and straight. She curled her fingers into her lap to keep from touching it. Her brain was filled with bubbles—light and fizzy—and her pulse galloped.

The belt released her. Mano took her hand and helped her out of the car. "*Mahalo,*" she said, careful to keep her head down. The rain struck her cheek, and she tucked her chin into her collar. She didn't want him to see the heat in her face. What an idiot she was! Her feelings for him had been so much a part of her for so many years she might never get over him. She thought she had, but she was fooling herself.

Mano's big hand touched her elbow, and she flinched. She managed a smile and then hurried up the stone steps to the restaurant with his fingers guiding her. The hostess met them at the front door and seated them by the stone fireplace. The room was narrow and filled with so many tables it was hard for the waitress to walk around. Candles on each table cast a soft glow around the room. Annie perused the menu to keep her eyes off the candlelight glinting on

Mano's hair. He was eyeing her over the top of his own menu. If she didn't know better, she'd think that was rapt admiration in his gaze.

"It's always so hard to decide what to eat," she said. "Maybe I'll get the leg of antelope filet."

"Ooh, feeling adventurous tonight, huh?" Mano grinned and closed his menu. "I think I'll get the lamb curry with mango chutney. But I want a taste of yours."

"As long as you don't eat it all. I'm hungry." In truth, she wouldn't be able to swallow a bite.

Mano ordered for them, then leaned back in his chair. "How did your dive go today?"

Annie told him about the adventure, glad for an excuse to watch him as she talked. He listened to her with the same intensity he applied to everything he did. She wasn't used to the undivided attention. "Did you ever dive to the volcano?"

He shook his head. "I've thought about it but never had the chance."

"I'll be going again if you want to come," she offered.

A smile lit his face. "I'd like that."

Silence fell between them, but it was the comfortable sort. The hard knots in her shoulders began to soften. Maybe she'd get through this evening without looking like a complete idiot. Or a lovesick teenager. Mano was displaying the graciousness she'd admired in him for years.

The waitress brought their dinner. Mano bent his head to pray, and Annie glanced around to see if anyone was looking, then lowered her head as well. His deep faith made her uncomfortable yet drew her as well. Maybe that was one of the special qualities he had. That same light seemed to be in Fawn. Annie's own light sometimes couldn't even illuminate a handful of fireflies.

Annie picked up her fork. The appetizing aroma awakened a hunger she'd thought she could ignore. The door opened, and wind blew the rain onto the floor. A couple rushed in from the pouring rain, and Annie glanced over to see Gina come in with her son slouching along behind her.

Gina stopped at their table while Jason followed the hostess. "I plugged in your data from the dive today, Annie. It's looking good. The earthquake swarms have increased all day. I think we might be seeing some major activity out there soon. I'd like you to go down again before it gets too dangerous."

Mano frowned. "It sounds like it already is too dangerous. Annie said there was so much noise down there today that it was hard to think."

Gina waved her hand in an airy motion. "I wouldn't hesitate to do it myself. She'll be fine."

Annie wanted to point out that Gina took too many chances, but she kept her mouth shut. "I'll be fine. When do you want us to go?"

"Did you get Jillian's computer model fixed?"

"That's the first thing on my agenda for tomorrow."

"Let me know when that's done, and we can make plans for the next dive." Gina hesitated, and her eyes flickered. "Where's your dad?"

"He went for pizza with Fawn."

"Isn't she a little young for him?"

Annie wanted to laugh at Gina's shocked tone. Gina had gotten a bad bite from the love bug. If she and her father married, where would Annie go? Fawn would be happy to share an apartment, but that wasn't the Japanese American way. It was more typical for a daughter to stay under her father's roof until she married. Annie's role would be upset though. She would no longer be the one to worry about her father's cholesterol or to fret when Leilani was out too late. That burden would be Gina's. The thought left her feeling hollow. How would she cope with not being needed by anyone?

Mano chuckled. "Fawn is just feeding Edega so Annie could come to dinner with me without guilt."

Relief lit Gina's eyes. "Annie is a good and dutiful daughter." She touched Annie's shoulder. "I'd better sit down. I'll see you tomorrow."

"Sounds like love is in the air," Mano said. He snaked out his hand and grabbed hers.

Annie curled her fingers though his and smiled. "Gina would be good for my father. He's been lonely since my mother's death." She studied his face. He could be someone to lean on. The thought appealed to her on one level but frightened her on another. Maybe she didn't know how to turn loose the reins of worry. Maybe that was her way of controlling her life.

She looked away. What would he say if she told him she'd been in love with him for years? Not that she would ever be brave enough to tell him. He released her fingers, and they finished their dinner. The warmth of Mano's hand under her elbow unsettled her as they walked back to his car.

She felt almost smug and definitely desirable on the drive home until her gaze touched the exotic skirt she wore. Leilani's skirt. Instead of trying to find her sister tonight, she'd stolen her skirt and makeup and was trying to steal an old boyfriend. Her sister might even be dead, though the thought made her chest constrict. Was she trying to *become* her sister? Could she have subconsciously been happy if Leilani was out of the way? She rejected the idea, but the magic of the night dissipated like the vog after a rain.

"Want to come in for some Scrabble?" she asked.

"Still a Scrabble fanatic, huh? I'm not a masochist. You'd pummel me." He grinned and got out to open her car door. "I'll take a rain check. I'm beat tonight." He helped her out of the car then stopped at the front door. "I had a nice time tonight. You're comfortable to be with, Annie."

Comfortable. Like an old shoe. It was hardly a compliment, but Annie decided it would have to do. She'd never be the type to make a man's heart beat faster. She'd never be Leilani. She whispered a hurried good night and raced inside to her bedroom where she scrubbed her face and took off Leilani's skirt.

fifteen

The small town of Na'alehu moved sluggishly in the late-afternoon sun. Tourists strolled the streets and poked their heads into small, quaint shops. Mano sat in his car across the street from the Shark Head Bar. He'd been told Tab Watson would be working tonight, and he had to stay alert though he'd like to lean his head back and take a nap.

Still no word from Tomi. Mano wondered if he'd gone to the bank yesterday by himself. A *mauka* breeze blew through the open window and lifted the hair on his head. The wind cooled the thin film of perspiration that dampened his face. The cooling action awakened him to the fact that he was hot. Too hot. As the realization came that his body was reacting, the alarm on his watch beeped. Maybe he should set it fifteen minutes ahead. All the activity might be throwing off his usual blood-sugar levels.

He dug out some cheese and munched it. The jitters began to leave, and his blurry vision cleared. With his brain once more focused, he turned his attention to the building. The employees began to arrive at the bar. An older man unlocked the building and opened the door for two women. Mano waited. The man didn't fit CeCe's description of Tab Watson. He unscrewed the top of his water bottle and took a swig. His gaze strayed down the street to the bank. Maybe he should have staked out the bank yesterday. Tomi might have shown up dressed in female clothing.

Mano straightened up when a tan pickup truck pulled into the parking lot across the street and parked. A man got out, and Mano held his breath. Kim Aki. Kim moved quickly for such a big man. He darted between two parked cars and hurried to the front door of the bar. Once he vanished inside, Mano got out and went to the door.

Could Kim be Tab Watson? He was big enough to be a bouncer. And he fit the description, though CeCe hadn't mentioned the birthmark on his face. At the door to the bar, Mano hesitated. Maybe now wouldn't be the best time to confront Kim. He might not want his employer to know his real identity.

A murmur of voices drifted out the open window. Mano sidled up to the window and listened, but he couldn't make out any of the words. Still, something in the tenor of one of the voices caught his attention. He peered through the window and saw two men standing at the bar. Kim's back was to the window, but there was no mistaking the man who faced the sunlight.

Tomi Tagama. He'd cut his hair short and dyed it blond. Not an attractive look for him, but it altered his appearance considerably. Mano started to pull away from the window, but Tomi's gaze met his. Tomi didn't betray Mano's presence other than with a mere flicker of his eyes.

Mano moved away from the window before anyone else could see him. Tomi knew he was out here. He jogged across the street to his car and settled behind the wheel to wait. There was probably a back way out of the Shark Head, but he didn't think Tomi would try to evade him, not when he likely needed help. He turned on the auxiliary power and found a Hawaiian music station that was playing an Amy Gilliom song. As the sound of her rich voice and Willie K's twelve-string guitar filled the car, he watched the front of the building.

Sure enough, fifteen minutes later Tomi darted out the front door and hurried across the street. He got in on the passenger side and shut the door.

"Are you crazy?" he hissed. "If Watson sees you, he'll be asking questions I don't want to answer."

"Who's Watson? The big guy at the bar?"

"Yeah. You know him?"

"I know him by another name," Mano said grimly. What game was the big Hawaiian playing? And how was Tomi involved? "He's the last one to see your sister. Did you know that?"

Tomi paled. "He never mentioned he knew Leilani." His voice cracked.

"I think you'd better tell me what's going on between you two," Mano said.

Tomi looked in the back of the car at the cooler. "You got any soda?"

"I've got water. Help yourself."

Tomi grimaced but reached into the back and pulled out a bottle of water. He took a swallow and shuddered. "Yuck."

"Quit procrastinating and just spit it out."

Tomi finally looked at him directly. "How much do you really know about my family, Mano?"

"Apparently not as much as I thought."

Tomi chuckled. "My dad built a little house forty years ago and has no idea of the gold mine he's sitting on."

"What are you talking about? The land isn't worth much."

"That's what I thought too. Look at HOVE. You can buy a lot out there for fifteen thousand dollars. But what would you say if I told you there's going to be a volcano theme park built out at Aloha Shores, along with a casino and a resort? That changes the value quite a lot, wouldn't you say?"

"I already heard about it. But what's that have to do with Watson?"

Tomi pressed his lips together. "Watson has connections with the casino. He's offered us three million dollars for the property."

"Your dad will never sell. What's it to you? Are you undercover?" Tomi looked away, but not before Mano saw pain darken his eyes.

Tomi shook his head. "I wish I were. It would be easier to get out of this than out of the mess I've made of things."

"So let's get you out of it."

"Spoken like the friend I know. Mano to the rescue. This is too bad for a quick fix, pal. A Band-Aid won't do."

"Just give the money back to the Iranians and forget the whole thing."

"The problem is, I need some of it." Tomi hunched his shoulders.

"You're not serious. You touch it, and you go to prison. What do you need with that kind of money?"

Tomi took another swig of his water. "I got a call last night. From Afsoon."

"I thought you said she was killed."

"That's what I thought. But she lived." He dropped his head. "You thought you deserted me, and now I find out I deserted her. She borrowed a car to drive me to catch a boat. We were on the end of the pier about to get into the boat when the ambush happened. The bullets were flying. She toppled into the water and was floating face down with blood coming out of her head. I was sure she was dead."

"So why call you now? And what about the money?"

"They'd told her I died. But she overheard her father talking to some flunkies and realized she'd been told a lie. I've got to get her out of there. And it's going to take some dough. A lot of it." He rubbed his hand through his dyed hair and left it standing in spikes. "Wouldn't it be poetic justice to use their own money to do it?"

"Sounds like you still love her."

"Yeah, I guess I do. Sap that I am." He sighed and looked down the street. "I've got to get to the bank."

"Tomi, you need to give that money back."

"I know." Tomi rubbed his forehead. "I don't know what I'm going to do."

"Where does Leilani fit into all this?" Mano decided Tomi had to know more about his sister than he was saying.

"She doesn't. That's what I don't get. No one's demanded anything of me. I still wonder if she's just run off with a boyfriend."

"What information do the Iranians want, exactly? You haven't been very specific."

"You know that tactical plan for how we would proceed if we ever found it necessary to invade Iran? They want me to write it all down for them."

"We'll never invade Iran."

"You and I know it, but they're not taking any chances after what happened in Iraq. And I can't give them what they want, of course."

"No, of course not."

Mano nodded toward the bar. "And Kim? Where does he fit in?"

"Kim?" Confusion clouded Tomi's face. He blinked, and his expression cleared. "You mean Tab? He's just the contact for the consortium that is building the theme park. Banos."

"You need to ask him about Leilani."

Tomi frowned. "The casino has nothing to do with Leilani, but I'll ask him. First, I've got to get that money off my hands. It's the key to getting us all out of this situation. As for Afsoon, I'll work on talking dad into selling the house instead."

"Even if you give them the money back, they're still going to want that information. They'll do whatever is needed to keep you under their thumbs. It's not going to be that easy, Tomi."

Tomi capped his water. "I'll figure out a way."

Annie sat on the hard wooden chair the detective offered her, with Fawn beside her. A drunk bellowed to be turned loose from the corner where he was being interrogated, and a woman with a blouse cut to her navel leaned over the counter and tried to talk the officer into not booking her for prostitution. Two kids hauled in for vandalizing a deserted house cried for their mothers, then one vomited on the nondescript vinyl tile floor.

"Where's Sam?" Fawn asked in a frustrated whisper. "We've been waiting for nearly an hour."

"If he doesn't come soon, we'll just leave and call him." Annie didn't think he would be much help anyway. She didn't know where to turn for answers. She chewed on her ragged thumbnail and tried to ignore the bedlam.

Sam finally appeared in the doorway. "Sorry to keep you waiting. Come on back." He escorted them to his office and pointed to two chairs that faced his desk.

Annie glanced around at the jumble of papers on the desk and the stacks of files on the floor. She itched to organize it all for him, but she had to be content with moving the stacks that inhabited her chair to the floor before sitting down. "You saw the report about our garage being broken into?"

"Sure did." He rooted through his papers. "So these guys threatened the family? Any specifics about Leilani?"

"No, but if they threatened to kill all of us, that surely means they have Leilani." She half stood, then sank back into the chair. "They shouldn't be that hard to find."

"You'd be surprised. We've got a whole raft of Arabs here on a tour right now. We've been talking to people. So far all we're finding are tourists." He narrowed his eyes and stared at her. "And why would some Arab men break into your house? I don't get it."

She couldn't tell him about Tomi. It was a mistake to have come here. "That's what we want you to find out." She rose. "*Mahalo* for your time, Sam. You've got my number." Her knees nearly buckled when she stood. She had to get out of here before he became suspicious.

He came around the end of the desk. "I hope to have some answers for you this week. Try not to worry."

He sounded kind and concerned. Fawn followed her to the door. Annie exited the police station like she'd been set free. "I don't know what I was thinking to go there," she muttered to

Fawn. "Of course he's going to wonder why some Arab men would target us."

Fawn examined Annie's face. "You need a break tonight. How about I come over and sacrifice myself on the Scrabble altar."

Annie laughed. "Again?"

"I'd do anything to cheer you up."

"You're a good friend." Annie was tempted to say no. She wasn't in the mood even for her favorite pastime. But Fawn was right—she needed to think about something else. She was helpless right now, at the mercy of the police investigation. Or lack of it would be more accurate. "Okay," she said.

Fawn waggled her eyebrows. "I'll bring some granola bars and my juicer. I just picked some new grasses. Very healthy. It will put a sparkle in your eyes."

"More likely a pain in my stomach."

Fawn punched her in the arm. "You'll love it."

"I'm supposed to meet Mano in about an hour. How about you come over around seven? I'll get some snacks on the way home."

Fawn made a face. "I'll bring the food. You're not a good judge of what's best for your poor body."

"As long as we get more than just grass and granola bars."

"Deal."

Annie dropped her friend off at her car in the parking lot and drove to town to meet Mano. She hoped he'd found Tab Watson. Frustration and helplessness combined to make her feel out of sorts and ill-tempered.

Volcano was filled with cars. The volcano had been putting on a lavish display today. Tourists and *kama'aina*, long-time locals, had flocked to the park to see it, and most of them ate here before they hiked out. She grunted in irritation at her inability to find a parking space, then managed to snag a spot someone else was vacating.

This wasn't like her. She told herself to lighten up, but she wanted to see her sister. And her brother, for that matter. Tomi still had a lot of explaining to do. She got out and went toward the bar where she was supposed to meet Mano. She saw a hand sticking out a car window and realized he was flagging her down. His new rental sat directly opposite the door to the bar.

As she neared the car, she realized he wasn't alone. Tomi sat in the passenger side. She jogged the last remaining steps and climbed into the backseat. Maybe she was finally going to get some answers.

Sixteen

nnie's face was flushed when she slammed the backseat door and looked at her brother. "Tomi. I'm so glad you're okay. But you've got to tell me what's going on." Her voice was controlled, but there was determination in the slant of her chin.

Mano listened while Tomi launched into the story. Mano watched Annie's face. It had to come as even more of a shock to her than it had been to him to find out that Tomi didn't walk on water. She'd adored her older brother for so many years. This mistake Tomi had made was going to have an impact on the entire family.

Mano was beginning to see more and more how Annie had been taken advantage of by her family. Without her, the Tagamas would have splintered from selfishness. She gave everything she had to ensuring their happiness and comfort. Her beauty was understated and shone from within in ways he was just noticing. She was worth ten of her sister. He'd sure been a blind idiot.

What would she think if he seriously pursued her when this was over? He gave himself a mental shake. There was no time now for romance.

Annie's eyes were clouded with confusion. "Afsoon is still alive? Are you sure she's not just trying another tactic to entrap you?"

"She's in trouble, Annie. I can't turn my back on her." Tomi pinched the bridge of his nose. "I've screwed up a lot lately. I have to find a way back. I don't much like the man I've become."

"Our sister is in trouble too. She should be your first priority. Not Afsoon." Annie's voice was agitated.

"Leilani may not even be connected to this, Annie."

"Then *where is she*?" Annie was nearly shouting. Mano had never seen her so upset. "You think it's some coincidence that she would disappear at the same time you magically come back from the dead?"

"I don't know. But you've got Mano to help you figure it out. Afsoon only has me. I have to help her."

"I think you've got your priorities skewed," Mano put in, struggling to keep his voice level. "We're talking about your missing sister. She's your responsibility too. I want to help, but step up to the plate, Tomi, and be a man."

Annie's shoulders slumped, and she leaned back against the seat, resigned to Tomi's stubbornness. "Sam says there are a bunch of Middle Eastern tourists on the island this week. Do you know what these men look like?"

"I have no idea. I wish I did," Tomi said. He rubbed his head. "You're right, though, we need to find Leilani. I just don't want to desert Afsoon."

"How much money will you need to go get Afsoon?" Mano put in.

"A lot. Probably at least fifty thousand."

Mano winced inwardly. "Do you have a plan?"

"Not yet. I'll need to bribe people to help me." He turned and looked into the backseat at his sister. "If I have to use some of the money in the account to pay it, I will. I'll figure out what to do to replace it later."

"You can't do that," Mano said. "Not if you want out of this mess."

"I can't abandon Afsoon." Tomi banged his head against the window several times. "I'm so stupid. I can't believe I got into this."

Mano couldn't either. Tomi had always had such a clear head. "What exactly did Afsoon say? Where is she?"

"She's in Tehran. Staying with a childhood friend at the moment, but her father's goons are looking for her."

"Why? Surely her own father won't hurt her."

"You know better than that, Mano. Women are expendable in that culture. Her father is livid that she betrayed him and has vowed to see her dead."

Mano sighed as his thoughts ticked through options. "Don't do anything yet. Let me see if I can call in some favors and get her out."

"Who's going to get her out, Mano? We can't ask navy people. They'll want to know more than we can tell them."

"I have some contacts I used when we were undercover. One of them is in Tehran. Asad. I helped him arrange to get his brother papers to come to the States. I think he might help."

Tomi straightened. "I should have known you'd think of something. You always do." He punched Mano on the arm. "*Mahalo,* buddy."

"No problem. I haven't done anything yet. I'll make some calls." He'd have to find Asad's phone number first. It was back on Kaua'i. He might have to make a trip home.

Tomi turned around in the seat and faced forward. "There's another way to get some money if I have to have it. We've got an offer for the land, Annie. Three million dollars."

She gasped. "That's not possible."

"A casino is coming in. We're not going to want to live nearby anyway."

"Father will never sell. You know that. He loves his property."

"Isn't he worried about the new magma chamber growing under it?" Mano asked.

Annie shook her head. "He refuses to believe Jillian's data. When he read the article Noah published, Father approved of the way Noah downplayed the danger."

"I've got to get to the bank." Tomi opened the car door.

"I thought you were afraid of being seen." Annie sounded worried. She got out and went to stand by her brother's open door.

"I've got a disguise like you suggested. Let me go grab it, and I'll meet you back here in half an hour."

The hug Tomi gave her seemed perfunctory to Mano. It must have felt that way to Annie too, because when she slid into the front seat, her eyes swam with tears. Mano reached across the seat and took her hand. She glanced up at him with a question in her eyes but didn't pull away. "I'm sorry," he said softly.

"This is going to kill our father," she muttered. "I don't know how to tell him."

"Don't. Let Tomi do it. This is his mess. You need to let him own it."

Annie was shaking her head. "He won't tell our father. Tomi has never been able to handle disapproval. It will be easier if I break the news, and we discuss what can be done. But to a Japanese man, honor is everything. Father will feel our name is dishonored when he hears what Tomi has done."

"If Tomi gives back the money, he may only have to endure a dishonorable discharge for going AWOL."

"Only?" She gave a faint smile. "Father will never be able to accept it."

He hated to see the pain in her eyes. "I wish I could help somehow."

She laid her other hand over his. "You're doing all you can to help me find Leilani. I'll never forget what you've done."

"It sounds like you're telling me good-bye." He grinned, not sure if he was joking or not. Her expression was one of finality and resignation.

"I can't imagine why you'd want to associate with us anymore. Not after Tomi let you believe you'd left him to die on the beach. If you want to go home and forget all about us, I'd understand."

"You're not getting rid of me that easily." A clean scent of flowers, maybe gardenia, drifted to his nose from the lotion on her skin. He badly wanted to pull her into his arms and kiss away her frown. Knowing she wouldn't welcome an embrace from him, he released her hand and settled back against his seat. "Have you had anything to eat?"

She shook her head. "I skipped lunch."

"I had a cheese stick, but I'm still hungry. How about a jerked-chicken sandwich?" He nodded toward the small café beside the car. "The sandwiches are pretty good here."

"I could eat a lu'au pig all by myself."

They got out of the car and went to the small open-air stand. The aroma of jerked chicken and teri beef made his mouth water. He ordered two sandwiches, fries, and mango tea. Annie tried to pay for hers, and he wouldn't let her. "My treat. And a fruit smoothie for dessert. There's a great stand just down the street."

He watched Annie as she ate. She devoured every morsel, then licked the sauce off her fingers. His fascination with her grew. He'd always heard that beauty was in the eye of the beholder, but he thought anyone should be able to see how lovely Annie was. The light in her eyes tugged at him, and he watched the curve of her lips and the slim line of her throat.

"You're staring," she said. A blush stained her cheeks.

"Sorry." He collected himself and glanced away. "You're so pretty it's hard not to." He glanced up in time to see a rush of red wash over her cheeks, and she dropped her gaze. She stood and went toward the car without answering. She got into the passenger side and slammed the door.

He went around to the driver's side. So much for pursuing her. Last night's date must not have affected her like it did him. It was obvious she had no interest in him beyond the help he could offer to find Leilani. Feeling more disappointment than he'd expected, he got in and fastened his seat belt.

nnie struggled with the guilt she felt. Last night, she'd almost become her sister. She didn't want Mano if he saw her as an extension of Leilani. The silence between them stretched out. She saw Tomi's familiar form loping toward the car. He carried a black satchel.

Opening the back door, he flung himself inside the car. "I've got to change." He pulled out a loud mu'umu'u and dropped it over his jeans and shirt. Taking out a long wig, he tugged it over his hair. "Can you put some makeup on me?"

"All I have is lipstick." She wished she had the makeup Fawn had given her. Annie rooted through her bag and pulled out the maroon lipstick she'd dropped in her purse that morning.

Tomi pulled away from her. "That's too dark. It will be hard to wash off."

He had a point. "How about just a touch?" He nodded and submitted to her dabbing a bit of color on his lips. "You need some, uh, shape to you," she told him. She suppressed a chuckle.

"Got it covered." He pulled out two small pillows and pulled up the dress, then stuffed the pillows under his T-shirt. Tugging the dress back into place, he preened. "What do you think?"

"You look hot," Mano told him. "You'd stop traffic." He winked at Annie.

Annie covered her smile with her hand. "Don't encourage him," she said. "How are you going to get them to give you the money? The name on the account is a man's."

"That's where I need you." He pulled out another dress. "We'll look like sisters when we go in and will stand out. Then we'll go into the ladies' room and pull off the dresses and stroll to the teller window as brother and sister. No one will be the wiser."

"You can't go into the ladies' room!"

"You can scout it out and make sure no one else is in there. Mano can stand guard."

"Oh, that will look good." Mano's grin stretched across his face. "I'll look like some pervert staking out the women's restroom."

"You fit the part, buddy." Tomi punched him in the arm.

Annie smiled to see them falling back into their old camaraderie. "It might work. There's rarely anyone in the restrooms." A giggle welled up, and she clapped her hand over her mouth, but it bubbled out anyway. "We're going to look ridiculous!" She grabbed the dress he handed her and pulled it over her head.

"I'm going with you," Mano said. "It will look natural for me to be escorting you."

They all got out of the car and began to walk toward the bank. Annie glanced at Tomi out of the corner of her eye. "You're walking like a man," she hissed. "Try a more fluid motion. Don't stomp."

"Yeah, sway your backside," Mano said. Tomi's swagger changed a bit. Annie began to laugh. "Your boobs are falling," Mano said with a fake leer.

Tomi grinned and hiked up his pillows. "Just get me to the ladies' room and out of this gear."

"Walk between us," Mano suggested. "Maybe no one will notice you walk like a sailor."

"I *am* a sailor," Tomi retorted.

Mano grinned and linked his arm with Tomi's. "Want to rest your head on my shoulder, darling?"

"You're sick," Tomi hissed.

Both men were laughing. Annie giggled. Maybe they could find their way across this lava bench of intrigue and danger to the way things used to be. She had to cling to that hope.

They reached the bank. "See anyone watching us?" she asked.

Tomi kept his gaze on the doors. "The black car parked in front of the fruit smoothie place." He started to open the door, and Mano stopped him.

"I'll be a gentleman and hold the door open for you two ladies," he said.

Tomi rolled his eyes, but stepped back and let Mano get the door. Inside, Annie glanced around. There were five customers. "The restrooms are down this hall." She led the way past the water fountain to the ladies' room. The building smelled of fresh paint and carpet from the recent remodeling. She liked the new seafoam green color that had replaced the institutional beige.

The hallway was empty. "Wait here a minute." She stuck her head inside and looked around the restroom, newly papered with hibiscus-print wallpaper. There were two stalls but no feet under them. She went back to the hall. "It's all clear."

Tomi ducked inside. "Stand guard at the door." He washed his face, whipped off the wig and dress, and stuffed them in his satchel. "Give me your dress." She pulled it off, and he put it in the satchel.

"I'll see if it's clear while you wash off the lipstick." She stuck her head out the door.

"I told a woman the restroom was full," Mano told her. "She looked at me like I was a slug." Though he was complaining, his grin told a different story.

She chuckled, then motioned to Tomi, who was wiping off his mouth. "All clear." They stepped out of the restroom and moved toward the teller window. They got in line behind a woman with two children. Mano began making faces at the baby on her shoulder and had the little girl giggling and hiding her face in a few minutes.

The mother turned around. "You must be a dad to be so good with kids."

"Not yet," he said.

Annie couldn't help but wonder what a child of theirs might look like. Mano's gaze caught hers, and she looked away, wondering if he could read her thoughts on her face. She was such a dreamer.

The woman in front of them concluded her business, and Tomi stepped to the window and produced his ID. "I've lost my bankbook on this account." He slid the number to her. "It's on a

New York bank. I want to move the money to a new account before someone finds it and gains access to my funds."

The teller looked at his driver's license and then back to Tomi's face. She punched some numbers into the computer. After a few seconds, she frowned. "Let me get my manager."

Annie's stomach tightened. Tomi's complexion had paled to a sickly yellow. "Maybe I should get out of here," he muttered.

"No, it's probably standard procedure," Mano said. "Just hold tight."

The back of Annie's neck prickled in spite of Mano's soothing, matter-of-fact voice. She wanted to finish this and get outside to the sunshine. Tomi's tension was getting to her. She glanced around but didn't see anyone watching them. "What about when we leave? Won't the men outside recognize us?"

Tomi shrugged. "We can put the dresses back on."

"Or just run for the car," Mano said.

"Come on, come on," Tomi muttered, glancing at his watch.

Finally the teller came back with an older woman. Tomi's face cleared. "Margaret, you can tell the teller who I am."

The woman's eyes widened. "Tomi Tagama. I couldn't believe it when my teller said someone came in yesterday claiming to be you. I called the police, but the man was gone by the time they got here. I froze the account and was going to call your sister." She glanced at Annie, then back to Tomi. "I can't believe you're here and alive. What a happy day." She reached across the counter and patted his hand.

"Good thinking, Margaret. Thank you. Can I please transfer the money to a new account?"

"Of course, of course." She moved to the computer and began the transaction. Minutes later she had him sign several papers and then handed him a new bankbook. "Try to keep better track of this one," she said with a teasing light in her eyes. "I didn't know the navy paid so well, Tomi."

He winked at her. "It's not my money. If I'd lost it, I would have been in deep doo-doo."

She chuckled. "I've missed you, Tomi. It's good to see you resurrected. I'm sure your family is ecstatic. I'm surprised news of your return hasn't spread all over the town."

"It will now, I'm sure," he said. Her laughter followed them toward the door. He paused and looked outside. Several olive-skinned men were approaching the bank. "Uh-oh, I'd better get out the other door." He turned and bolted for the hallway by the bathroom.

Annie ran after her brother, but he'd vanished out the exit door. She poked her head out, but all she saw was an empty alley. Mano joined her, and she slumped against him. "He's gone."

He touched her elbow and guided her down the alley in time to see the men enter the bank. She glanced at the parked cars. "They all seem to be inside. Let's make a run for it while we can."

Mano guided her down the street. "We probably better tell Sam that Tomi is back in town. He's going to hear about it, and he'll be furious we've kept him in the dark."

"I suppose." Annie stopped. "We'd better figure out what we're going to tell him though. We can't tell him about the money."

"No, we can't."

"We'll just say Tomi was picked up by some Iranians and just now made it back to the States. It's the truth."

It would have to do, but she knew Sam would be suspicious. "Lead the way." They went down the street to the police station.

Sam was at the front desk when they arrived. He smiled when he saw them. "I was just going to call you. I got a call from someone who said they saw your sister in Hilo yesterday with a man. She was laughing and seemed happy. It looks like I was right all along."

Annie closed her eyes then opened them again. "Thank you, God. Who was this caller?"

"It was her friend, CeCe."

"CeCe? Why didn't she call me? That makes no sense."

Sam shrugged. "She said Leilani asked her to get me to call off the dogs. I'm sure she knew I'd tell you."

"I don't understand why Leilani didn't call me. I'd better talk to CeCe."

"Go right ahead."

Annie turned, then remembered why they'd come in the first place. "There's something else. I wanted you to hear it from me first."

"Oh?"

"Tomi isn't dead after all. He was picked up by some Iranians and just now made it back to us. Isn't that wonderful?" She forced herself to gush to make sure Sam wasn't suspicious.

Sam's face brightened. "You're kidding me! Where is he?" His smile was genuinely delighted.

"I'm not sure, but I'll tell him to stop by and see you."

"I can't wait to see him." Sam beamed. "Great news all around for your family. I'm glad this has ended so well on both counts."

Annie could tell he was congratulating himself on being right about Leilani. But something didn't sit right with her. She and Mano chatted a few more minutes, then exited the station.

"We need to see CeCe now," Mano said as soon as they stepped into the sunshine. "This stinks like dead mackerel."

Seventeen

nnie glanced at her watch. "CeCe's probably at lunch now. She and Leilani always used to go to the Kilauea Iki Overlook with their lunch. We could try there." They got in the car, and passing through a shower in the rain forest, drove to the park. Several vehicles were in the parking area at the overlook.

"There she is," Mano said.

CeCe sat on the stone fence. One foot swung carelessly back and forth as she talked to another young woman about her age. "And I told him no way was I going to give back the ring. If he was going to dump me, I was getting something out of the relationship. Of course that just made him livid." She licked a piece of peanut butter from her thumb.

"CeCe, we need to talk to you," Annie said, breaking into the conversation before CeCe could draw another breath.

CeCe's eyes widened. "Annie. Hi." She sounded breathless, and her giggle came out nervously. "What are you doing here?"

"We just talked to Sam. He said you saw Leilani."

The other girl got up. "I'll be in the car." She hurried away as though she wanted nothing to do with the conversation.

"That's right." Her head bobbed up and down.

"Who was the guy she was with?"

"Um, I don't know. I didn't recognize him." CeCe looked away, back toward the rain forest surrounding the outlook.

Annie grew cold, though the breeze was warm and fragrant. "What was she wearing?'

"Uh, let's see. That new red and black aloha top with black denim shorts. Those ones I've tried to get her to let me borrow."

Annie crossed her arms. "That's not possible. That top is still in her room."

"Oh, is it? Maybe she bought one like it." Her voice faltered, and she stood and brushed crumbs from her shirt. "I've got to get back to work."

"You didn't see her at all, did you, CeCe? Why would you lie to Sam?"

"Don't tell him." CeCe's voice rose. "Tab will . . ."

"Tab Watson? He told you to lie?"

CeCe nodded. "He wanted to get Sam off his back. He thought if you were convinced Leilani was all right, the cops would lay off."

Tab Watson. The last person to see Leilani alive. Nausea roiled in her stomach. Did that mean Leilani was dead?

"Don't say anything, please," CeCe begged.

"Why would you lie for Tab?"

"Well, we've gone out a couple of times," CeCe said.

"I thought you said he didn't appeal to you," Mano put in.

CeCe shrugged. "I lied, okay? He says he preferred me to Leilani all along, but Leilani was more forward, and he thought I didn't like him."

"Oh brother," Mano said, his voice heavy with disgust. "Let's go, Annie." He pointed at CeCe. "You tell Aki that if he's hurt Leilani, I'm going to take him down."

"Who's Aki?" CeCe asked as they walked away.

Mano whirled. "Ask your boyfriend why he uses an assumed name. His real name is Kim Aki."

Annie could feel Mano's anger coming off in waves. Was it because CeCe had said Leilani was a flirt, or was it because of the lies? She wished she knew what his feelings for Leilani were now. "What's this about Tab Watson being Kim Aki?" She got in the car.

Mano slammed his door. "Me and Aki have had a run-in before. He's trouble, and I have a feeling he's involved in this up to his neck. I'm going to have another talk with him later." He glanced at his watch. "What about that place where Leilani and Tomi had their clubhouse? Let's go check it out."

There was nothing better to do. She nodded. "It's out toward our house."

He started the car, and she directed him. They were both silent as the town fell behind them. "There," she said. "Turn here." She pointed to a dirt track that was practically obscured by overgrowth. "Take this about two miles in toward the volcano."

"Seems too spooky a place for kids to hang out. This is on your property, isn't it?"

She nodded. "At the northern edge."

He slowed the car, but it still jolted when it hit the potholes in the lane. "No one's been out through here in a while. The last rain washed away any tire tracks."

"She could have walked," Annie pointed out.

"Leilani's not exactly one for physical exercise. This is a long way back."

"I think I know my own sister better than you do," she snapped. She looked away. He was going to think she was a shrew. She told herself she didn't care what he thought of her, but she knew it was a lie. She cared. Way too much. "Sorry," she said softly. She pointed. "There's the lava tube they called their clubhouse."

He stopped the car and twisted in the seat to look at her. "Look, Annie, let's get this clear between us. You've been prickly ever since I told you that I thought you were pretty. I'm not a womanizer. I don't say things I don't mean. When a man gives you a compliment, you're supposed to say *mahalo*, not turn it into some kind of big production where you question his integrity." He got out and slammed the car door.

From the set of his shoulders, she could tell he was mad. Could he really be over Leilani? Was that even possible? She was afraid to hope. Her emotions were too raw to handle one more problem.

She let her gaze travel over his husky build. Pure Hawaiian, full of the aloha spirit of giving, and passionate about the people and things he loved. For a moment, she let herself dream about what it would be like to be one of the things Mano Oana loved. It was too wondrous to fathom.

Annie got out of the car and went to stand beside him at the opening to the cave. She touched his arm and felt the firm muscles under the skin. "Sorry, you're right. I know you better than to think you'd lie to me."

He turned to look down at her. Before she could think about it, she reached up and touched his cheek, then stood on tiptoe and brushed her lips across his. She heard his swift intake of breath, then he caught her in his arms. She closed her eyes when his kiss gained in intensity. She'd never been so thoroughly kissed. In fact, the only time she'd been kissed by someone other than a family member had been in third grade when Johnny Choo kissed her for putting a Band-Aid on his leg.

She wasn't prepared for the onslaught of emotion that left her shaking when he finally released her. "Wow," she whispered.

His dark eyes regarded her with amusement and something she thought might be tenderness. "I think I'd like to try that again when we have more time."

Heat flared in her chest and spread to her face. "Fawn and I have a big Scrabble tournament on for tonight. Want to come?"

"Can I get you in the moonlight afterwards?"

"Maybe." She smiled, her heart as light as the honeycreeper that soared from the tree above her head.

Mano walked along the rough *a'a* lava rock toward the lava tube. Black gravel crunched beneath his boots. Little vegetation had returned to the area, and the sparse landscape was like another world. Light shone from the other end of the hollow tube and illuminated the length of the enclosure. Filmy roots dangled like spiderwebs from the ceiling.

"I can see how this would be intriguing to kids." He stooped to enter the tube.

"Watch the stalactites," Annie warned. She pointed to the rock formations that hung like black icicles from the ceiling. The floor was flat and level with high water marks on the walls.

Annie pointed out a depression in the side of the lava tube. "Look, someone has been here."

Blankets, a cooler, and some Styrofoam cups lay on the smooth floor. Tucked away like this, they almost escaped Mano's notice. There was nothing to indicate who the items belonged to. He glanced at her. She wore a closed expression, and he wondered about her childhood and how she'd lived in the shadows of her more flamboyant siblings.

He smoothed the blanket out. "This is our clubhouse now. Sit down." He sank onto the blanket and folded his legs in front of him, Indian-style. "I've got a macadamia-nut protein bar we can share for our little picnic." His alarm beeped on his watch, and he shut it off.

A smile tugged at her lips, and the distant expression vanished from her eyes. "You're nuts." She joined him on the blanket. "You didn't even check for scorpions or lava spiders."

"They wouldn't dare interrupt our good time." He unwrapped the protein bar, broke it in two, and gave her the bigger half. "A repast fit for a princess."

She tucked a strand of silky black hair behind her ear and accepted the candy. "Sugar-free. I didn't know you were a health nut." She smiled at him. "And Leilani was always the princess. I was the wicked witch."

"You're too pretty to be a witch. They have crooked teeth and warts." The dim light inside the lava tube cast a misty, ethereal halo around her. It seemed like he'd just met her, and yet he knew her so well. All the qualities he'd seen subconsciously were no longer hidden from him. She took a bite of her candy bar and didn't answer, and he knew he'd embarrassed her again. He wondered when she'd last had a compliment. "Your father must be very proud you chose to follow in his footsteps," he told her.

She met his gaze. "Tomi was the one who was supposed to do it. Father groomed him from the time we were small. But Tomi has no patience for the meticulous work of geological studies. It bored him."

"And you love it."

She nodded. "The earth holds so many secrets. It's my job to tease them out, to coax the stones and strata into revealing our past and how the earth came to be."

"I don't think I'd have the patience either. I just turn to the Bible and know that God created it all."

She leaned her head back against the smooth, black wall. "It's exciting to see how the Bible lines up with science."

"It's science's job to line up with the Bible."

She blinked. "Uh yeah, sure."

He wondered what her spiritual life was like. He knew her family attended church, but science had always been more important than anything else to the Tagama family. He started to say something else, but Annie held her finger to her lips.

"Shh."

"What is it?" he whispered.

"I heard something. It came from the back."

They both got up and crept to the back opening of the lava tube. It was barely large enough to crawl through. A thud came through, faint and to the left of the lava tube. "Let's check it out," Mano whispered. He wiggled through the opening, then helped Annie step out of the tube. "I think it was this way."

Annie's breathing quickened, and he knew she was scared. And no wonder. The light was going now, fading fast with the coming of twilight. The sound of the waves crashing on the rocks beyond the hill sounded like a dragon gnashing its teeth. Hardly anyone ever came out here. It was Tagama land, though they never would have stopped a casual tourist from strolling the grounds.

This didn't sound like a tourist. The noise was a furtive, dragging sound, as though someone didn't want to be heard or seen. Mano wasn't sure why he was certain of that fact, but he was. He clasped Annie's hand and wished he'd brought his gun. Or a knife. He stopped and picked up a sharp rock. It was better than nothing.

"Maybe we should call Sam," she whispered.

Mano shook his head. "No time." He released her hand. "Stay here. I'll be right back."

"I'm coming too." She stayed close to him.

He didn't argue. The sound had stopped now, but the air had a watching and waiting quality. There was no telling what they would find behind the line of scrubby shrubs. It was now or never, though. The last of the light would be gone in a few more minutes.

He grabbed another rock and tossed it into the darkness of the trees. There was a sudden *whoosh* of wind, and he heard the sound of someone running away. "Hey. You there! Wait." He plunged into the cool shade of the palms, then stumbled as his feet contacted something in the path. It was too soft to be a rock.

Annie uttered a cry and put her hand over her mouth. He stared down into Noah Sommers's face. Mano knelt and touched him. Too late. From the coldness of the body, he knew the man had been dead awhile. Dog tags lay beside the body. He didn't touch them but could see the name engraved on them. Tomiko Tagama. "Call Sam," he said.

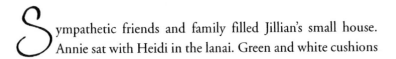 ympathetic friends and family filled Jillian's small house. Annie sat with Heidi in the lanai. Green and white cushions

on wicker furniture crowded the narrow room. Plumeria bloomed outside the screened-in area, and their fragrance drifted in, though she couldn't see them in the dark. She and the little girl sat on the wicker loveseat. Heidi hadn't cried yet. Annie thought it probably hadn't soaked in yet that she'd lost her father. Mano was with Jillian in the living room, and the low tenor of his voice drifted through the door. The sound comforted Annie.

No one wanted Heidi around while Sam was asking Jillian questions. It probably didn't look good that Noah and Jillian were estranged. Jillian would never have killed Noah, but Annie knew the police would be investigating the whole situation. Where did Tomi fit in? She refused to believe her brother could have had anything to do with the murder.

She picked up Heidi's hand. "Want to play a game?" she asked.

Heidi shook her head. "Can we pray for my dad?"

It was a little late now, but Annie didn't point that out. She was pretty rusty at the praying thing.

"I asked Jesus into my heart last year," Heidi confided. "He'll take care of my dad."

"I was your age when I asked Jesus too," Annie said. She remembered the frilly red dress she'd worn that day and how her heart pounded so hard she thought she could see it bounce against her dress. She'd pressed her hand over it to keep it in place, and her teacher thought she was getting sick.

Where had that excitement gone? Little by little, other things had crept in. It hadn't helped that her parents cautioned her not to let religion take too strong a hold on her life.

Heidi tugged at her hand. "You want me to pray?"

"I think that would be good," Annie said. A strange sensation swept over her, a yearning that she found hard to recognize. Mano had mentioned God earlier in the day as well. It must be nice to have that kind of close relationship with God, that kind of peace and certainty. She went through most of her days without giving God a thought.

What did she have, really? An obscure job studying volcanoes, a family that hardly noticed her unless the laundry needed to be done, and no social life to speak of. She stirred restlessly on the wicker sofa. Maybe Fawn was right—about everything.

Heidi gripped Annie's hand and prayed a halting yet somehow confident prayer for God to watch over her dad and to take care of her mom and her. The trust and total belief in Heidi's voice gripped Annie by the throat. She tried to be strong for her family, but she wished she could let go. Maybe there was more, something deeper, that she was missing.

Heidi nestled against her, and soon her rhythmic breathing told Annie that she'd fallen asleep. With her arm around the little girl, Annie was wedged into the cushion. She heard a car door slam at the front of the house, then the sound of an engine starting. Maybe Sam was done with Jillian.

The quality of the air changed. The sensation that she wasn't alone brought her head around, and she saw the shadow of Mano's bulk in the doorway. "She's asleep," Annie whispered. "How's Jillian?"

"Devastated and blaming herself for not listening when Noah wanted to talk."

"You can't blame her after what he did."

"I know, but she is. I called Jesse and Kaia. They're on their way and should be here by midnight, along with our mother. My grandfather is still not feeling well, so Bane will stay with him."

"You sound tired." The lanai was too dark to see well, its only illumination the dim spill of light from the house. But she heard the fatigue in his voice. His usual confidence seemed subdued.

He moved into the lanai and sank onto a chair that faced her. The light from the house touched his face, and she saw the weary lines around his eyes. "Is Jesse doing okay?"

"He's upset, of course. He really liked Noah."

"Does Sam have any idea what happened?"

Mano shook his head. "Noah was shot in the back of the head from close range. Definitely murder. Sam's trying to find Tomi."

"Tomi had nothing to do with it."

"You have to admit it looks bad that his dog tags were by Noah's body."

"There has to be some other explanation. Do they suspect Jillian?"

"I'm sure they'll look at her too. Did she have an alibi? Did you see her today?"

Annie shook her head. "No alibi. She was out by herself at the lava fields all day."

He grunted. "That's not good."

"You're going to wish you'd never come here on leave," she blurted.

"Not a chance," he said softly. "I wouldn't want to miss being here and helping out."

She could feel his stare, taste the way his gaze traveled over her face and lingered on her lips. She knew he couldn't forget the afternoon any more than she could. She didn't know if that was good or bad. Either way, she wasn't in his league, and when she hit the bump back to reality, the fall might destroy her.

Eighteen

The area buzzed with the news of the murder. Annie wasn't able to get much work done over the next day with coworkers stopping to ask how she found the body. She parried the discreet and not-so-discreet questions about how Tomi's dog tags happened to be there.

She took a bite of the granola bar she'd pinched from Fawn and stared at her computer screen. None of the numbers made sense to her tired brain.

"Annie?" Gina stood in the doorway. "Monica had a flat after lunch. The earthquake swarms have increased. I need you and Fawn to get some lava samples." She glanced at her watch. "If you take the ATV, you should still be able to get out there and back by four."

Lava samples. Annie stood, and her sudden movement knocked papers to the floor. She knelt and scooped them up. "I—I can't, Gina. Please don't ask me." The papers in her hands shook.

"If there was anyone else to ask, I would. But Monica won't be back today. And Shawn is on the other side of the park working on a broken GPS receiver. Obviously, Jillian won't be in for at least a week. Besides, the only way to get over this fear is to face it, sweetie. You can do it."

The compassion in her boss's voice made Annie's eyes burn. "You're right. I know you're right." She took a deep breath. The key to the ATV was on the top of her filing cabinet. She picked it up.

"Good girl," Gina said with approval in her voice. "Fawn is already outside."

Annie wouldn't have been surprised to see her knees knocking together. She went down the hall and out into the parking lot. Fawn was strapping their equipment to her ATV. Her eyes widened when she saw Annie. "Isn't Shawn coming?"

Annie shook her head. "No, Gina wants me to do it. And Shawn is on the other side of the park."

"Are you going to be okay?"

"Do I have a choice? If I want to be a scientist, I've got to get over this. Otherwise, I might as well quit now and find another line of work."

Fawn squeezed her hand. "I'll be praying for you. You can do it."

Annie returned the pressure. "I need all the prayers I can get to do this." She got on her ATV and put the key in the ignition. Fawn got on the other one, and they drove out over the lava flats. They passed tourists walking along the trail to the vent. The odor of sulfur grew as they followed the trail.

"This is as far as we'd better take the machines," Fawn shouted.

Annie nodded. She stopped her ATV and shut off the engine. Her muscles froze, and she couldn't seem to make herself get off the seat. Her gaze traveled over the ropey lava. Where were the weak spots? She saw a fumarole. That was one place she would avoid. Another spot had an indentation that made it appear unsafe.

"Annie?" Fawn put her hand on her shoulder. "I can't carry everything by myself."

Annie nodded and forced herself to move. She and Fawn donned protective clothing, fire helmets, and boots. She hadn't been in this gear since the accident. Her heart fluttered against her ribs like a caged wild bird. She stopped and bent over. Bile burned the back of her throat, and she gagged.

Fawn touched the back of her neck. "Breathe deeply," she instructed. "In and out."

Annie did as her friend instructed. Gradually the nausea passed. "I'm okay now," she said weakly. "*Mahalo.*" Aware of the interested stares of tourists, she grabbed her equipment. "Let's go." She eased herself out onto the bench. Trying to breathe through her mouth to minimize the stench just made her throat burn more. She dug out her gas mask and put it on, but that just made her panic rise, so she ripped it off and endured the odor.

The ground gave beneath her boots, like there was Play-Doh under the crust on top. But Annie knew from past experience that what lay beneath the hardened layer was much more dangerous. "I can't do it," she said suddenly. "I can't." She turned and ran back to the ATV. When she reached the machine, she vomited the contents of her stomach at the tires.

Fawn was at her side moments later murmuring soothing noises. "It's okay. Let's get back to the observatory. Shawn and I can do this tomorrow."

"Gina will be so mad at me." Annie squeezed her eyes shut at the thought of the disappointment she would see on her boss's face. But there was no way she could go any closer to the fire.

When they got back to the observatory, Gina was in the hall talking to another worker. Her smile faded when she saw Annie and Fawn. "You look terrible. What happened?"

"She's sick," Fawn said, her eyes challenging Annie to deny it. "She threw up, so we came back."

"Sick or frightened?" Gina walked to meet them.

"I can't do it," Annie blurted. "You might as well look for a replacement for me. Give my job to Monica." She burst into tears and ran out of the building. Her vision was blurry as she jammed the key in the ignition. She drove aimlessly out to the water, out to Ka Lae, the southernmost point in the United States. The ferocious winds here caused the trees to grow bent over.

Annie was surprised she could still walk upright, as bent and tattered as she was by the winds of change that were sweeping over her life. Her career was over. Monica would take her place at work, and Gina would take her place with her family. What would she do? How could she find meaning in her life? She fell to her knees while the wind whipped her hair around her face. God was still there for her, Fawn said. He was the one constant she could always count on. Why had she forgotten that?

She lay facedown in the tall grass. She smelled the earth, the sky, and the grass in a comforting aroma of God's creation. She was his creation too. He would know where she belonged. Her tears soaked the roots of the grass and nourished it, even as she was nourished by the Lord's love that seeped down into her heart. In his arms was home and nowhere else. She wanted to make a new start with him.

The next morning, Annie honked the horn outside Fawn's house. She smoothed the navy slacks she wore. These pumps were killing her feet, but she seldom wore heels. She'd put on navy trouser socks to hide the scars on her feet, but her limp was more pronounced in these shoes.

Bougainvillea covered the front of Fawn's small house. Herbs grew in raised beds in the yard and rambled up a white picket fence like something out of a Thomas Kinkade painting. The front door opened, and Fawn came running out. Annie didn't think she'd ever seen her friend in a skirt. The black ankle-length skirt was topped with a flower-print silk top that flowed down to her hips at an angle.

"You look nice," Annie told her.

"So do you." Fawn fastened her seat belt. "I hate funerals."

"Me too. But we need to be there for Jillian." They rode in gloomy silence for a few minutes. "Have you talked to Jillian this morning?"

Fawn shook her head. "I didn't want to bother her. Her brother is here. They haven't been able to get hold of her sister."

"She's in the Peace Corps, isn't she? Somewhere exotic."

"Poor Jillian," Fawn said moodily. "I remember a couple of years ago thinking how she and Noah were the perfect couple." She glanced at Annie. "Speaking of the perfect couple, I haven't heard the dish on how your date went with Mano the other day. We've been too busy to talk."

Annie turned the radio down. "I think it went okay. I had a good time."

"That's all? What about romance? Did he kiss you? Did he say anything about another date? Come on, you're killing me here!"

Annie grinned. "If you'd go out on a date yourself, you might not be so nosy." Her cheeks burned. There was no way she was telling Fawn about the kiss at the lava tube. She had a feeling Mano regretted it by now.

"I still would." Fawn poked her in the ribs. "Come on, dish."

"He said I was comfortable to be with." She wrinkled her nose. "*Comfortable*. That's something you want from your Lazyboy, not from a woman, isn't it?"

"That's good though," Fawn said eagerly. "Feed him some good food, and he'll be thinking marriage before you know it."

"You are such a dreamer." Annie winked at her. Fawn could always be counted on to lift her spirits.

"You know you love him," Fawn said. "Even if you're not admitting it to yourself."

"Oh, I'm admitting it. I've tried to get rid of how I feel, but it won't go away. Not that I have any real hope." Talking it out, her cheeks cooled. Once Leilani returned, Mano would forget he ever kissed Annie.

"There's always hope. He might be the exact one God has in mind for you. I've seen the way he looks at you."

"You need glasses." Annie wished she could believe it, but Mano could have anyone. Why would he even notice someone like her?

"You shortchange yourself, and I'm sick of it. Sick of it, you hear?" Fawn stuck out her tongue. "Did he ask you out again?"

"No. But there's been no time. We've been too busy trying to figure out what's happened to Leilani and trying to get Tomi out of his mess."

"Are you scared? I am a little. I've been double-locking my doors. It's been hard to sleep. Noah's death kind of rattled me."

"Everything in my life has rattled me lately," Annie said. "I don't know where I'm going anymore or what my life is supposed to be about." Fawn didn't answer, and Annie glanced at her. "Spit it out. You've got something on your mind."

"It's because you're leaving God out of it, Annie. You've lost your vision and can't see the forest for the trees. You're always going to feel lost until you put God back at the center. He has to be the core equation. When was the last time you read your Bible? A year? Two?"

Annie tried not to get defensive, but her hackles rose anyway. "I've been busy. My research hasn't been going well, and I need to spend every minute on it." She should tell Fawn about her earlier talk with God.

"Have you ever stopped to think that maybe God is trying to get your attention? God doesn't like it when we put something else in his place. You've put your family above everything else in your life. The order is supposed to be God, family, then career. You've got it all out of whack."

"I don't have anything in his place. I still pray." She tried to recall when she'd last prayed and talked to God like a friend before today. Most of her prayers consisted of complaining about what a failure she was. When was the last time she even opened her Bible? Annie couldn't remember.

"I'll shut up for now, but you need to think about it," Fawn said as Annie pulled into the parking lot of the Black Sands Funeral Home.

Annie didn't answer. She knew she should tell Fawn about her first steps back to her relationship with the Lord, but it rankled that her friend could see so clearly what she'd missed for years. She parked next to Mano's car.

"Don't be mad, Annie. If I didn't love you so much, I wouldn't have said anything."

Annie's irritation melted at her friend's soft plea. "I'm sorry, Fawn. I know you just want what's best for me. You're right. I'll try to do better." She was always trying to do better and failing at something. It should come as no surprise. She released her seat belt and grabbed her purse. "Let's find Jillian. She's going to need all the support she can get today."

Mano realized he'd been watching for Annie the minute he saw her come in. He stopped midsentence and forgot what he was saying to his sister.

Kaia turned to see what he was looking at. "So that's who caused that moonstruck expression on your face. You're a goner, big brother."

"She's like a baby sister to me," he protested. He knew better though. He'd never been tempted to kiss Kaia like he was tempted to Annie.

"Uh-huh. I don't believe a word of it." Kaia started toward Annie and Fawn.

Mano followed her. Annie's straight black hair was pulled back from her face with clips, and she had a touch of color on her lips, just like on their date. Every time he saw her, she drew him more. She seemed to glow with vitality in the red top she wore.

"Hi." She smiled up at him.

How did she do that? He felt as powerful as King Kamehameha when he was with her. She barely reached his shoulder and looked as fragile as a ginger lei. "Where's your dad?" That was a stupid question. She made him scatterbrained.

She blinked and her smile faded. "He's coming with Gina."

He tried to recover his wits. "Love is still in the air, huh?"

"Looks like it." She turned to Kaia. "How's Jillian doing?"

Kaia nodded toward the casket. "Not good. Heidi is taking it really hard too. Jillian is still torn up over not hearing his reasons for what he did. I don't think she's slept at all."

"Does Sam have any idea who killed him?" Annie's lips trembled.

"Tomi is his main suspect." Mano shifted, wondering why he was feeling so on edge. Was it Annie's presence? His agitation was increasing. Sweat beaded on his forehead. He had breakfast, didn't he? He couldn't remember if his watch alarm had gone off to remind him. He couldn't seem to move his tongue right, and his thoughts were slow. He probably ought to eat something. He put his hand in his pocket and came up empty. Had he left his candy in the car? He couldn't wrap his mind around the questions.

He started toward the door and stumbled. His vision was fuzzy, and he felt he was walking in lava that was hardening around his feet. "Are you okay?" he heard someone ask as if from a great distance. The words he tried to form wouldn't congeal in his mouth. He stumbled again, then fell to his knees.

Annie was instantly at his side. "What's wrong?"

She tried to help him stand, but his head was spinning. "I need some candy or orange juice," he whispered.

She grabbed her purse, opened it, and dumped the contents on the floor. Mano was vaguely aware of people gathering around them. If he didn't feel so sick, he'd be mortified, but all he wanted now was something sweet.

Annie shoved a piece of hard candy in his mouth. "It's old, but it's sweet."

Sour apple flavor flooded his mouth, and he sucked on the sugary treat. He prayed for the reaction to pass so he could get to his feet and gather his dignity again. Annie was on one side of him, and his sister was on the other.

Jesse, Kaia's fiancé, moved her out of the way and grabbed his arm. "Can you stand, buddy?"

"Give me another minute," he mumbled. His vision sharpened, and his thoughts began to present themselves in logical order again. He wondered if he'd said anything stupid. He glanced at Annie but saw only concern, not disgust or pity. Pity was something he couldn't stand. He put his head between his knees and began to feel better. Raising his head, he grabbed Jesse's hand.

Jesse hoisted Mano to his feet. "Steady."

"I'm good now."

"Maybe we should call a doctor." His sister sounded fretful.

He was going to have to tell them. His gaze sought Annie's, and he took strength in the concern he saw there. He looked away. Better not to see the pity and disgust come. "I'm fine. It was just a—a low blood-sugar reaction."

"What do you mean? You have hypoglycemia or something?" Kaia demanded.

"More than that. I have diabetes." He heard Annie's tiny gasp but couldn't bring himself to look at her.

"Diabetes?" Kaia grabbed his arm. "How long have you known? And why didn't you tell me? Does Bane know, or the rest of the family?"

Mano shook his head. "I haven't told anyone. That's why I couldn't remember what happened when I lost Tomi in the water. I had a severe diabetic reaction. Blacked out. I had several more before I figured out what was wrong. I just found out for sure a month ago. I'm still figuring out how to manage it."

"Don't badger him," Jesse said. His shrewd gaze lingered on Mano's face. "Hard to admit a weakness, huh?"

"You got it." Mano was feeling stronger by the minute.

"Oh, you men make me so mad!" Splotches of color stained Kaia's face. She stared at Jesse with fire in her eyes. "It's not unmanly to admit a weakness. Mano is as strong as a whale. So what if he has diabetes? It doesn't make him a weakling."

"It's hard to deal with finding out your body is betraying you," Mano said. "I guess I didn't want to admit even to myself that there was something I couldn't lick." He finally dared to look at Annie again. Still no pity. If he wasn't still so befuddled, he might actually believe there was some love in her expression as well. He shook his head slightly to clear it.

"Why didn't you tell me that's what happened when you were trying to save Tomi?"

"I didn't want your pity."

She flinched. "What's your prognosis? I don't know much about diabetes." She sounded worried.

"I'll be fine. I just have to take insulin shots and monitor my meals. I messed up this morning. I was in such a hurry I didn't eat right. I'm okay now."

"Good, because the funeral is about to start." Annie took his arm in a matter-of-fact way. "I want to sit at the back and see who all is here. They say a murderer usually returns to his victim. Maybe whoever killed Noah is here."

Annie's heels sank into the soft, uneven ground, and she stumbled. Mano caught her arm, and she gave him a grateful smile. Most of the mourners were beginning to disband after the interment ceremony. She had seen no suspicious characters at the funeral, just close family and a few of Noah's friends.

Mano drew her toward a lovely Hawaiian woman who stood off to one side. "*Makuahine*, I'd like you to meet Annie. Annie, this is my mother, Faye Latchet."

His mother? Annie had heard his mother had deserted him when he was a kid. But there was no mistaking the resemblance. Mano had her eyes.

Faye held out her hand. "I've heard so much about your family. I'm sorry to hear about the problems you've all been having."

Annie shook her hand. "*Mahalo.* Are you going to be on the island long?"

Faye patted her son's hand with obvious fondness. "I was going to leave this afternoon, but I might hang around a day or two and make sure Mano is going to be okay. I heard about the low blood-sugar attack that happened before I arrived."

"I'm fine." Mano waved his hand. An irritated frown crouched between his eyes. "I hate people to fuss over me. Just drop it."

His mother's uncertain laugh touched Annie. Their relationship must be fragile. She glanced toward Mano to reprove him, but a movement caught her attention. A big man stood on the grass by a mausoleum. He wasn't looking at the structure though, he was staring at the group under the awning. Could it be Tab Watson? "Mano, who is the man back there? Is it Tab Watson?"

Mano turned to look, then his frown deepened. "Sure is. Or rather it's Kim Aki, his real name." He turned back around. "I don't want him to see me until I'm ready to talk to him."

The color in his mother's cheeks waned. "Aki? The same one who was involved with Kaia's kidnapping?"

"Yeah, that's him."

"Why isn't he in jail?" She started toward Aki, but Mano grabbed her arm.

"He turned state's evidence."

Faye was glaring at the man, and Annie had to cover her smile with her hand. She was like a bantam hen ready to defend her chicks. Maybe they were alike, in spite of their obvious differences of dress and elegance. Annie caught Mano's eye, and he grinned and winked at her. He put his arm around his mother. "Let's go back to town, and I'll buy you a fruit smoothie."

Annie cast a last look over her shoulder at Aki, but he'd left. She wondered if he was the one who had killed Noah.

Nineteen

After the fruit smoothie, Mano, Annie, and Fawn dropped his mother at the airport, then went back to the funeral home. Annie's SUV wouldn't start when they arrived, so Mano volunteered to take her and Fawn home. They dropped Fawn off, then drove to Annie's. The two hardly spoke on the way home. Mano seemed to be able to sense her mood, a rare ability. She liked the way she could be quiet around him without any discomfort.

She dropped her purse on the end table. "Want some coffee?" she asked him.

He grimaced. "Your coffee is like tea. I'll fix it."

He went toward the kitchen with the natural movements of someone who had been at home here for many years. Annie didn't want to think about how well he fit into her life. His presence here was temporary. She sat on the couch and leaned her head back. Wilson chirped at Annie's feet. "I'm fine, Wilson." She lifted her head and looked at the mongoose. Once he knew he had her attention, he ran in a circle chasing his tail, then ran straight up the wall. She laughed, and he ran to her and climbed into her lap. She ran her fingers over his sleek head.

She didn't know what was going to happen to Tomi. Had the men at the bank followed him? Was he in danger? When he turned up, he'd explain how his tags got to Noah's body.

Soon the aroma of coffee began to drift into the living room. "Smells strong," she called.

"It will help us think," Mano said, carrying two steaming cups into the room. He handed one to her.

She took it and sniffed. "I'm not sure I'm up for shaving my legs tonight."

He burst into laughter. Wilson raised his head in alarm. Mano's grin was still wide when he nodded. "Try it. You have good Kona coffee, and even strong, it's not bitter."

She took a cautious sip. He'd laced it with a hefty dose of sugar and milk. "It's good," she said.

He grinned. "Told you. I'll make a real coffee drinker of you yet."

She wished that meant he'd be around to affect her that way. Averting her gaze, she sipped at her drink.

"You're doing it again."

"Doing what?"

"Pulling into yourself. Shutting me out when I say anything about being part of your life."

But what part? That was the trouble. She wanted more from him than he would give, she was sure of it. Before she could frame an answer, the doorbell rang. Glancing through the window, she saw the mailman standing on the walk. She scooted Wilson off her lap, and he growled in protest. She gave him a reassuring pat and went to the door. "Hi, Paul."

"Got a registered letter for you, Annie." The mailman handed her a green card to sign.

She scribbled her name, took the letter, and waved good-bye to Paul. The return address filled her with dread. Aloha Bank. She stared at it in her hand, wanting to put off the inevitable as long as she could.

"You okay?" Mano stood in the entry to the living room.

"Fine." She ripped the letter open. Scanning the letter, she inhaled.

"Bad news?"

"Yeah." She rubbed her forehead. She might as well tell him.

The whole town would know soon enough that she had failed to help her father keep the land that had been in their family for over fifty years. "The bank is foreclosing."

He took the letter from her fingers and glanced at it. "You still have thirty days to pay the back payments and penalties."

"The penalties are almost as much as we owe."

"Highway robbery." Mano sounded disgusted.

"I have to figure out a way to pay it. We can't wait and let the casino pick it up for peanuts after the bank forecloses."

"I could help you."

Annie was touched, but she didn't want him to see it. "I can't let you do that."

Mano handed the letter back to her. "Have you talked to your father about it?"

"He's always liked me to handle the finances." She hated handling the money, but she'd never been able to tell her father. If she'd only been honest about how bad she was with finances, they wouldn't be in this fix.

"This isn't your fault, Annie. Your father is the man of the family. It was his responsibility, and he should be involved in figuring out the answer. He wanted the money for his research. Maybe he could pay it back with grant money."

"Maybe." Annie went down the hall to the living room. She knew better than to expect any help from her father. He would be sure to lay the blame firmly at her feet.

Mano grabbed the jumper cables out of the garage; then he and Annie returned to her Nissan. He got it started, then followed her home to make sure she made it safely. As he drove, he thought of what he could do to help her. He couldn't pay the mortgage off, but he could at least get it caught up.

When she pulled into the driveway, he stuck his hand out the window and waved, then drove away. Glancing at the clock on the dash, he realized his mother should have gotten back to Kaua'i by now. He pulled out his cell phone.

"Hey, *Tûtû Kâne*, how are you feeling?" he asked when his grandfather answered the phone.

"Mano, I was just talking about you. Your mother is here too."

"Checking up on you, huh? You'd better listen to her."

"Oh, she's making me toe the line."

"Bane said you'd been a little under the weather. Have you been to the doctor?"

"I just got back. I'm fit as a fiddle. It was just the beginning of an ulcer. Your mother has me on apple-cider vinegar morning and evening, and some enzymes. I'm already feeling better."

"Great! Listen, could you do me a favor? You or *Makuahine*?"

"Your mother is riding herd over me pretty hard, so maybe you'd better let her do whatever you need."

"Sure, put her on."

He heard the sound of fumbling and his grandfather calling loudly. Mano's mother came on. "Missing me already, Mano?" Her voice was teasing.

"Always. Listen, I need to have some money transferred from my savings to checking. My bankbook is in the safe in my old bedroom. Could you transfer five thousand dollars for me?"

"Sure, son. But is everything okay? Do you have enough? I can give you whatever you need."

His mother had been trying to make it up to the three kids for her abandonment when they were children. She didn't seem to understand that they'd forgiven her and still loved her.

"I've got enough."

The worry in her voice softened. "I'm being a mother hen again, aren't I? Sorry."

"It's okay. So, when can you run over to the bank for me? I really need access to it right away."

"I can do it now while your grandfather takes a nap."

"I'm too young to nap like a baby," Mano heard his grand-father call. He grinned. "Tell *Tûtû Kâne* if he's good you'll bring him a new whoopee cushion."

His mother chuckled. "That would do it." He heard the sound of her steps. "Let me make sure I can find the bankbook." There were more noises, then he heard her give a grunt of satisfaction. "Here it is. I'll go now."

"Great." He thanked her and closed the phone, started the car, and drove to town. Along the way, he watched for Tomi's familiar slender form, but he passed only a family of hikers. He'd tried to keep his worry from showing to Annie, but he thought Tomi was in real trouble. And Mano wasn't sure how to get him out.

He parked at the bank and saw the same car Tomi had pointed out. Maybe that meant Tomi had eluded the men. Mano got out and started toward the bank. He heard quick steps behind him, but before he could turn, someone took his arm in a tight grip.

"We'd like to have a word with you."

Mano tried to jerk his arm free and looked to see who accosted him. There were two of them, both Middle Eastern from their looks. The one who had hold of Mano's arm had bulky muscles and was dressed in black.

They propelled Mano toward their black Ford. The back pas-senger door was open. Mano knew he needed to get out of this now. He pretended to trip, and the man's hand on his elbow slack-ened. Mano wrenched his arm free and whirled to run to the bank. There were security personnel in there. He sprinted up the steps and through the glass front doors into the lobby.

When he burst into the bank, he looked around for the secu-rity officer. The man's head jerked up, and his eyes widened when Mano slid to a panting halt in front of him. His hand went auto-matically to his gun.

"Outside," Mano gasped. "Call the police. Two men tried to abduct me."

The security officer grabbed his radio and called it in. Mano went to the window and looked out, but the black Ford was gone. The men must have known he'd call the police. What could they want with him? Maybe to see if he knew where Tomi was holed up.

"The police are on their way, sir," the security officer said. "Are you injured?"

"No, I'm fine." Maybe he should have talked to the men. He might have been able to find out more information. No. It wouldn't have been safe to allow himself to be pushed into a car.

Sam came running through the door. He stopped when he saw Mano. "Oana, what happened?"

"Two thugs tried to force me into their car." Mano described the car and the men.

"Any idea what they wanted? Could it be navy related?"

"I don't think so. I think they might be the ones who broke into the Tagama house."

Sam barked orders at a couple of his men, who hurried outside to look around. "You have any idea why a couple of Arab men would be breaking into homes and trying to abduct you?"

Mano ignored Sam's sarcastic tone. "I think they wanted to know where Tomi is."

Sam nodded. "I'm listening."

Mano was going to have to be careful. He didn't want to get Tomi in even more trouble. "They seem to be after him for some reason." That was lame. Sam was going to want to know why he thought the men were after Tomi.

"Some SEAL mission." His eyes bright, Sam straightened. "Maybe they planted Tomi's dog tags."

Mano knew when special ops got in someone's blood it was hard to get it out. Sam had been a SEAL for six months before he injured his knee. "Maybe. There's something else. I've seen a man

in the Aloha Shores and around town who calls himself Tab
Watson."

"The last person to see Leilani."

"Right. His real name is Kim Aki. And he was involved in a plot
to blow up a munitions cache at Barking Sands a few months ago."

Sam raised his brows. "You think it's related?"

"I don't know, but I'd like to go with you to question him."

"I do my own investigative work." Sam turned to speak to
his men.

At least he wasn't going to have to explain about Tomi any fur-
ther. Sam had jumped to an assumption and seemed eager to help
Tomi now. But Mano would have to find a way to force Sam into
taking him to talk to Aki. He went to the desk and told the teller
he wanted to catch up the Tagama mortgage. Fifteen minutes later
he was five thousand dollars poorer, but richer for the contentment
that flooded him at finally doing something to help Annie.

Annie dressed for worship with a sense of adventure. For the
first time that she could remember in years, she actually
wanted to go. She'd read her Bible two nights straight now and was
beginning to see that her priorities were all wrong.

She went to the kitchen. Wilson followed her. His squeak was
the one he used when he was hungry, so she fed him first, a mixture of grubs and larvae she bought at the pet store in Hilo.
Sometimes he ate cat food, but he preferred his natural diet. He
growled softly as he gulped down his food, then looked up to her
for more.

"That's it, you little piglet. If you're good, I'll give you a bite of
my egg." She put the skillet on to heat and got omelet fixings out
of the refrigerator.

Her father came into the kitchen. "I overslept. You should have
woken me."

He'd been out late the night before with Gina. "I tapped on your door. I thought I heard you say *okay.*" In fact, she was sure he'd answered her. He'd probably gone back to bed.

"You were mistaken." He settled at the table. "Get that animal out of here."

Annie sighed and scooped up Wilson, who squeaked in protest. She stashed him in her bedroom, then hurried back to the kitchen to pour coffee for her father. She needed to tell him about the foreclosure notice. Wetting her lips, she tried to decide how to bring it up. She didn't want to upset him when he was about to get to work. She stirred cream into his coffee, then went back to the stove. Maybe she should tell him tonight instead of this morning. She was such a coward.

Wilson dashed under her feet. She must not have latched her door. He had something in his mouth. He nudged her leg, then dashed past her. She recognized the red seal on the top of the paper and realized he had the letter from the bank. "Wilson, give me that." She made a grab for him, but he evaded her and ran up her father's pant leg.

He sputtered hot coffee on his shirt as Wilson burrowed into his lap. "That stupid animal. I want you to get rid of it." He shoved Wilson onto the floor. The mongoose dropped the paper on Edega's feet then broke into a series of barks. Edega frowned. "What's this?"

As her father leaned down to pick up the paper, Annie leaned back against the stove and closed her eyes. The fireworks were about to begin. She should have told him right away. He hated secrets. She opened her eyes and squared her shoulders. "I was just about to tell you about that."

He smoothed the letter out and began to read it. His frown turned ferocious when he realized what it was. "Foreclosure! A Tagama doesn't lose his land for nonpayment. How is this possible?"

"Our expenses here are just so high," she began.

He held up his hand. "This never happened when your mother was alive. I expected you to be able to handle things in her place."

"We didn't have a huge mortgage when Mother was alive," Annie said.

He shook his head. "Don't make excuses, Annie. You should have come to me about this before we got to this stage."

"I tried," she burst out. "But you wouldn't listen to me." He didn't make Leilani kick in any money toward her upkeep, but she and her father pooled their resources. Still, it wasn't enough. With Leilani's help, it might have been.

"I always listen. Don't try to make excuses for your failure and blame someone else." He pushed away from the table. "We must take care of this. How much money is in the bank?"

"Not enough." He wasn't going to listen. She wanted to crawl back into bed and drag the covers over her head.

"How much?" he demanded. She told him. "That's not enough to even make one month's house payment."

"I know." She shoved her hair out of her face. "That's what I'm saying. We don't make enough money to keep up this kind of high payment. You thought you'd get grant money back in to pay what you took out, but it's never come."

"But what are we going to do?" His tone was that of a bewildered child.

She lifted her head and looked at her father. "Tomi says he's had an offer for our property. Three million dollars."

Her father gasped, and his eyes bulged. "That's not possible. Who would offer so much money?"

"A casino is coming in and turning this area into a resort destination with a theme park and housing subdivision. They want it right away though. They intend to break ground very soon, so we have to move quickly."

His eyes grew thoughtful. "If we lose the house, they would buy it for practically nothing from the bank. Why would they just not wait for that?"

"They probably don't know we're in trouble. And even if they did, it would take time to foreclose. They don't have the time to waste."

"Let me think it over. I don't like to be rushed into a decision. Tomi is back now. Perhaps he will help me decide. And speaking of your brother, why has he not come to see me? You have seen him several times, yet he makes no visit to see me. He dishonors me."

"He's been . . . taking care of urgent business. I'm sure he'll be here to see you soon." Her father was never going to listen to her. Annie watched him turn away and exit the room the way he always did when he was finished with a conversation. She pinched the bridge of her nose and wondered how she was going to fix this. If the offer to buy the house slipped away, they could lose everything.

Twenty

ano jogged to keep up with Sam. Rain drizzled on his face and ran in rivulets down his neck. They'd parked at the road and had to walk through thick rain forest along the trail to Kim Aki's shack. Mano's shirt was drenched from brushing against the dripping tree ferns. Though Sam really hadn't had any choice after the navy honchos learned Aki was back in the spotlight, Mano decided to be diplomatic. "*Mahalo* for letting me tag along, Sam."

"Cut the crap, Oana. I don't want you here, and you know it. Just don't get in my way."

"So much for an olive branch. You wouldn't even know about Aki if I hadn't told you. You might show a little gratitude."

"Gratitude? For a wild-goose chase? So an enemy of yours is here under an assumed name. Big deal. That probably has nothing to do with Leilani running off."

"He was the last person to see her. Another thing you should know—I saw him outside Noah's cabin the other day. You don't want to believe Tomi had anything to do with Noah's death any more than I do. What if Aki killed him?"

Sam stopped and turned to face him. "And you're just now telling me?"

"I forgot until now." His face burned. He hated these memory lapses more than anything.

Sam snorted. "Likely story. I don't want any more interference in my cases. First you get involved in Leilani's disappearance, and now this."

"Don't forget about Leilani now that Noah is dead. Something has happened to her."

Sam held up thick fingers. "One, she's done this before, Oana. Two, there's been no ransom note or anything else that would lead us to think foul play was involved. What makes you all so sure this stunt of hers is unique? And three, people have seen her since she disappeared."

He should tell Sam about CeCe's lie. A shadow moved up ahead before he could tell the officer. Mano squinted. "There's Aki now."

Sam turned and thrashed forward through the last bit of forest. "Mr. Aki, I'd like to have a word with you."

Kim Aki whirled and crashed through the tree ferns that lined the path. Mano sprang after him, but Aki knew the area better and vanished in a stand of koa trees that towered over the underlying vegetation. He and Sam thrashed through stag's tongue, woodfern, and 'olapa for fifteen minutes before giving up.

"What a waste of a morning," Sam grumbled.

They returned to the squad car, and Mano glanced at the detective's face. He was finally beginning to realize that Sam did care about the Tagama family, but he was genuinely worried about his other cases. "How about we settle our beef here and now? If we can't be friends, I'd at least like to be civil."

Sam slung himself into the car, and Mano got in on the passenger side and shut the door. Sam gripped the steering wheel.

"We're never going to be friends, Oana."

"Leilani has dumped both of us. There's no reason for us to be at each other's throat. She's moved on. Happens to the best of us."

"I think she would have married me if you hadn't come into the picture with your flashy uniform and smooth ways." Sam flexed his fingers.

"If she was going to be flighty, wouldn't you rather find that out before you married her?"

Sam glared at Mano "You knew she was dating me."

Mano knew he should have an answer for Sam's accusation, but he didn't. He shrugged. "Look, we could argue this all night. She burned us both. Can't we put her behind us?"

Sam blinked, and the florid color faded from his face. His jaw flexed, and he turned to stare out the window. "It's a little late now."

"Better late than never."

"I'm fine now," Sam said. "I've got a new girl, and I don't have time to waste on looking for Leilani Tagama. She'll turn up." He started the car and put the transmission in gear.

"Can we call a truce?" Mano asked.

"I guess. Leilani trashed us both pretty well. She didn't stay with you long either."

"About a month." Mano grimaced at the reminder. He'd been so stupid over that girl. She taught him not to trust a pretty face. As Sam pulled out, Mano's thoughts wandered to Annie. She might be an exception. He saw a movement from the corner of his eye and craned his neck to look. Aki's face disappeared back into the brush.

"Stop!" Mano shouted. "Aki is there."

Sam wrenched the steering wheel and pulled to the side of the road. Mano jumped out and ran into the thicket of Hawaiian huckleberry. Sam followed, thrashing and cursing as he got caught in a tangle of climbing screw-pine vines. Ahead of them, Aki stumbled over a mound of *a'a* and went tumbling into a tree fern. He staggered to his feet, but he'd lost his advantage. Mano tackled him.

"Calm down," Mano panted. He wrestled Aki's hands behind him, which was no easy task, because the man had to outweigh him by sixty pounds.

Sam reached them. "Let him go, Mano. We just want to ask you some questions," he told Aki.

The big man rolled to his back and sat up. "I haven't done anything. What do you want?"

"For one thing, for you to stop when a police officer tells you to," Sam said sternly. He grabbed Aki and hauled him to his feet.

Mano got up as well. He and Sam exchanged a wordless glance, and Mano read the warning in the detective's eyes. He moved off to the side to give Sam room to handle the interrogation.

Sam took out his notebook. "Name."

Aki glared at Mano. "Kim Aki."

Sam looked up. "You've been going under an assumed name. Why?"

"Trying to stay out of the spotlight of yahoos like Oana over there."

Mano ignored the big man's glare. He studied Aki's body language. Head thrust forward, arms crossed defensively, poised as if to flee any minute. The man was hiding something. Mano was sure of it.

Sam grunted. "What spotlight? Do you have a record?"

"No." Aki's response was instant. His smile held a trace of triumph.

"He was offered a deal for testifying against his dad," Mano put in.

Aki bunched his fists. "See what I mean? How can I start a new life with that hanging over me? So I just changed my name."

"Changed it or assumed a new one? Let me see your ID." Sam held out his hand.

Aki reluctantly got out his wallet and handed the detective his driver's license. "I assumed it."

"Then where'd you get the documentation for this license?"

"I got sources." Aki's lips had a sulky twist.

Sam sighed. "Look, we want to know about Leilani Tagama. Where did you see her last?"

"About a week ago. We went out for drinks. I took her to her car afterwards. It was parked where she worked."

"And that was the last you saw her?"

Aki nodded. "She was just fine when I left her."

"What time was this?"

"About two in the morning."

Leilani was a partier. It looked like that hadn't changed. Mano itched to question Aki but forced himself to stay silent.

"Did she say where she was going when she left you?"

"Straight home."

Sam scowled. "Did she have another boyfriend?"

"Her and me weren't like that. We'd only been going out a few weeks. We weren't serious."

"A friend says she saw you with Leilani a few days ago in Hilo. What do you have to say about that?"

Aki clenched his fists. "It's a lie. I haven't seen her."

"Were there any other men in her life?"

Aki shrugged. "Not as far as I know, but you never knew with Leilani. She liked to keep men guessing."

Ah, they had him. "You're talking like she's dead," Mano said. "You're using past tense."

Aki flushed. "It's just a figure of speech."

Sam's eyes narrowed with suspicion. "I think you'd better come downtown for a few more questions. Like what you were doing outside Noah Sommers's house."

It was about time Sam pounced with that line of questioning. Mano was certain Aki was involved with Noah. Whether he had killed him remained to be seen, but there was something between the two men.

Aki held up his hands. "Don't be framing me for that murder. It wasn't me."

"I just want to ask some questions," Sam said.

Aki nodded, and they started toward the patrol car. When they reached the road, Aki made a sudden move to the right. He jerked his arm out of Sam's grasp and bolted for the forest.

"Stop!" Sam gave chase with Mano on his heels. Ten minutes later they gave up. "We'll find him," Sam said grimly. "Every cop on the island will be looking for him."

"What's your take on this now?" Mano asked him. "Still think Leilani just ran off with a boyfriend? I think Aki is in this up to his ears."

"Maybe. Or he might be tied to Noah's death." Sam started the car. "But I'll look into it a little more."

Finally. "Where can we start?"

"There's no *we*, Oana. This is my job. Let me handle it." Sam dropped the gearshift into drive and headed toward town.

Twenty-one

Annie stood in the doorway to Gina's office. She wasn't sure whether to act as if she still had a job or to throw herself on her boss's mercy and beg for menial work.

Gina looked up from her perusal of a graph. Her face lit with relief and something else that Annie couldn't read. "I wasn't sure if you'd be coming back in today or not. Come in, sweetie, I want to talk to you."

At least she wasn't mad. Annie stepped into the office and sat on the edge of the seat, gripping her knees.

"You look like you're about to hear a death sentence." Gina smiled and went to the small rolling cart against the wall. "Want some tea?"

"Sure."

Gina heated two mugs of water in the microwave, dropped a tea bag into each, and handed one cup to Annie before taking her seat again. Annie used the reprieve to try to calm her jitters. Was that unknown emotion regret for letting Annie go, or something else?

"I've been thinking about what you said," Gina said, taking a sip of tea. "And I realize I was pushing you too hard, too fast. I don't want to lose you, Annie. You're too good of a scientist for me to stand by and let you throw it away. I want you to see a therapist and try to get over this fear."

"I don't think that's necessary," Annie protested. "I just need a little time. Let me do it in small stages instead of sending me right out to the most dangerous areas."

"I'm not sure we have that kind of time. I need you up to speed as soon as possible. The earthquake swarms likely mean something big is about to happen. I need the whole staff fully functional and operating as one."

"Even a therapist can't work miracles overnight."

"True." Gina took another sip of tea. "How about we compromise? Over the next two weeks, I want you to enter an area where you feel frightened, even if it's only for a few minutes. Don't do any work there, just go to the brink and evaluate your reaction. If you find the fear is lessening, we'll assume you can conquer this by yourself."

It was a good offer, and Annie knew it. Though fear soured her stomach, she nodded slowly. "Okay. It's good of you to do this, Gina."

The older woman played with a pencil on her desk. "I'm no stranger to fear, Annie. I know what it's like to feel your heart shrivel in your chest."

Annie couldn't imagine tiny but intrepid Gina afraid of anything. "I don't believe it," she said.

Gina looked up. "My childhood was a nightmare. I had a father who brutalized me and my sister. I remember hiding in the closet and praying he wouldn't find me. I decided when I was a teenager that I wasn't going to let fear control me any longer. I don't want to see you bow to it."

Annie tried not to show her shock. Gina seemed so calm and put together. Sometimes she seemed too controlled, though now Annie could see why. Gina would be good for her father. "I'm sorry, Gina. I had no idea."

Gina waved her hand airily. "It's all in the past. You're like me in many ways, Annie. Even in your family life. I've noticed your father is a little hard on you. You need to remember that you're a strong woman. You don't need his approval. Make your own way."

"My family needs me," Annie said weakly.

"I think you overestimate your importance to them. They'll survive without you. You need to look out for yourself. No one else will."

Gina had it all wrong. Insulating herself against hurt was no way to live. But for the first time, Annie was beginning to realize that being a doormat wasn't what God intended either. Was there a happy medium where she could open herself to her family and yet be her own person as well? She wanted to rush home and look through the Bible to find out.

Gina interrupted her thoughts. "As long as we're in agreement, you can get back to work. I want you to go out as far on the lava as you can go today. Then come back here and work on your data. And get that formula fixed for Jillian."

"Okay." Annie rose and went toward the door. She hesitated. "*Mahalo* for everything, Gina. I hope things work out with you and my father." Gina smiled without answering, then bent her head and went back to studying her graphs. Annie went down the hall, checked her e-mail, then went outside. She had to go out on the lava bench.

Someplace dangerous, but not too dangerous. She got on her ATV and drove out across the rock. Though she didn't like the thought of going back to where she'd vomited the other day, she had to face her fear. She got as far as the path but couldn't make herself get off the vehicle. Maybe Gina was right and she needed professional help. She turned around and went back to the observatory.

Annie frowned as she stood in front of the seismograph two hours later. The earthquakes were increasing at the rift. She'd never seen so many in a twenty-four-hour period. She went to the bank of computers on the other side of the room and began to call up data that she could check. Wilson batted at the mouse, then tried to nibble on the cord. Her father had been unusually grouchy about him, and she decided to keep him out of the house.

"Forget it, mister." She nudged him away. He squeaked, then hopped to the floor and went to the sofa by the door that they used for guests. He raced up the sofa and perched on top to look out the window.

"You're frowning." Fawn had come into the room behind her. "Is something wrong?"

"All these earthquakes make me a little uneasy." Annie showed her the data.

Fawn perused it, then handed it back to her. "Looks like we might be about to have another eruption. Maybe Mauna Loa is ready to sound off again."

While it was impossible to predict eruptions, Mauna Loa was said to be "overdue" for one. The volcano had erupted thirty-nine times since 1832. In the last century, the events had occurred every one to twelve years. This latest lull, however, had gone on since 1984. The islands breathlessly awaited a new light show.

Annie's excitement rose. "Maybe." She looked back at the computer. "With this much activity, though, I wonder if we might get an explosive event."

Jillian came into the room as she spoke. "You think? I've been wondering about it."

"Don Swanson proved there have been some in the past," Annie pointed out. "It could happen again. And my father's data shows the same thing."

Jillian leaned over Annie's shoulder and looked at the computer. "Looks like we'll be getting something. Let's pray for a nice, gentle flow that doesn't hurt anyone."

Wilson growled, and Jillian turned to look. "I don't know how you get away with bringing Wilson in here. I'm surprised Monica hasn't complained."

"She has, but Gina told her to mind her own business,"

Fawn put in with a sly grin. "And Annie doesn't bring him every day."

Annie got up and grabbed her purse. "I think I'll go put out some new GPS receivers on Mauna Loa."

"Speaking of receivers, did you get Orson Kauhi to agree to let you plant them in his neck of the woods?" Jillian asked.

"No, but I'll go to talk to him about it while I'm out." She picked up Wilson and headed for the door.

"I still need your help on that computer model," Jillian called after her.

"I know. Later, I promise." She kept going, grabbed some GPS receivers, and headed to her SUV. Maybe she could get somewhere with her neighbor if she went out by herself. Orson might be more amenable to a woman alone. He'd always been more courteous to women. She stopped at her house and dropped off the mongoose, then drove on down the road to the Kauhi property. She parked where the road ended and walked up the hillside. It was a hard climb over the jumbled black lava rock. The hillside could have been a play yard for a giant tossing balls of lava rock.

At the crest of the hill, she paused and looked around for her neighbor. The air was still and silent but fragrant with the scent of flowers. The extreme silence gave her the willies. She saw movement to her left, so she began to wander toward a small structure. As she neared it, she realized it was a *heiau*. Constructed of lava rocks, the small structure held an altar. Orson knelt before it. A lei circled an offering of fruit and vegetables. He was chanting as he bowed. A *ki'i* frowned over the scene.

Annie clasped her arms around her and waited. How could he think praying to a god made of wood would gain him anything? Watching him, she was struck again by what Fawn had said to her about idolatry. Had Annie herself been worshiping at the feet of the god of her family? Had she really let her desire to be needed become her god? She was afraid her friend was right.

And the yearning would so easily creep back in. Though she'd begun to read her Bible every night before bed, she sensed it wouldn't take much for the old habits and attitudes to take over her life again. Recognizing how much she loved her family, she knew her tendency was something she was going to have to guard against a long time, maybe all her life.

She shook away the thoughts as Orson rose. Dressed in traditional hula costume with ti leaves and a shell lei, he wore a contented smile. He turned and caught sight of her. The beatific expression on his face changed to a scowl. "I told you not to come here."

"What god are you worshiping?" Annie blurted, her horrified gaze still on the temple.

"You have lived on the island all your life and still do not recognize Ku?" Orson shook his head. "How typical of the young ones."

"Ku likes human sacrifice. How can you worship him?" Annie half expected to see blood dripping from the altar.

"Only on certain holy days. Ku's four days of worship are here. Are you offering yourself as a sacrifice?" Annie backed away, and he smiled. "You can't take a joke? I wouldn't hurt you, Annie. We're neighbors." He said the words almost gently.

She dragged her gaze from the *heiau*. "Did you introduce Leilani to Ku worship?"

He studied her for a moment without answering. "Your sister is searching for meaning for her life. How could I not show her?"

He *had* gotten her involved. Annie's excitement rose. "Do you know where she is?"

"I haven't seen her." He picked up a walking staff and began to walk back toward his cabin.

Annie fell into step beside him. "The mountain has been shaking lately. I really need to put out some GPS receivers. I promise to pick them up in a few days. I won't leave them here indefinitely."

Orson stopped, and his dark eyes glared out of his face and into her eyes. "I have told you no before."

"I know, and I'm sorry to keep bugging you, but this is really important to my career." She told him about the dramatic increase in recent activity, then fell silent. She hated to beg. He was quiet, and she thought he was going to refuse her again.

Then he nodded slowly. "Show me where you want to put them."

"I'll get them from the Nissan." She hurried back to her SUV and grabbed the receivers. Her foot ached from all the walking, and she was limping heavily by the time she got back to Orson.

"You are limping," he observed.

She nodded but didn't explain.

"Your sister said you now fear the rivers of fire."

"Leilani mentioned my accident?"

He thrust his staff into the hard, rocky soil and followed her up the mountain. "The old gods were trying to get your attention."

Annie gave an involuntary shiver. All this talk of gods—demons, to her mind—made her want to run back to her vehicle.

He noticed her shudder. "You are a fearful girl, Annie Tagama. You must conquer your fears."

At least he was right about that. Annie wished she could be brave and strong like Fawn. Maybe someday. They reached the first spot she needed to get coordinates on. She showed Orson what she planned, and he consented to letting her plant the receiver. They walked the hillside together, and she marked the spots. She'd never been this high on this side of the mountain. There was so much to discover up here. Unexplored lava tubes, hot springs and pools, old fissures . . . it was a volcanologist's dream. Now that the ice was broken between her and old Kauhi, maybe he'd let her look around once in a while.

She and Orson walked back down toward his cabin. Annie saw movement at the front door. "Looks like you have company."

Orson scowled. "Not for long. I've told them three times I will not sell my land."

"Who wants to buy it?" She suspected she knew.

"They want to put a casino here. It's sacrilegious!"

Annie glanced toward the road and recognized the big car that was parked behind her Pathfinder. Evan Chun must be here. She was tempted to hang around and see if he'd talk with her, but after glancing at her watch, she realized she needed to get back to the office and work on Jillian's computer model. And she had to get home on time. Her father would be flustered if she was late tonight. He was planning on taking Gina to a slack-key guitar concert at seven, and he wouldn't be able to find the right shirt without her.

As she drove past her home, she wondered again what she was going to do if her father remarried. The thought of not being needed anymore terrified her, though she knew it was time she learned to live her own life.

When she reached the observatory, she stopped by Gina's office and got the file she needed. She took it to Jillian's office and seated herself in front of the computer. Annie began to go line by line and check the formulas in the model.

After an hour her eyes ached and her head throbbed. It had to be here somewhere. Some equation had to be wrong. Something was throwing the entire computer model off-kilter. She'd back-tracked through all the formulas and had only five more to review. Maybe she should start at the beginning and go through it all again.

She glanced at the root formula and then blinked. It had been right here in front of her the whole time. The spreadsheet drew its results from the basic temperature and gas-mixture formula. That formula was transposed. No wonder the model wasn't working. With the foundational equation wrong, nothing could come out right.

She corrected the formula, then launched the model. It began to spew out data that, for the first time, made sense. Annie smiled.

24 Black Sands

Fawn had been saying something similar about Annie's life. When something else is in God's place, nothing comes out right. Annie's life was meant to be lived with God at the center of everything, the driving force of everything. Instead, she tried to hold onto some control. God wanted to be her all, the reason she lived and breathed. She bowed her head and surrendered.

M̶ahalo for the ride, buddy." Tomi stood lightly on his toes with his hand on the car door as if poised for flight. He glanced around, then got in with Mano.

"I wanted to talk to you anyway." Mano pointed his car toward the Tagama house. "You vanished after Noah died. That's looking real bad. Where are your dog tags?"

"My tags?" Tomi's eyes widened. He felt his pocket. "I must have dropped them someplace."

"Like at the murder scene."

Tomi went white. "They were found by Noah's body?"

"Yep. And Sam is looking to talk to you."

"I had nothing to do with it! I don't even know Noah, not really." His face fell. "I've been set up!"

"Maybe." Mano rubbed his forehead. "I have no idea how we're going to get you out of this one, Tomi. You've got the Iranians after you and now the cops."

Tomi leaned his head against the window. "Maybe I should just go to the cops. Throw myself on their mercy. I want to talk to my dad first though."

They'd reached the Tagama house. "Let's go," Mano said. He shut off the engine and got out.

"There might be yelling," Tomi said.

"Yeah, but having someone along might help keep it to a dull roar."

"My hero," Tomi said, grinning as he slapped Mano on the back.

The two men went to the front door. Tomi pushed open the door. "Annie? Are you here?" He stepped inside, and Mano followed.

The aroma of teri beef made Mano's mouth water, and he realized he'd skipped lunch. He and Tomi went toward the kitchen. Wilson dashed under their feet, and Tomi nearly stumbled. He caught himself and mumbled, "Stupid mongoose." They stepped into the kitchen.

Annie stood at the counter sliding beef onto wooden sticks for kebabs. A lock of hair had fallen forward and touched the gentle curve of her cheek. The heat of the stove brightened her face with a hint of color. She looked up and saw them, and her blush deepened.

Something in Mano's chest expanded, filling him up from the inside. He couldn't explain it to himself how he knew, but he realized in that moment he loved Annie, really and truly loved her in a way he never expected. She was beautiful outside but even lovelier inside. In the past, a woman would catch his eye because of her shape or her smile or her eyes. But with Annie, he'd been attracted first to her spirit. Weird, but true.

He couldn't drag his gaze from hers. It was all he could do not to shoulder Tomi out of the way and take her in his arms. Before he could figure out what to say, Edega came in from the garage.

"It's about time you showed your face, Tomi," he said.

Twenty-two

atching her father embrace her brother, Annie wondered if she was invisible to them. The two of them needed no one else. Tomi was her father's favorite in so many ways, in spite of Edega's rebuke. And that was as it should be, maybe. Tomi was the only boy, and her father looked to him as holding the future of the Tagama name.

Did he even see her as his daughter—or as anything more than his secretary and maid? Annie didn't think so, but she found that she didn't mind. Not anymore. She wanted to please God now. Her glance moved to Mano, and she realized he'd been staring at her. The expression on his face nearly made her gasp. Could that be—yearning? She must be tired.

"I just talked to Sam," Mano said. "Still no sign of Leilani, but he figured out that CeCe lied. He needs to talk to Tomi about those dog tags, though. Tomi says he hasn't seen Noah."

"I knew Tomi wouldn't hurt anyone." Annie rubbed her forehead. "Maybe everyone is right and Leilani is just off on a lark. You'd think we would have heard something by now." Something crashed behind her, and she whirled.

Wilson wore as guilty an expression as was possible for a mongoose. The plate of teri shish kebabs lay on the floor. He sniffed, then crouched as though to jump down and explore the food on the floor. "Don't you dare," she said. She swooped him up, and he wiggled to get away, but she held tightly. "What am I going to do with you?" she scolded.

"Toss him to the dogs?" her brother suggested.

Mano stepped forward and scratched Wilson on the head. "He just wanted a bit of that tasty food. Didn't you, Wilson?"

The mongoose squeaked and nuzzled Mano's fingers, then crawled up his arm and down the neck of his shirt. Mano's eyes widened, then he grinned and caught Wilson before he crept past his neck to his stomach. He fished him out and held him up to stare in his face. "I think you need to go to mongoose training."

"I've had it with that animal," her father said. He grabbed Wilson by the nape of the neck. The mongoose growled in protest as Edega stepped toward the door.

"No!" Annie jumped between her father and the door. "Give him to me."

"You should never have been allowed to raise this thing. He's going outside where he belongs."

Annie faced him. "He's mine. You have no right to get rid of him. I'm not a child." She tried to take the mongoose, but her father held it out of her reach.

"You will obey me in my house. I should never have let you bring that animal in here."

"Then maybe it's time I had my own house." Wilson was her solace, her companion when loneliness stalked her. She sent Mano a silent plea, and he stepped forward and plucked Wilson from her father's hand and deposited the mongoose in her arms. "*Mahalo*," she whispered, then ran for her bedroom.

Ignoring her father's angry shout, she dashed down the hall and slammed the door behind her. Wasn't she allowed to have a life of her own, things of her own, a pet? She'd given up everything for her family. They had no right to dictate her life to this degree. Her chest heaved. She wanted to throw something, but she kept Wilson tucked under her chin and tried to control her distress.

She should pray. The thought came out of nowhere, but she obeyed it anyway. She had to let God be the boss, the center. Her life was to be about pleasing him now, not herself. The tension began to ease from her body as she turned her hurt and confusion over to her real authority.

She heard a sound when she lifted her head. Wilson moved at the soft knock on her door. "Annie?" Mano called. "You okay?"

Hearing Mano's voice, she realized the angry shouts from the kitchen had ceased. She opened her door. "I'm fine."

"How about you, me, and Wilson go eat by the water? I'll get a pizza."

He was so dear and so thoughtful. His shoulders spanned the doorway, and his expression seemed almost tender as he looked down at her. She wished she could believe it. "What are Tomi and Father doing?"

"Salvaging the shish kebabs." He grinned, and she laughed. "I think your dad is sorry and ready to apologize."

"He doesn't know how to apologize." She smiled to let Mano know it didn't bother her. She followed Mano to the living room. As she stepped into the kitchen, she heard her brother say, "We might as well sell, Father. We won't want to share our home with a casino." Sadness lodged itself like a lava rock in her chest.

"The bank is foreclosing anyway," Tomi continued.

Her father turned to look at her as she approached the table. "I see you told your brother you've lost the land that has been the Tagama property for generations."

Annie decided she wasn't taking all the blame for this. "I didn't know what to do, how to save the house. Tomi has told you about the offer for the property."

"I entrusted your sister with the family finances, and she has made a fiasco of them. If she'd only told me there was a problem, we might have averted this."

Annie stifled her gasp. It was his idea to get the mortgage in the first place. She'd insisted then they couldn't afford to repay it. She didn't know how to answer his outrageous accusations. "I'm sorry,

Father," she said finally. "I'm not like my mother. Money management is not one of my strengths. But you knew we had this problem." Mano put his hand in the small of her back, and the touch of support allowed her to lift her head. "Besides, I told you when Mother died that you should handle it."

"I relied on you for that. It is your job."

What was her job? Annie didn't know anymore. She'd thought it was important to be needed by her family, but she was merely a doormat for them to wipe their feet on. They didn't appreciate her work, none of them. She focused on her brother's face. "And if we sell the house, how long would we have to move out?"

"I've talked to the CEO of the casino. We'd have six months. They will pay cash and expedite the sale. But they want to do it now, this week."

"It goes against my grain to be forced," her father said, holding up his hand. "We have no choice. Better to sell and be known as shrewd investors than to give it away to the bank and let the casino have it for a fraction of its value. Tell them we'll do it."

Mano's hand dropped away from her back. "Uh, there's something I'd better tell you now while you're still deciding. I got your mortgage caught up. You've got a little breathing space to decide what to do."

Annie should have known, should have suspected he'd do something like this. "You spent five thousand dollars of your own money to pay the mortgage?" she whispered.

He nodded; then his gaze went to her father. "So make your decision on what's best for you. Don't be pressured into something you don't want."

Indecision swept over her father's face. He glanced at his son. "If we don't do it today, Father, we'll lose the deal, and they'll buy other land."

The older man nodded. "Very well. Call them." He stared at Mano. "*Mahalo* for your care for my family. I'll make sure you're repaid." His back was bent, and he looked like he'd aged ten years as he walked out of the kitchen.

Tomi watched him go. "It's hard for our father to accept change. I wish we could just stay here too. But he wouldn't be happy with all the traffic from the casino around. It's for the best." He slapped Mano on the back. "You're a good friend, buddy. *Mahalo.*" He went to the phone. "I'll call and make the arrangements. Aki gave me the number."

"No problem." Mano's gaze was on Annie while Tomi dialed and started talking.

She peeked at him from under her lashes. He should have been born during the warrior days of the early Hawaiians. He was a hero to her in every definition of the word. "*Mahalo*, Mano," she whispered.

"I was glad to help." He shifted, and she knew the thanks were making him uncomfortable. They waited in silence for Tomi to finish.

After he hung up, Tomi mussed her hair. "Little Annie hates change, just like Father," Tomi said.

She sniffed, letting him know with her expression that she was wounded. She wanted to laugh and shout with the joy that infused her. Their financial troubles were over. Her playful brother was back again. "Don't push your luck."

He slung his arm around her. "You think we can salvage those shish kebabs? I'm famished."

"You're always hungry." She glanced at the discarded food and shook her head. "I wouldn't want to eat them. Why don't we order a pizza, and you can get us caught up on what's happening. Have you talked to Afsoon?"

Tomi's open, expectant expression grew guarded. "Yeah. It's become really hard for her to stay a step ahead of her father. She's afraid she's going to be discovered any moment. I've got to get her out."

"Right." Mano said urgently. "Because of the murder, I didn't get a chance to check with my contacts. I'll do that now." He pulled out his cell phone, called his mother, and asked her to go through his safe again for his address book. She promised to call him back with the number.

"*Mahalo*, buddy," Tomi said.

"Don't thank me yet. We still don't have her out of there."

"With you on the job, she will be."

"Who's up for Scrabble while we eat our pizza?" Annie asked.

Tomi groaned. "Anything but that."

"Have you forgotten everything I taught you while you've been gone?" Annie teased.

"It was a welcome reprieve."

They played Scrabble while they ate their pizza. Annie beat both men in all three games. Tomi finally leaned back in his chair, then stood. "I'm going to bed. I can't take another whupping. Besides, the casino is sending someone over early tomorrow to pay for the property and have Father sign the papers. They ordered the title work months ago. Can you believe that? It will all be done tomorrow."

"And we have six months to find another place to live." Annie looked around. She'd lived here all her life. She watched Tomi go down the hall to his room. It had been so long since he slept in that familiar bed. If only Leilani were here as well.

"Let's walk by the water," Mano suggested. "I need to walk off that pizza." He stood and held out his hand.

Annie hesitated, then let him tug her from the chair and lead her out the back door.

The moon was big and bright. "The full moon will be here tomorrow," Mano said. Wilson trotted behind them to the water. The surf rolled in on waves of white foam. Mano and Annie sat on a flat rock that had just enough room for the two of them.

Annie made a face. "I hate to be out on the night of a full moon. I know it's just superstition, but I remember all the stories I heard about the dead walking about on the night of the *akua* moon."

Akua meant gods, and in the old Hawaiian religion, the gods could be seen walking about on that night and could kill a person. Mano smiled at her. "We'll go for a walk tomorrow, and I'll show you I can protect you." The waves just missed their feet, then were dragged back to sea. He breathed in the scent of the ocean.

"*Mahalo* for coming to my defense," she said.

"You're welcome." He'd do anything for her.

"Why did you pay the mortgage? We wouldn't have been able to pay you back if we didn't sell."

"I didn't expect to be repaid. I wanted to do it." Lame, lame. Why couldn't he just tell her he loved her? She couldn't do more than laugh at him, and he'd been laughed at before. It was no big deal. He leaned down and grabbed a stick. "Fetch, Wilson," he said. He tossed it out toward the white foam the sea had left behind.

The mongoose growled and dashed after the stick. He carried it back with an air of triumph, then curled around it. "He's not giving you a chance to get it," Annie said, smiling. "What a selfish little pig."

Kind of like me, Mano thought. He wanted Annie all to himself as well.

"Wilson needs to learn from your generosity," she said. "You're a good friend."

"You're much more than that to me." She went still, and he wondered if he'd picked a bad time to get into this. But he'd come too far to back out now. He took her hand, and she looked up at him. Her lips were slightly parted, and he took that as encouragement. "I love you, Annie." That was as plain as he could make it. He tipped her chin up and bent his head. Her kiss tasted of garlic and tomatoes. And longing. Her arms came around him, and he tasted the love on her lips.

Then it was over. Annie tore herself out of his arms. "Don't," she said piteously. She put her hands over her face.

"What's wrong Annie?" He tried to pull her hands down, but she turned her back to him. Her shoulders heaved.

"Just forget it," she said. "I couldn't bear to disappoint you." She jumped to her feet and ran toward the house.

"Wait, Annie!" Mano fumbled to his feet and tried to go after her, but Wilson dashed from under his feet and tripped him. He fell to the sand while the mongoose ran nimbly after Annie. Mano groaned when the back door slammed. No one had ever accused him of understanding women.

Twenty-three

Annie propped her chin on the top of Wilson's head. He seemed to sense her agitation, because he didn't struggle to get away but curled against her chest and nuzzled his nose into her neck. Her tears dripped onto his fur. What was wrong with her? Mano would think she was crazy to run off like that. She loved him so much it hurt, but she couldn't give in.

He deserved someone beautiful, someone he could be proud to be with. She remembered the one date her sister had fixed her up on, and how the guy seemed embarrassed to be seen with her. She wasn't pretty and vivacious. She glanced at her bare feet, and the scars made her cringe. The thought of Mano someday being sorry to be with her made her mouth go dry. Better to cut it off now. If Annie didn't know Mano better, she'd think he was teasing her. But he seemed sincere.

There was a tap on her door, and Wilson wiggled out of her grasp and ran to the door. He pawed at it and growled. Annie thought about not answering. She wasn't in the mood to talk to any of her family. She glanced at her watch. It was after nine.

"Annie? It's me."

Fawn's voice was a welcome relief. "Coming," Annie called. She went to the door and unlocked it, then stepped back to allow her friend to enter. "What are you doing out so late?"

"I was coming home from Bible study and wanted to ask how your talk went with Gina." Fawn's eyes widened when she glanced into Annie's face. "What's wrong?" She lowered her voice and shut the door behind her.

At her friend's sympathetic voice, Annie's tears flowed fresh. "Mano says he loves me," she whispered. She covered her face with her hands and turned away.

"And that's cause for tears? What on earth is wrong with you?"

"I should have known even you wouldn't understand. You're beautiful."

"So are you." Fawn grabbed Annie's wrists and forced her hands down. "Mano isn't the kind of man to say something he doesn't mean. You've loved him for years. You should be rejoicing."

"He deserves someone beautiful and talented. Someone who will be an asset to him."

"And you're all that. You've let your father's attitude color your perceptions too much. A real man isn't looking for an ornament but a partner to love." She gave Annie a slight shake. "Your outward beauty will fade, but your lovely character will bloom. You've got a caring spirit that is appealing to everyone, Annie. You just don't see it. The man who marries you will be getting a real treasure."

Annie began to smile. "You're prejudiced." She wished she could believe Fawn. Mano was so handsome and wonderful, but Annie loved him too much to saddle him with someone undeserving.

"Maybe a little. But it's true." Fawn plopped on the bed. "So what did Mano say? Dish, girlfriend."

Annie laughed. "I can't talk about it." Her cheeks burned. "He was very romantic though." It was best not to even think of what he'd said, how love had radiated from his eyes and voice.

"Ooh, I love romance." Fawn glanced out the window. "Is he still out there?"

Annie shook her head. "I heard him drive off a little while ago. He probably thinks he's had a lucky escape."

"You're going to go see him tomorrow and tell him how you feel."

"I can't." Her palms grew sweaty at the thought. "He'll forget all about me soon."

"No, he won't. You're going even if I have to go with you. You're being completely unreasonable. If a man like Mano tells you that he loves you, you're supposed to believe him. I don't understand why you put yourself down so much. You're just as lovely as Leilani, just in a less flashy way." Fawn stood and dragged Annie to the mirror. "Look at yourself. Shiny black hair, large beautiful eyes, slim and shapely. And you're even lovelier on the inside."

Annie didn't see it. She saw a small, nondescript woman with no redeeming features.

"It's all your family's fault," Fawn said angrily. "I've never once heard your dad compliment you. Tomi never has either. We women base too much of our worth on what the men in our lives seem to think."

Annie had never thought about that, but she supposed it might be true. "I didn't have any admirers in school either though," she pointed out.

"Because you've been trained to fade into the background. You have always been so unassuming, no one noticed you. It's about time you got over your fears and went after what you want. In this case, you don't even have to go after it. God has dropped your heart's desire right in your lap."

"He has, hasn't he?" Annie began to feel a flutter of hope for the first time. The concept seemed foreign to her. She'd heard so much about service while she was growing up that it seemed impossible to think God might want to give her something.

"I think that's why you've let your family and your need to be needed become your god," Fawn said.

"I thought about what you said, and you're right. I realize I'll probably have to guard against that forever. It's the one area where I feel competent and in control, like I'm making a difference." She told Fawn about the computer's faulty formula and the epiphany it had given her.

"Good. God wants to be the most important thing in our lives.

He wants to be our first passion, our first thought in the morning. He wants to be what gives our life purpose. For you, your family was most important. And that was wrong. I think it's because you have the wrong view of God and who he is. You think good living is all about being a servant, and while that's important, you forget that he really wants to be your best friend. You don't delight in him, and enjoy the daily communion with him."

Annie wasn't sure she'd ever delighted in God the way Fawn was talking about. She couldn't remember a time when she wasn't worried she was failing everyone around her, and that she needed to try harder. "How can I do that?" she whispered. "He's first in my life now, but how can I be a friend?"

"Tonight when you go to bed, just tell him you love him and want to spend time with him. Read your Bible and listen to what he says. Read the Psalms and just praise him for being there for you. And try actually asking for something for yourself, some way you'd like to grow. You might try asking for the courage to believe in yourself the way he believes in you."

Annie nodded. "I'll try. I've been reading my Bible." She couldn't imagine talking to God so easily. It seemed presumptuous. God was God and she was just—Annie. But the surge of hope couldn't be ignored. She would try it.

The phone rang, and Annie went to get it. "Tagama residence." There was a buzz on the line, then she heard the discordant sound of a voice altered by a synthesizer.

"Annie." The voice was sibilant like a snake's hiss. "Time is up, Annie. Say good-bye to your sister." The line clicked and the voice was gone.

Annie stood frozen with her fingers gripped around the phone. This couldn't be happening. She dropped the phone and covered her face with her hands.

"Who is it?" Fawn asked. She picked up the phone and put her ear to the receiver.

"He's gone," Annie whispered. "The voice. The voice said that time was up. It said to say good-bye to my sister." Maybe she hadn't heard that right. She gulped and looked up at Fawn. "We have to find her, Fawn."

Mano couldn't stand the thought of going back to his hotel room, not after what had happened with Annie. It wasn't too late to go to Jillian's and talk to Kaia. She was a woman; maybe she could make sense of Annie's behavior. He drove the deserted road to the Sommers's house.

Jesse answered Mano's knock on the door. "Hey, buddy, what brings you out this way?" His smile faltered when he stared at Mano's face. "Is it that bad?"

"How long did it take you to understand Kaia?"

Jesse grinned. "Who says I do? Is this about Annie?"

"Yeah, I thought I'd get Kaia's take on it." He followed Jesse into the living room.

"I'm afraid you're out of luck. Kaia thought Jillian needed a distraction. They've gone to hula class. Can I help? Though I don't claim to be an expert on the female psyche."

Mano sat on the couch. Checkers started to jump onto his lap, then sniffed his pant leg. The cat hissed and then shot under the sofa. "Checkers must smell Wilson."

"Yeah, he terrorizes the poor cat." Jesse sat in the chair opposite the sofa. "So what's up?"

"Tonight I told Annie I loved her. She ran into the house."

"Before or after she kissed you?"

"How'd you know she kissed me?"

"Buddy, I've seen that besotted look she gives you when she thinks no one is looking. That's a woman in love if I ever saw one. Did you scare her?"

"I don't know what I did. I kissed her, and she kissed me back.

Then she shoved me away and wailed, 'no,' and ran into the house."

"Women don't know their own mind half the time," Jesse said. "Tell her again tomorrow, and it will probably be fine."

"You're a lot of help," Mano said with a grin. His cell phone rang, and he glanced at the caller ID to see that it was his mother. "Hi," he said, answering it. Jesse motioned that he was going to the kitchen to make coffee. Mano nodded.

"I've got the number you wanted, son," his mother said. She rattled off the number, and he jotted it down on his notebook then stuck it in his pocket. "*Mahalo, Makuahine.*" He hesitated before he rang off. Maybe she'd have some idea. "Can you answer a question for me about women?"

"Women in general or one woman in particular?" She sounded amused.

"Annie. If a woman cares about a guy, would she run away if he told her he loved her?"

His mother was silent for a minute. "I think she's afraid, Mano. From what I could see, she seemed the typical middle child who always wants to please her parents. Her father seemed the kind who is never pleased. That can generate a lot of fear in a woman's heart. She may feel she can never live up to expectations. Going into a relationship, the expectations of the other person are as high as Haleakala. She probably is afraid of failing you."

"But I love her." It shocked him to confess his feelings to his mother, of all people. But she seemed to understand.

"Then woo her gently. She'll respond."

"*Mahalo.*"

"You're welcome. It seems I didn't return to your life too late to give some advice once in a while."

He could hear the smile in her voice. "Love you, Mom."

"I love you too, Mano. Sleep tight."

He clicked off the phone and whispered a prayer of thankfulness that he had a mother in his life again after all these years. The clock on the mantel said it was almost ten. It would be early afternoon in Tehran. A perfect time to call. He dialed the number and waited.

"Asad, my friend, it's Mano."

"Mano, my good friend. Too long I have not heard your voice." Asad's voice was as vibrant as Mano remembered it.

"I need a favor." Mano explained the situation.

"To my family you have given a new life. Such a small request I could never deny. I will set it up and let you know when the package is ready to be picked up."

"You're a good man, Asad."

"I am honored, my friend, to be of service."

Mano disconnected the call. He thought about calling the Tagama house to tell Tomi but then rejected the idea. It would be soon enough to tell him once the rescue was set up.

S am had come and gone with the old familiar promise to do what he could to find Leilani. He questioned Tomi while he was there, and Annie could see he still suspected Tomi of the murder. She didn't believe Sam would find Leilani. Not any more. It was going to be up to her to find her sister. Tomi paced the living room floor, and her father seemed even more shrunken and older after hearing what the caller said. He shuffled down the hall to bed after Sam left. Annie longed for Mano, but she resisted the urge to call him.

A notebook in her hand, Fawn sat beside her on the sofa. "Okay, let's make a list of what we know. See who our possible suspects are."

"Tab Watson was the last to see her," Annie said. "The Ku cult she's involved with. Or the casino people." Fawn's eyes questioned this last one.

"They've got our house now," Tomi said. "And wouldn't they have used her to strong-arm us into selling?"

Annie shrugged. "It's just that we know Tab works for them." She looked at her brother. "And I can't ignore that she disappeared right before you showed up. This seems to be tied to you."

Tomi shook his head. "Other than the Iranians, I can't think of anyone who would have a grudge against me. And why pick on Leilani?"

"I'm adding the Iranians to the list anyway," Annie said. She rubbed her forehead. "I want to check out the cult. If we could just attend a meeting, maybe we could find out something."

"Kauhi likes me. Maybe he'd take me to a meeting," Tomi suggested.

"I want to go too," Annie said.

"Let me see if I can talk him into it. He's up until late. I could run over there right now."

"I'm coming with you." Annie rose. "I'll never be able to sleep anyway." She followed her brother to the door.

"Me too," Fawn called.

"This isn't your problem," Tomi said. "You'd better let me and Annie handle this."

Love was the pits, Annie decided, looking at Fawn's crestfallen face. She wanted to be with Tomi, and he was too dense to even see it. Mano's face floated before her mind's eye, but she wouldn't think about him. She couldn't bear to disappoint him.

She didn't say anything on the short drive to Kauhi's. Tomi parked the car in the bright moonlight. "Let me do the talking," he said.

"Okay." He helped her along the boulders. He paused on the path to the cabin and held his finger to his lips. She nodded, and he knocked on the door.

The door creaked, then swung open to reveal Kauhi dressed in warrior garb with his face painted. Annie saw a dozen other men and women crowded behind him in the room. She stifled a gasp.

Kauhi's glower was all the more ferocious with the paint on his face. "You are trespassing." His anger waned when he saw Tomi and recognition lit his features. He nodded to Tomi. "Take your sister and come back another time."

"We'd like to talk to your friends about our sister."

Annie recognized the girl who worked at the fruit-smoothie stand and the man who worked at the gas station in town. The others were strangers. "Please," she said. "Have any of you seen my sister, Leilani?"

Their closed faces told her nothing. She tried to crowd past Kauhi, but he blocked her path. "Your sister is none of our concern. She was not serious about her worship, and we expelled her. Look for her somewhere else. We are readying for our holy night tomorrow." He closed the door in their faces.

Annie beat on the door for several minutes, but it remained closed and barred to her. Just like her sister's fate.

Twenty-four

A holy day tomorrow. Annie turned it over in her mind. Tomorrow would be the night of the full moon, the *akua*. She and Mano had just talked about it. She shivered. "I think we don't have much time to find Leilani," she whispered to her brother. "If tomorrow is a holy night, she may be sacrificed then."

Tomi glanced at her. "If that's even what's happening. I can't imagine someone going so far in today's day and age. It's ridiculous."

"What else could it be? There's something else. I'd dismissed it, but it keeps nagging at me. In that first phone call I got where the voice was altered, the person boasted that they'd sent Mother to hell."

"What? Why didn't you tell me?"

Annie wasn't sure why she hadn't talked about it. "For one thing, it was preposterous. We have a suicide note from her. So it was a lie I didn't want to think about. But what if whoever has Leilani really did have something to do with our mother's death? Maybe she was forced to write the letter."

"Do you still have it? Maybe we should reread it."

"It's in my room."

Tomi parked in the driveway. "Go get it while I call Mano."

"Mano? What for?" She yearned to see him, to know that she hadn't hurt him too badly, but she didn't think she was strong enough yet. Avoidance would be better at this stage.

"I want to see if he made any arrangements for Afsoon."

Annie relaxed. At least he wouldn't be coming over tonight. "I'll get the letter." She went inside. Wilson greeted her at the door.

She picked him up and carried him down the hall. Her father's room was dark. What a blessing that they didn't have to explain anything to him right now. She dropped Wilson on the bed and went to her jewelry box. Though she didn't have much jewelry, she treasured the few pieces of her mother's that Leilani hadn't cabbaged. And the letter was in the top compartment.

She lifted the lid and pulled it out. Though she hadn't been able to throw it away, neither had she been able to read it since the terrible night she'd found it. The envelope was creased and stained, and she always wondered if her mother had been weeping when she wrote it.

Tomi appeared in the doorway. "Find it?"

"It's right here. What did Mano say?" She sat on the edge of her bed.

Tomi dropped into the armchair by the door. "He got hold of his contact. The guy is going to call when she's ready to be picked up." He nodded at the envelope in her hand. "Read it to me."

She didn't want to. The thought of reliving the horror sickened her. Her fingers were stiff as she pulled the single sheet of paper from the envelope. Her mother's familiar handwriting made her eyes blur. She blinked rapidly until her vision cleared.

"My dear family," she began. "I'm so sorry this sorrow must come to you. It appears the only honorable way out for me. At the volcano, I will find the strength to save you all. Always remember how much I love you, and remember me with fondness. Your loving wife and mother." Annie looked over at her brother.

Tomi's head was bowed. "I never got a chance to say good-bye. I was gone when the funeral happened. In Iran, I read the paper online and found out what had happened. I've been so stupid. This was my fault. She was despondent over my supposed death."

Annie rose from the bed and knelt beside him. "Don't say that, Tomi. She was grieving you, but rereading this note, I'm not so sure she killed herself."

His head came up at her words, and he stared at her through eyes wet with tears. "What are you talking about?"

"It doesn't sound like a normal suicide note, Tomi." She stared down at the letter again. "This part about finding the strength to save us all at the volcano. At the time, I assumed she meant to save us from herself and her depression, but now I'm not so sure. What if she went to the volcano for a different reason?"

"You're grasping at straws. What possible reason would she have for going out there? And what could it possibly have to do with Leilani's disappearance?"

Annie slumped. She didn't know. Who knew what was in her mother's mind?

Annie read the Psalms as Fawn had suggested, then asked God to help her conquer her fears. Though a strange peacefulness descended on her when she turned out the light, her subconscious had a different agenda. She barely slept all night. Her dreams were punctuated with scenes of her mother calling to her from a lava lake. Her gut told her Leilani's disappearance was tied to their mother's death, though she couldn't see how the two were connected. Getting ready for work in the morning, she decided she couldn't let it ride. Though she wasn't ready to see him, Mano had a logical mind. Tomi was too guilt-ridden to be much help.

The doorbell rang as Annie put the last plate in the dishwasher.

"I'll get it," Tomi called. He bounded to the door and admitted two men in suits.

Annie joined Tomi and her father in the living room. The men went over the details of the sale pointing out the clause allowing the Tagamas to stay in the house for six months. Her father hesitated, then signed the paper slowly. The men handed over the check and left.

It took only half an hour to sign away their way of life. Instead of elation, all she felt when she looked at the large check was trepidation. Her life was going to change, and she didn't know if she could handle it. She glanced at her watch and realized she was going to be an hour late to work. She grabbed Wilson and went out the door.

Rain drummed on the roof of her SUV. Moisture dripped from ferns and trees along the route. The rain forest was living up to its name today. She called Mano from her cell phone on the way to the observatory. He answered on the first ring. "Mano, it's Annie." It was all she could do to choke out the words.

"Annie. Are you okay?"

Typical how his first thought was of her safety. "Yes—no, I don't know. I need your logical mind on a problem. Could you meet me for lunch?"

There was a pause. "Sorry, I was swerving to avoid a mongoose in the road. Not Wilson, by the way. Sure, I can meet you. In fact, why don't I bring lunch to you, and we'll have a picnic if it quits raining?"

At the last picnic, they'd shared their first kiss, but she refused to dwell on that. "Okay. Just come to the observatory. We can eat out on the observation deck."

"Fish tacos okay?"

"Love them." She ended the call and wiped slick palms on her jeans. It was stupid to be so nervous. While tossing and turning last night, she'd mulled over what Fawn had said about getting over her fears. She wanted to try, especially with Mano, but what if she failed him? Still, she couldn't think that way. Living meant embracing the possibility of pain, and she didn't want to just exist any longer.

She parked and carried Wilson through the downpour into the observatory. Flinging water on the floor when she stepped inside, she hurried down the hall toward her office. She sat at her desk and fired up her computer. The phone rang. She glanced at the display.

Banos LLC. Was there a problem with the sale? Her hand hovered over the handset; then she picked it up. "Hawai'i Volcanoes Observatory."

"I'd like to speak to Jason Sarris." The voice on the other end was gruff.

She didn't know whether to feel relief or disappointment that the call wasn't about the house. "He doesn't work here."

"I realize that, since he's our employee. But I'm having trouble tracking him down. He's not answering his home phone, and this is an alternate number I have for him."

"His mother works here." Annie was becoming more and more curious. Could Jason be involved with the casino project? How strange no one had ever mentioned it.

"Could I speak to her?"

"She's not here either. Did you try her house?"

"Of course I did. I just said I couldn't get him."

Annie flinched at the man's testy tone. "I could have her call when she gets in."

"Don't bother. I'll track him down."

The phone on the other end clattered in her ear. She returned the handset to its cradle. If only Mano were here now to talk this out. Could Jason be the one behind it all? She remembered him saying he'd seen men outside their house; she'd wondered then if he was stalking Leilani. She should take a hard look at him.

She looked at her computer. No time like the present. She launched her Mozilla browser and typed in BANOS LLC CASINO. Hundreds of hits popped up. She began to go through them one by one, marveling at the width and breadth of the company. They had projects in dozens of countries and many of the states. She ran across a blog of someone who railed about the company's scare tactics to get him to sell his property. Annie pinched the bridge of her nose. That hadn't been the Tagamas' experience with Banos.

People began to file into work. She closed her browser and pulled up her data. Working would help the time pass until she could talk this over with Mano.

The aroma of the fish tacos made Mano's stomach rumble. At least that's what he told himself. It was better than admitting his heart echoed with loneliness. Woo her, his mother said. How should he go about wooing someone who was as likely to take flight as a Hawaiian honeycreeper?

He parked beside Annie's Nissan and ran through the rain. Muddy water splashed on his legs and over his feet clad only in rubber slippers. Just inside the door, he shook the rain from his hair and went to Annie's office. Annie sat at her computer wearing an intent expression. Unobserved, he let his gaze roam over her face.

Small, even teeth caught her lower lip in an expression of intense interest. Her busy fingers twiddled a paper clip. She was so tiny, so perfect for him. He just had to convince her of that. She looked up, and color ran up her neck to her cheeks.

She dropped the paper clip and stood. "You startled me." She swept her hand toward the window. "So much for our picnic, huh?"

"I was sure it wouldn't dare rain on our day." He stepped into her office.

Her gaze turned uneasy, and she nodded toward the door. "Shut the door, would you?"

"Sure." Something was up. He saw it in the stiffness of her shoulders. He hoped she wasn't going to tell him she didn't want to see him anymore. "What's wrong?"

"Jason Sarris. I found out today that he works for the casino developer."

"Gina's son? How'd you find out?" Mano opened the sack of food and handed her a fish taco and chips.

She took it. "A guy called this morning from Banos LLC looking for Jason. He said he was Jason's employer."

"It's unlikely they'd hire workers when they're still six months away from ground break."

"And the night we stayed with Gina, I talked with Jason the next morning. It sounded like he might have been a little obsessed with Leilani. Like maybe he'd been stalking her. We've never really checked him out."

"No, you're right," he agreed. "I'll go have a talk with him, and we can talk about it tonight over dinner." He said the last with a hopeful tilt to his eyes.

She laughed, a soft sound that gave him hope. "Okay. But I'm cooking."

"I can fix a mean salad."

"In that case, you're on." The color came to her cheeks again.

When he left her half an hour later, he was whistling. The sun had finally come out, and its rays sparkled on the wet vegetation. He drove out to the Sarris house, but no one answered his knock. He got back in the car and thought. What about Aki? If Jason really was involved with the casino plan, maybe he and Aki were connected. It was worth a try.

He drove to Aloha Shores and stopped in front of Aki's house. A yellow Volkswagen was parked in the driveway. Aki's or Jason's? Mano got out and went to the front door. No one answered his knock. He decided to go around to the backyard. The sloping yard contained only pots of herbs and a few lawn chairs. Where could they be?

He went back around front. Maybe they were just ignoring him. Subtlety would get him nowhere. He went boldly to the front door again and pounded with his fist. "Open up, Aki. I know you're in there. I'm not going anywhere until I talk to you. I can come back with Sam if you'd rather."

He pounded so hard, the glass in the front windows rattled. Finally, he heard footsteps, and the door swung open.

Kim Aki's face was red, and the birthmark stood out in livid relief. "Knock it off, Oana. You'll have the neighbors out with their guns."

Mano tried to see past his bulk but spied only a living room that looked like it hadn't been cleaned in months. "This will only take a minute. I'm looking for Jason Sarris."

"Don't know him."

Aki tried to close the door, but Mano stuck his foot out and shoved the door with his shoulder. He caught the big man off balance, and Aki stumbled back. Mano pressed his advantage and stepped into the living room. "Sarris, I know you're in here." He strode down the hallway carpeted in black, though it was so littered with crumbs the color was nearly hidden.

Aki roared and barreled after him. Mano turned aside, and Aki fell against the door at the end of the hall. The door sprang open and revealed Jason standing in the middle of the room with a gun in his hand. His face was white, but the hand he used to bring the gun up to point it at Mano's chest was steady.

Mano stopped and held up his hands. "I just want to talk."

"I should call the police and have you arrested for trespassing," Aki said, getting to his feet.

"Go ahead." Mano's attention focused on the gun. "I'm sure they'd like to take a look at the gun. It looks like the same caliber that killed Noah Sommers. Why'd you shoot him, Jason?"

"It wasn't me," Jason said.

"Shut up!" Aki glared at the younger man. Jason blanched even more.

Mano couldn't believe he'd actually found Noah's murderer. "What about Leilani? Where is she?"

"I haven't seen Leilani," Jason said.

"I said shut up!" The cold stare Aki used on Jason made him take a step back. Aki turned back to Mano. "I think we'd better go for a little ride."

"Not in this lifetime." Mano bent over at the waist and rushed the larger man. His shoulder hit Aki's stomach, and the two men tumbled to the ground. He was vaguely aware of Jason tossing the gun aside and running from the room. The men thrashed on the floor until Aki finally heaved Mano off. He gained his feet and looked around. He swore, then jumped for the door.

Mano staggered to his feet and tried to go after him but tripped over a boot left in the middle of the floor. By the time he got to the front door, the yellow car was gone and neither Aki nor Jason was anywhere in sight.

He fished out his cell phone and called Sam. "I've found Noah's murderer," he told him. "Come to Kim Aki's house. I'll wait for you here." He shut off the phone and turned to explore the house before the police arrived. But try as he might, there was nothing to indicate Leilani had ever been here.

Twenty-five

Leilani dreamed of walking with Annie along a black-sand beach. Annie's hand was leading her like when they were children. When she awoke, a hollow sense of bereavement assaulted her. Would she ever see Annie again, ever be able to thank her for all the things she'd done?

Being trapped in this dimly lit place was like being lost between life and death. She'd spent most of her time thinking about how selfish she'd been. Had she apologized even once for all the shirts she'd ruined that belonged to her patient sister? Or had she ever even told Annie she loved her? Leilani couldn't remember a time when she'd acknowledged the quiet sacrifices she'd seen Annie make over the years. Things like giving her and Tomi the largest cuts of steak, like asking their mother to buy Leilani a new outfit even if it meant Annie dressed in styles that were outdated long ago. Instead, she'd whispered with her friends about Annie's lack of good taste.

She heard something at the front of the cave and glanced up. They were coming back. She gasped when Tab dragged her to her feet. He untied her, then marched her out of the lava tube. She blinked in the bright light, though it was later in the day than she'd thought. His tight fingers hurt her forearm as he marched her down the hillside to a pool of water.

"Wash," he said.

Why had she ever been attracted to him? She waded into the water and began to splash it onto her body. The refreshing moisture brought her senses alive in time to realize this was the sacred pool of Ku. She moaned and tried to run from the water, but he grabbed her and threw her back in.

M ano had called to tell Annie that her hunches had been correct. Not only was Jason involved with the casino, but he and Aki were implicated in Noah's murder. The police were looking for both men and had taken the gun to check ballistics. He was going to have to skip dinner, but he'd be over later in the evening.

Fawn offered to assuage her disappointment by coming over to keep her company. Annie hoped Mano's delay would mean that Leilani would soon be found. Surely Jason and Aki wouldn't do anything to her sister now that the police were on to them.

Fawn stretched. "I'm bored. Let's do something."

"Scrabble?" Annie suggested. "I already thumped the guys in three games."

Fawn groaned. "Not Scrabble. I'm in the mood to organize or something."

Annie brightened. She was always in the mood for cleaning. "I've got all those boxes of Tomi's possessions that Mano brought me. We could unpack them and put them away for him."

"Perfect. Lead the way." Fawn got off the bed and followed Annie down the hall.

Annie hadn't been in Tomi's room since she cleaned last week. His futon was unmade, and two drawers hung half-open out of the black-lacquer chest. A T-shirt dangled from the Kyoto lantern. "It didn't take him long to mess it up." The boxes were piled in the closet. She hauled them out into the middle of the floor. "I'm not sure what all is in these."

Fawn opened a box and began to root through it. "Looks like books and toiletries in this one."

Annie opened another box. "This one has pictures and scrapbooks. Tomi is a terrible pack rat." Wilson snatched a small album from her hand and dragged it under the bed. "Wilson, come back here with that." She flopped on her stomach and scooted under the bed to retrieve the album before the mongoose could chew it up. He growled but gave it up and scampered out the other side of the bed.

Annie scooted back out from under the bed and sat up. The book was open. "Oh, this is one of his scrapbooks of the year he had the diving business." The year before he joined the navy, Tomi had bought a boat and taken divers out to the volcano to dive. She propped her back against the bed and began to flip through the pictures. Her heart hurt at the sight of her smiling brother, carefree and happy and unsuspecting of the trouble that would soon plague him.

The girl and man standing with Tomi in the next picture looked vaguely familiar. She glanced at the newspaper article on the facing page. It documented a dark day in her family's history. Tomi had dropped the divers at the volcano, then left as was the standard practice. A dive boat couldn't anchor in the waters at the volcano because the ash would foul the engines, and the high water temperatures would cause them to overheat. When Tomi came back for them, he couldn't find the buoy that marked their position. He'd scoured the region for over two hours before it got dark. Then he called in the Coast Guard. The two had drowned.

She glanced back at the picture and stared into the girl's dark eyes, then gasped. "Fawn, look."

"What's wrong?" Fawn sat on the floor beside her.

Annie shoved the album onto Fawn's lap.

Fawn studied it. "I've seen them before."

"Me too. It's Gina's husband and daughter."

"You're kidding." Fawn glanced at the newspaper article too. "The family brought a wrongful death suit against Tomi, didn't they?"

"Yeah, but it was thrown out because the buoy was defective. Tomi wasn't at fault."

"How odd that Gina has never mentioned it."

They both absorbed the implications in silence. Annie didn't want to think of what this discovery might mean. "Could Gina have taken Leilani?" she asked slowly. "For revenge?"

"I can't imagine her doing something like that," Fawn said. "But I don't understand why she's never told you who she is."

"This doesn't feel right." Annie got up. "Let's go talk to Gina."

"Not without backup. Call Mano. He'll be glad to go with us. In fact, I'd better stay here. If you're not back in an hour, I'll call Sam."

"Maybe we should call Sam first."

"And tell him what? It's possible that their deaths are just too painful for Gina to talk about. We might be barking up the wrong tree."

"Maybe." But Annie didn't think so. Something was very wrong with this picture. Gina had been too close to them to have kept it secret this past year. She grabbed the phone and dialed Mano.

"Mano, can you get away? Something has come up."

"What is it?"

"It's better to show you."

He was silent a moment. "The investigation here is almost wrapped up. I'll be there in fifteen minutes."

Annie clicked off the phone. "He's on his way," she told Fawn.

"I have another idea." Annie went to the computer in the corner and called up Google. She put in BANOS ALEX SARRIS. She followed several links and found one that made her eyes go wide. Before his death, Alex Sarris had been CEO of the company. "Look," she told Fawn.

Fawn bent over behind her to read it. "Oh, Annie, I think this proves it. She hasn't said anything about her connection to the casino either. Let's see if your dad knows anything," Fawn suggested.

Annie frowned. "I hate to upset him."

Fawn put her hands on her hips. "You listen to me, Annie Tagama! It's time you let your father be an adult and take the responsibility for his own life like a man. This is not your burden. Your job is not to keep anything unpleasant from touching him. You either go out there and talk to him, or I will."

Annie knew she'd do it too. She held out her hands. "I know you're right, but my mother wanted me to keep things running smoothly. I want to honor her." Annie wasn't sure why she so feared her father's displeasure. She supposed it was in her mental makeup to hate upsetting the peace. "Let's go talk to him," she said. She led the way down the hall and found her father watching TV in the living room. "Where's Tomi?" she asked him.

"He went to the store after soda."

Annie sat on the arm of the chair and clasped her hands in front of her. "I need to ask you a question."

Her father muted the television. "All right. You look very serious."

"It's about Gina." Annie wet her lips.

He held up his hand. "It's too soon to know where things will lead with her. I like her very much, but we're just beginning our relationship. And no matter what happens, there will always be a place for you."

"Um, that's good to know, but it's not what I need to find out."

He frowned. "What's this all about then?"

"I was going through Tomi's things and found a picture. You remember that diving accident where he couldn't find the divers by the volcano?"

"Of course. Our honor was questioned."

"Did you know that it was Gina's husband and daughter who died that day? And her dead husband was CEO of Banos."

From her father's thunderstruck expression, she knew Gina had never mentioned it. The dread in the pit of her stomach grew, and she knew she had to talk to Gina.

M̃ano's car hugged the curves of the narrow road that led to Aloha Shores. The full moon illuminated the barren lava fields on either side of the vehicle. He glanced at Annie. She sat clutching the side of the door. He wanted to bring up the emotions that hovered between them but knew now wasn't the right time. Not while she was intent on hearing Gina's explanation.

"I still can't believe it," she mumbled. Wilson snored as he slept on her lap.

"I think she likely just didn't know how to tell you all about it."

"But don't you think it's weird that she'd date my dad and mother me when she was upset enough with Tomi to bring a wrongful death suit against him? And what about those phone calls saying that Tomi is going to pay for what he did? I thought it was about the money, but now I'm not so sure. She didn't tell us about the casino connection either."

"I want you to be careful not to ruin your relationship with Gina over this when it may have nothing to do with Leilani's disappearance. It could be that her good will toward you is just her way of trying to make up for the suit against Tomi."

Annie nodded. "I know you're probably right, but something feels wrong about it. She's had a year to tell us. Surely she could have found the right time."

"Maybe." He still wasn't convinced. Turning the wheel, he approached the subdivision. It was after nine. Too late for a social call, but Annie wouldn't rest until they'd talked to Gina. He stopped beside her house. The outside light was on, and one small lamp inside shone dimly through the living-room window.

"It looks like she might not be home. Her car isn't here either." Annie deposited Wilson on the seat, then followed Mano to the door. She knocked. There was no answer, and she tried three more times before giving up.

"Any idea where she might be?"

Annie shook her head. "I don't know much about her social life. We need to find her tonight."

Mano had been thinking. "Remember what you said about hating the night of the full moon?"

She nodded. "I thought maybe the Ku cult was going to sacrifice Leilani tonight. I'm almost relieved to think Gina might have her instead." Her face was turned up to him to listen.

"This is the night offerings are made to the *akua*, the Hawaiian gods. The calls you've been getting have hinted that Leilani is the one who will pay for whatever Tomi did, right?"

"Yes." Her eyes widened. "You think Gina could be involved with the cult too?"

"Maybe. Gina is gone. Maybe it's a leap to think they could be connected, but it somehow makes sense."

"We have to find her!" Annie grabbed his arm. "Mano, I'm scared. What if you're right and we have to find her now—tonight?"

He took her hand, and they ran toward the car. Where they'd look next, he wasn't sure, but they couldn't stand around waiting for another clue to drop into their laps. Annie ran to her side of the car and jumped in. He got in and started the engine. "How about we go see Kauhi? He seems to be our only real connection with the cult."

"Hurry!"

He dropped the gear shift into drive and punched the accelerator. Careening around curves, he made the trip to Orson Kauhi's in ten minutes. The glowing numbers on the dash said it was nearly nine thirty. They had only two and a half hours to figure this out if he was right, and he prayed he wasn't. Unless they got a real break, it would be impossible to figure out which *heiau* was to be used.

Annie was opening her door before he brought the car to a complete halt. Her limp was pronounced as she raced over the loose rock to Kauhi's cabin. Mano grabbed his gun from the glove box and tucked it into his belt, then caught up with her before she got to the house. "Hang on," he whispered. "He's likely to shoot us both."

"I don't care. We have to make him tell us where they have her."

"If they have her. I could be wrong."

"But you might be right." She went to the door and pounded

on it. "Orson, it's Annie. I have to talk to you." She kept pounding, but no one came to the door. Tears glistened in her eyes when she finally turned around and stared up at him. "What if he's at this ceremony too?"

Mano didn't want to tell her it was hopeless, that he didn't know where else to look. Rubbing the back of his neck, he turned to stare out over the lava field. "Let's assume they're at a sacrifice. They'd surely use the volcano itself. Where are the hot spots right now? Are there any big skylights or open craters?"

She nodded. "A few. The biggest one is out by the ocean."

"That might be important to them. Can you take me there?"

It looked like she was biting her lip hard enough to draw blood. "I'll try," she whispered. "We can drive part of the way there, but we'll need my SUV."

They hurried back to the car and drove down the road to the Tagama house, where they exchanged his car for her SUV.

"I'll drive," Annie said. "I know where I'm going." She drove along Devastation Trail to a rutted lane of crushed lava rock. "Hold on, it's going to get bumpy."

Mano grabbed the hand rest on the door. Wilson squeaked and wiggled against Mano's hold. The Pathfinder lurched along the one-lane road. One wheel hit a pothole, and he thought they were going to be hung up, but the SUV plodded on.

Finally Annie stopped the vehicle. "This is as far as we can go on wheels. We'll have to walk from here. It usually takes me two hours to walk it in the daylight."

Mano looked at the clock again. Nearly ten. He winced. "Let's go." He had grabbed his flashlight from his car, and Annie took another from the glove box. She joined him at the front of the SUV. The moon was so bright they didn't need their flashlights to see the path in front of them.

"I'm surprised we don't see other sightseers," he said. He realized he had Wilson in his arms and handed the mongoose to Annie.

She tucked the animal into her shirt. Mano patted his pocket to make sure he had his gun.

"This is a spot we don't tell the tourists about. It's too dangerous." Her voice quavered.

He could feel her fear and wished he could take it away. If he could find the spot by himself, he'd tell her to stay back, but he needed her. "You can do it, Annie." He squeezed her hand. She squeezed back but didn't say anything.

His breath rasped in his throat from the exertion. The breeze brought an occasional whiff of sulfur to his nose. They were rushing faster than was safe, but they had no choice if they hoped to get there before midnight. And what if they got out there and no one was there? He realized he should have called Sam. What was he thinking? They'd been so intent on rushing to Leilani's rescue, all rational thought had left his head.

He paused at the top of a hill. Annie's exhausted panting made him worry. "Rest a second." Digging his cell phone out, he clicked it on and waited for a signal.

Annie shook her head. "Don't bother. You can't get a signal out here."

"I was going to call Sam."

"I thought of that too. But Fawn will have called him by now."

"She won't know what to tell him."

"She knows enough to tell him to check out Gina."

"He won't know it's crucial to look tonight. Besides, what if it's not Gina at all? There's no guarantee she's involved with the cult. Maybe I was grasping at straws."

"I still think it's her, Mano." She stopped and grabbed his arm. "Wait, I just remembered something. She has a collection of Greek figurines. Her favorite one is Nemesis. The goddess of revenge." She grabbed his hand. "It's Gina, Mano!"

"Let's go." He grabbed her hand, and they ran across the hardened lava again. The air was beginning to get hotter, and now he could taste the sulfur in the air, feel it burn his nose and throat.

They jogged for what seemed forever. The illuminated dial on his watch said they'd been traipsing over the lava field for nearly two hours. "It's just over that hill." She pointed, and he saw the glow.

"Come on." He tugged on her hand, but she pulled out of his grasp.

"I can't." Her voice sounded strangled. "I can't go up there."

Before he could answer, the ground shook under their feet and tossed them to the ground. The jagged lava rock cut his palms, and his cheek stung. He swiped at it and touched moisture. Blood. "Are you okay?"

She struggled to a seated position. "Just go. I can't go up there."

He didn't have time to argue. "Go back to where you can get a cell phone signal. Call Sam and tell him to get up here." She nodded, and he took off toward the glow over the hill. He hated to leave her behind, but they had only minutes before midnight. He reached the crest of the hill and moved into the valley. The stench was stronger, and he could feel the instability of the ground under his feet. He hurried toward a large black rock, then peered around it.

A *heiau* had been erected near the edge of a giant skylight. Several figures were crowded around the slab altar. A white-robed figure lay there. She wasn't moving. At first Mano feared he was too late, then he saw Leilani's head move in a dreamy motion. He realized that she'd been drugged.

The nearest figure held a long, curved knife aloft. He was going to have to move fast. Slipping his hand into his pocket, he reached for his gun. There was nothing there. He checked the other pocket and came up empty again. It must have fallen out when he fell. He'd have to fake it. Glancing around, he saw a rock that had the right shape and grabbed it.

"Stay right where you are!" he shouted. He advanced toward the group.

The figure with the knife turned around, and he inhaled sharply at the sight of Gina, her hair perfectly coiffed as always.

Twenty-six

Stupid and cowardly. Annie paced with Wilson in her arms. She'd gotten through on the cell phone after moving only a few yards and called Sam. Though he'd been skeptical that someone like Gina could be behind Leilani's disappearance, he promised to come out as soon as he wrapped up an attempted robbery investigation.

What if Mano needed help now? Annie turned and looked back out over the lava field. She used to hop along that rugged landscape like a feral sheep. Now she was as timid and awkward as the *nene*, the Hawaiian goose that roamed this area. She wanted to throw off the fear that held her rooted to the spot, but she wasn't sure how. What was it that Fawn had told her? Something about fear and God. She thought a moment, then the verse came to mind.

For God has not given us a spirit of fear, but of power and of love and of a sound mind.

She'd always been proud of her mind. Her intellect was one area in which she excelled. God had given her the ability to think. She needed to use it now. This fear that paralyzed her was not from God.

Praying the whole way, she put one foot in front of the other and started back down the trail to where she'd left Mano. Fawn had called it stepping out in faith. She had promised that if Annie would do it, God would be faithful to help her. And to Annie's surprise, her faltering courage grew stronger, and her fear lessened. She picked up the pace and began to move as quickly as she could.

She stumbled across something, and it clinked. It didn't sound like a rock. She flipped on her flashlight and swept the ground with the beam. A glint of metal caught her eye. A pistol. She picked it up and looked it over. It looked like Mano's. That meant he was without protection. She started off again, running as fast as she dared. Mano needed her help.

She reached the top of the hill and paused. The fear began to creep back when the stench of sulfur grew strong and the fumes burned her eyes and throat. Her foot began to throb. Across this area of instability, the ground could give way with no warning and plunge her into the molten lava. She didn't think she could go through that again.

Wilson nipped at her chin as if to tell her to go on. Praying harder than she'd ever prayed before, she edged closer to the lava bench. A steam fissure released just to her left, and she bolted back to the top of the hill. She could feel the heat from here. Mano was out there somewhere though. What if he was hurt or injured? She should never have involved him in this. He wasn't equipped to handle this terrain. But she was a volcanologist, she reminded herself. She knew how to handle herself out here.

She started back into the valley again. The heat grew more intense as she moved closer to the red glow in the distance. The ground moved under her feet like a grumbling stomach. She could feel the bench shift and move like something alive. Sometimes she thought the lava had a mind of its own. She'd seen it do crazy things over the years, all of it impossible to predict. All she could do was go on and pray the ground stayed firm beneath her feet.

A rumble from the bowels of the earth crescendoed, and the rolling tossed Annie to the ground just as another fissure opened up. Wilson slipped out of her shirt and ran away. "Wilson, come back here!" The scalding steam burned the hair from her arms as she quickly scrabbled away. The skin on her arms stung like a sunburn. She had to find Mano and get off this unstable shelf. There was no sacrifice going on back here. No one in their right mind would be this close to the volcano.

She cupped her hands around her mouth to call to him when she heard a sound off to her right, behind a large rock. Creeping to the rock, she peered around it. A giant skylight lay before her. A fountain of lava, as well as steam and vapor, spewed from it occasionally. A *heiau* crouched too close to the fissure for safety. Mano was brandishing what looked like a gun at the people standing around the altar.

Annie tried to make out the faces of the figures, but there was too much vog and haze. Then she noticed the white form lying on the altar. The spill of dark hair cascading over the edge of the stone slab stabbed Annie with panic. Leilani. It had to be her sister.

There was a shuffling, sliding sound behind her. She whirled in time to see a figure rise up and leap toward her.

Get your hands up where I can see them," Mano ordered. He gestured with the rock and hoped it was dark enough for all to mistake it for a gun. "Drop the knife, Gina."

The older woman stood with her eyes wide, then her gaze flickered to something behind him, then back again. "I think you'd better drop your gun, Mano."

Mano stiffened when he heard a sound behind him. Then Annie called out, "Don't do it, Mano." He turned and saw Annie being shoved toward him by Kim Aki.

"Let go of me." She jerked in the big man's grasp.

Aki seemed surprisingly gentle as he propelled her along. He stopped and pressed a gun to Annie's head. "Drop your gun, Oana."

Mano had no choice but to release the rock he held. It thudded to the ground. They still seemed unaware all he'd held was a rock. He held his hands in the air. "Let her go, Aki."

Aki lowered the gun and pushed Annie forward. He gripped her by the forearm with one big hand. As Annie neared, her gaze went past Mano to the figure lying on the slab. "Leilani," she gasped. She jerked her arm loose from Aki's grip and ran to her sister. Leilani was moving about, but her eyes were still unfocused from whatever drug Gina had given her. Annie slipped her arm under her sister's head and tried to help her to sit.

Gina jerked her head toward the women. "Get her out of the way," she told Jason.

Mano moved to intercept Jason, but the young man pointed a gun at him. "Go ahead. I'd love to put a bullet in your chest," he sneered.

Mano raised his hands and stepped back. He didn't want to risk Annie getting shot. Jason grabbed Annie's arm and dragged her away from the altar. He shoved her onto the ground near a large rock. She rubbed her arm and stared up at him, then looked over to Mano with a plea in her eyes.

Mano clenched his fists and searched for a plan, any plan, to stop Gina.

"Gina, I know about your family," Annie said softly. "I'm so sorry. But please don't do this to Leilani. She had nothing to do with their deaths. She's innocent."

Gina's eyes glittered in the moonlight. "So were Michelle and Alex. They were just having a good time. Your brother killed them. He took my daughter and my husband. Now his sister will join his mother in paying for his sin."

"Mother?" Annie's voice broke. "What about my mother?"

"You really thought she'd kill herself? She never seemed the type, so I was surprised when everyone bought that story." Gina gripped the knife and moved closer to the altar where Leilani lay.

Annie rose slowly. "You killed my mother? You threw her into the volcano?"

She closed her eyes, and Mano knew she must be thinking of

the horror her mother went through. He itched to move, to do something.

"It seemed a perfect justice," Gina said. "She put up a good fight and even got away for a while. We chased her over the lava field, though, and the bench gave way. I took that as confirmation that I was doing the right thing."

"Why did she come out here?"

"She recognized my name when I first arrived and went to the observatory to talk to me. When she was told I was out at the volcano, she followed me out here. She had a picture of my family." Tears shimmered in Gina's eyes. "To tell you the truth, I really didn't want to hurt her. If she'd listened to reason, I would have let her go."

"You couldn't let her go. She would have told everyone," Annie said softly.

Tears began to leak from Gina's eyes. "You're right. But she was a mother like me. I was already beginning to love you like a daughter, Annie. I hated to cause you pain." The tears stopped. She straightened her shoulders. "It had to be done."

"You made Mother write the suicide note, then threw her into the volcano." Annie's voice was choked. "You've got your revenge. You don't need Leilani too."

Gina shook her head. "I hadn't planned to take her, but she was going to accuse my idiotic son of stalking her. I couldn't let that happen. When I realized the *akua* moon was coming, it seemed perfect to save her for that. Besides, once Leilani is gone, we can build a new family. Your father, me, and Jason."

"What about Tomi?" Annie asked. "And me?" She glanced up at Mano and discreetly showed him a pistol in her pocket. She must have found the one he lost.

Gina smiled. "He'll be in jail where he belongs. I don't want him dead. I want him to suffer for what he's done."

"And me?"

Gina frowned. "If you had just stayed out of things. You've spoiled it all. I really loved you, you know." Her voice sounded pained.

"You loved me so much you tormented me with those strange phone calls. That was you, wasn't it?"

Gina glanced at Jason, who scowled and looked away. "Jason has been a little jealous, I think. Is that what it was, Jason?"

"First Michelle, and then Annie," he muttered. "You never loved me, Mother."

"You're just like your father. Weak and whining. I never wanted any sons. Only daughters. Strong daughters like me." She looked back at Annie. "And like you, Annie. I never wanted to raise a man to mistreat women like my father did."

Mano had put the pieces together. "You're planning to frame Tomi for Noah's murder, aren't you? We already know your husband was the CEO of Banos before his death."

Gina's smile widened. "You're smart, Mr. Oana. It's the perfect plan. Much better than killing him. Once the gun that killed Noah is found among Tomi's belongings, the police will know they've found their man."

"Noah told me about lying for the casino. That was all going to come out, wasn't it? So you had him murdered, and if you can frame Tomi, you'll kill two birds with one stone. Your plan has a flaw, though. Did your stooge tell you that he lost the gun? The police have it. They're going to figure it all out."

Gina's smile faded, and she glared at her son. "Is this true, Jason?"

He shuffled his feet. "I didn't have a chance to tell you."

Mano looked at Aki. "What's your part in all this, Aki? Money?"

Aki shrugged. "Of course."

"I despise incompetence," she muttered. She looked at Annie. "Why did you have to come out here, Annie? You are so much like

Michelle. You were her replacement in my heart. But I can't let you live to tell anyone. I'm sorry. It didn't have to be this way if you'd just kept your nose out of things."

While Gina was talking, Mano began to edge closer to Annie. "I need to sit down," he said. No one seemed to object, so he squatted beside Annie. Her arm moved slightly; then she pressed the gun into his hand.

"I won't tell anyone," Annie said, standing. "Just let Leilani and me go, and things will be like they were before."

Gina laughed. "I can see you think I'm crazy, Annie. Maybe I am, but not in a way that makes me stupid. This is about revenge, not madness. You saw my statue of Nemesis. She's my role model. An eye for an eye and a tooth for a tooth, isn't that what your Bible says? Nemesis takes justice very seriously. And so do I. This is about justice for Michelle and Alex."

"But why like this? You're not even a religious person." Annie moved toward Gina, then stopped when the older woman held up her hand.

"It seems fitting. And the lava will destroy the evidence. When the *heiau* is found, the police will naturally assume it's the work of a cult." She moved toward the altar. "But I don't have any more time to chitchat. It's almost midnight."

She stepped to the left of the altar and smoothed the white layers of Leilani's dress out.

"No!" Annie shouted. She jumped up and started toward the *heiau*. Taking advantage of the distraction, Mano leaped to his feet. Aki moved to intercept Annie. He grabbed her arms and wrenched them behind her back.

"Tie her up. I don't want any more distractions," Gina snapped. She lifted the knife.

Mano was glad his military training involved so much nighttime target practice. He prayed for accuracy as he brought the gun up and fired. The gun bucked in his hand.

The bullet struck Gina's hand. She reeled and fell and dropped the knife. Clutching her wrist, she screeched at the men, "Get him, you fools!"

Aki released Annie and turned toward Mano. Annie shrieked and leaped onto his back. She began to pummel his back and pull his hair. He wheeled around in a circle trying to dislodge her, but she clung to him like an octopus.

Jason moved toward Mano, but the SEAL shook his head. "I'll shoot your mother if you move."

"Go ahead, what do I care?" Jason continued to advance.

Mano swung the gun around and shot him in the leg. Jason howled and fell to the ground.

Annie screeched, and Mano backed up to put himself in a position to fire. He trained the gun on Aki. "Jump out of the way, Annie!" In a flash, Annie dropped off Aki's back and danced away before he could touch her. Aki held his hands up. "Sit on your hands," he told Aki. The man complied, watching the barrel of the gun. Mano gestured to Annie. "Get the knife."

She hurried to her sister. The knife was lying close to the fissure. She paused, and Mano knew she was too frightened to go closer to the open pit of fire. He glanced at Gina. She was still nursing her wrist. "Never mind," he called. "Get Leilani out of here."

She helped her sister sit up. "Come on, Leilani, it's time to wake up." She patted Leilani's cheeks.

Leilani shook her head groggily. "Annie?" Her head lolled back.

Annie shook her gently. "Wake up, Leilani, we have to go home."

"Bring me that rope when she comes to," Mano said. "I want to tie up this guy. You'll need help getting Leilani out." He turned his head and saw Gina stagger to her feet.

"You've spoiled everything!" Gina turned and stumbled toward the knife.

"Stop her!" Mano yelled. He didn't dare let his attention stray from Aki. Jason was still moaning on the ground. The earth rolled under their feet again, and the fissure spit a fresh fountain of lava and a roiling stench of sulfur. The quake brought Mano to his knees. Aki jumped to his feet, then turned and raced away. Mano struggled up, but the big man had vanished around a rock. The sheriff could track down Aki. He leaped toward Gina, who was bending toward the knife. The ground convulsed again.

Annie was seated on the stone altar with her arm around Leilani. "Hurry!" she called.

Gina's hand was almost on the knife. Mano started to fire, but another quake knocked him down once more, and the gun flew off into the dark. He patted the rough shelf of *a'a* for the weapon, but it eluded his grasp. There was no time. He stood and ran toward Gina. She seized the knife and turned toward the women. Holding the knife aloft, she ran shrieking toward the altar. The blade began to arc toward Leilani.

Mano put on another burst of speed. He wasn't going to make it. Then, with a ferocious growl, Wilson leaped out of the darkness to Gina's shoulder. He bit into her skin, and the knife fell from her hand.

"No-o-o," Gina moaned. She flicked the mongoose off her shoulder and threw herself at the knife as it skittered on the slick rock toward the open fissure. Just as her hand touched the knife, the ground heaved. She sailed into the air. Her legs and arms flailed as she tried to find something to hang onto, then with a last, despairing shriek, she plummeted into the fiery waves.

Mano halted and tried to find his balance. He wanted to pray for her soul, but knew she was beyond that. She'd chosen her path, one of vengeance and retribution. The ground was swaying under his feet as if it were alive. His hair crackled with electricity. They had to get out of here. He moved toward the women. "Let's go!"

Annie shuddered and buried her face in Leilani's hair. Mano

reached her and lifted Leilani into his arms. "Come on. You lead the way."

A loud rumble built under them, vibrating like a cage that contained a ferocious beast. Terror gripped Mano by the throat. "Hurry!"

Annie blinked and seemed to come out of the trancelike state she'd been in. She gazed at the gaping wound in the ground. Fountains of burning rock spewed into the night sky like a deadly Roman candle. She leaped in front of Mano. "We have to get to the sea. It's our only hope." She turned and called for Wilson. The mongoose dashed toward her. He climbed her leg, and she tucked him into her shirt. "Let's go."

"What about me?" Jason wailed. He staggered to his feet.

"Help him!" Mano struggled with Leilani in his arms. They couldn't leave Jason here to die. Annie grabbed Jason's arm, and they began to move over the rough lava rock. Leilani was small, but the extra burden of her weight was no small matter as Mano struggled to find enough oxygen in the hot, sulfuric air. Ash began to rain down around him. He heard several thuds and turned to see the volcano spewing rocks as well as lava.

"It's an explosive event," Annie panted, still hanging onto Jason. "We all knew it might come. Pray we don't get a pyroclastic surge. This way." She led the way down the slope toward the ocean.

They stood on a cliff and looked down into the water. Rocks were raining down behind them with more fury now. The ash cloud that billowed from the volcano blocked the bright moonlight. One boulder landed only two feet from them and lay smoldering. The water was twenty feet below, and there was no path down. "Now what? Is there a better access point?" He wasn't sure of this plan. If the lava reached the water, it was sure to parboil them.

"There's a ledge right down there." She pointed. "We can climb down to it and jump."

"Jump?" Was she nuts? He stared down at the whitecaps. "We don't even know how deep it is here."

"I can't jump," Jason howled.

"I've dived here. It's deep enough." She shoved Jason toward the edge. "Go, or you'll burn!"

Jason moaned but did as she said, slinging his wounded leg over the edge. He slid to the rock shelf below. Annie followed him.

Full of misgivings, Mano waited until she was down, then lowered Leilani to the ledge. The younger woman was finally beginning to awaken. Once Annie had Leilani, he joined them. The racket above them increased until it was almost impossible to be heard.

Annie pointed down. She leaned toward him and put her lips against his ear. "I'll go first so I can get to Leilani."

He nodded. Looking into her eyes, he wanted to say something profound and loving, but he couldn't think with the explosions going off.

Annie pressed her lips to his. "I love you," she said. Then she pulled Wilson from her shirt, turned, and they both plunged over the side.

Mano leaned over to watch and saw the splash that she made. Then her head bobbed up in the hazy moonlight. He saw Wilson swimming beside her.

Leilani backed away, shaking her head. She was awake enough now to be frightened.

There was no time to reassure her. He grabbed her and flung her over the side. Leaning over, he watched her fall into the sea. Annie was by her side in moments.

"You next," he told Jason. He didn't wait for a response from the young man. Giving him a shove, Mano sent Jason sailing over the edge. He saw him splash into the water.

A huge boulder came rolling toward him. It was still sizzling. He dove over the side of the ledge just a moment before it reached him.

Twenty-seven

The water was already hot. Off to her left, Annie could see lava dripping into the sea like a bloody fountain. The hiss and crackle as it hit the waves was deafening. Ash rained everywhere. She tried to support her sister, but Leilani was thrashing about in the water and wailing.

"Hush," Annie said. "We've got to swim." She released her sister and made sure she was swimming, then looked around. Mano was just to her right with Jason. She pointed down the coast. "There's a landing about a mile down that way," she called. A mile. She didn't know if she could make it. Her foot throbbed.

She reached under the waves and struggled to undo her wet laces. The heavy boots weighed her down, and she gulped in a mouthful of seawater mixed with ash. Trying again, she finally kicked free of them. Wilson paddled nearby. He loved a swim, but even he seemed to realize the danger that threatened them. Annie's head went under the water again. The heat of the water was beginning to get uncomfortable.

Steep rocky cliffs rose straight up from the water. There was no safe place to come ashore. They began to swim toward a speck of light in the distance. Annie knew there was a house on the hill near the landing she had in mind. It seemed so far away. She didn't see how they could make it. The wind blew tiny fragments of ash, cinders, and Pele's hair—lava so fine it was like spun glass—onto her head. Called tephra, the various forms of lava was a sign to Annie that the volcanic eruption was shooting fountains of lava high into the wind.

Mano and Jason came alongside Leilani and Annie. "You doing okay?" Mano panted.

"I don't think I'm going to make it," Leilani whispered. "Go on without me."

"If only Nani was around," Mano said.

Nani. Annie glanced over at Wilson. "Wilson, call Nani." The mongoose barked and kept paddling. "Nani, call Nani." Wilson barked again, but Annie knew it was doubtful that the dolphin would hear him. They were going to have to do their best to get out of this on their own.

The volcano's fury increased. The mountain began hurling rocks that struck the water all around them. "Dive," Mano yelled. "Swim underwater as far as you can."

Annie had little breath left, and she was sure Leilani was in the same predicament. But she took a gulp of air and dove under the waves. Her feeble kicks did nothing to propel her forward. She kicked out again, and finally began to make slow headway. Coming up for air, she gasped in a lungful and stared wildly for her sister and Mano. There was no sign of them in the boiling cauldron of waves.

Annie fought back the fear. They were probably still under water. She struck out in an overhand stroke, then saw her sister's long hair trailing in the water as her head broke the surface. Moments later, Mano came up as well. Then Jason's head popped up. Just ahead she could see Wilson paddling for all he was worth. He was still barking for Nani.

It was getting hard to breathe with all the ash in the air. The heat scorched her lungs, and Annie was beginning to realize they wouldn't make it. She decided that was okay. God was with them, no matter what happened. She paddled in place and turned to look back at the mountain. A fabulous light show was going off with fountains of lava being hurled into the night sky. Tiny flecks of burning lava lit the sky like fireworks. If this was her last sight on earth, it was one guaranteed to confirm God's awesome power.

Something nudged Annie's arm, and she looked down. A dolphin bumped her with its nostrum, then another surfaced, and another. They were swimming in a pod of dolphins. She grabbed hold of the closest one's dorsal fin, and the animal pulled her through the water at a fast clip. She started to let go to grab Leilani but saw another dolphin was already helping her sister. Mano had hold of Nani, and he scooped up Wilson as he passed. Jason grabbed a dorsal fin as well. The four of them zoomed away from the danger.

The water temperature began to cool slightly. Fifteen minutes later they were in calm waters just offshore from the landing. When her feet touched bottom, Annie gave her dolphin rescuer a final, thankful pat and let go. She waded toward shore where Mano and Leilani were already waiting. Every part of her body ached, but they were alive. She could hardly believe it. On the sand, she stopped and looked back at the mountain. It was still spewing fountains of lava. The sight was even more beautiful now that they weren't in the thick of the ash.

Mano rushed to meet her. "Are you okay?" He cupped her face in his hands, and his gaze searched hers.

"I think we're all in one piece." She drank in the devotion on his face. Wilson poked his head out of Mano's shirt and broke the moment's poignancy. Mano dropped his hands as the mongoose scurried down his arm to meet Annie. She laughed and took her pet, then stepped past Mano to where Leilani sat on a large lava rock. Jason lay on the ground a few feet away, his chest heaving with exertion.

Leilani had her face in her hands. Annie sank to her knees in front of her sister. Leilani's eyes looked dark and enormous in the moonlight, and Annie thought they must be dilated from the drug. "We need to get you looked at. I'm not sure what they gave you."

"I'm okay." Leilani hesitated, then threw her arms around Annie's neck. "*Mahalo*," she whispered. "I've learned a lot through this, Annie. I've taken so many things for granted in my life, especially you. I want to be different from now on." Tears leaked from her eyes, and she sniffled.

Annie hugged her back. She couldn't speak. "Let's go home," she said.

A nnie's skin burned and stung. They probably all had first-degree burns, maybe even second-degree in some places. She could feel some small blisters on her upper arms. But they were lucky to be alive. No, not lucky. Blessed by God's providence. She stopped and put her hand on Mano's arm. "Let's thank God we're alive. Would you pray for us?" All but Jason knelt together on the cinders, and Mano praised God for bringing them safely through the maelstrom of fire. His arm was pressed closely around Annie, and gratitude swelled in her that he was here, safe and whole. And that he loved her.

Behind them, the volcano still spewed, but they were at a safe distance now. The ground trembled beneath their feet, but Annie knew God's hand held them steady. They left Jason where he lay on the sand. He wouldn't be able to walk without help, and they could send Sam back for him.

They trudged toward town. By the time they arrived, dawn was lightening the gloom, though heavy cloud cover from the eruption hovered low overhead. Crowds lined the streets. Vans with equipment and supplies were already speeding out to the site to see the extent of the eruption. Mano waved at Sam.

Sam's gaze took in their state. "What happened to you?" he asked.

"It's a long story." Mano told the detective about Gina and her part in Leilani's abduction. Sam sent a car to pick up Jason.

"You're saying Adele was murdered by Gina as well? Talk about an old-time harpy, just like in the old Greek myths. We picked up Aki, by the way." He clapped Mano on the shoulder. "Good job."

Annie was drooping. She wanted to crawl into bed and close her eyes. "Where are my father and brother?" Wilson was already sleeping inside her shirt.

"I haven't seen them," Sam said.

"Maybe they're at the observatory. I'm sure Father is anyway." She clasped her arms around herself. She hated to be the one to tell him about Gina. Even if it was too soon for his heart to have been touched, his honor would be tarnished by his association with her.

Sam motioned for another officer. "Run these folks home, would you?"

"My Nissan," Annie said, suddenly realizing her SUV was probably destroyed.

Leilani slipped her hand into Annie's. "You can have my car."

Her sister's Ford Mustang was her pride and joy. Annie squeezed her sister's fingers. "I'll just get another one."

"I don't know what I would have done if you hadn't come, Annie," Leilani said in a small voice. "I'll never be able to repay you."

"Your love is enough." Annie kissed her sister's cheek, then they all crowded into the back of the patrol car. In front of their house, she and Leilani got out.

"Where to now?" the officer asked.

"I'll get out here. That's my car," Mano said, pointing out his car in the driveway. He climbed out and went toward it. He stopped and came back to Annie. "We're both too tired to think. All I want to say to you can wait until tomorrow night."

"Come for dinner?" she suggested. Her heart swelled at the promise she saw in his eyes.

"If you let me help."

"You can keep Wilson out of things."

His smile lit his tired eyes. "Deal." His gaze searched hers. "I'm going to have to call navy security and straighten out the mess with Tomi tomorrow. He might be arrested until it's all squared away."

Annie gulped. She'd hoped the worst of the ordeal was over. "Can I come?"

"It would probably be easier on Tomi if you didn't."

"Will you call me when it's over?"

"I'll come tell you in person." He dropped a kiss on the tip of her nose, then went to his car.

Mano sat in Sam's office in a cracked vinyl chair. Ash lay thick on the furniture, and his throat still burned. Tomi sat beside him. Two navy security officers were waiting to take Tomi into custody when Sam finished his interrogation. A preliminary necessity only, Mano hoped. It was nearly five.

"So let me get this straight. Gina's dead husband was CEO of Banos. He'd begun negotiations to build the casino here and died with his daughter while diving. Gina blamed Tomi for the deaths and came here to get her revenge. Noah altered research that would have shown the development was on unsafe ground so that the conglomerate could go ahead with the sale of land to developers and homeowners."

Mano nodded. "Noah was killed when Gina's associates thought he was going to renege and spill the beans. They'd be stuck holding worthless land."

Sam grimaced. "They are anyway. They own most of the land the lava is spilling onto now. It looks like Aki actually pulled the trigger. At least that's what Jason tells us."

"And Gina planned to pin the murder on me," Tomi said. "Jason and Aki were going to plant the gun among my things. She killed my mother."

"Your poor mother never had a chance." Sam's eyes drooped, and he blinked rapidly.

Tomi bent his head and just nodded. Mano swallowed the lump in his throat. He'd loved Adele Tagama like a mother, and he could only imagine how devastated her children were at the realization of how she really died.

"What about the calls to Annie, the ones with the altered voice?" Sam asked.

"Jason. He was jealous of how much his mother loved Annie."

"Some love. She was going to kill her."

"I think she really cared about Annie in her own way. Killing Annie wasn't something that she planned to do."

Sam drummed his fingers on the desk. "What about this money in the bank?"

Mano looked up at the security officer. "Planted there by some Iranians who were trying to blackmail Tomi into giving them some intelligence. With him in custody and the whole thing in the open, they won't have any option but to go back to their own country."

"I'd like to find them first," Sam grumbled.

Mano wished the detective luck, but he knew the men had probably flown out this morning when the news began to leak.

The security officers shifted restlessly. Tomi stood. "I think these men are ready for me." He gripped Mano's hand. "I heard from Afsoon this morning. She's in Egypt. When she gets here, she can corroborate my story. *Mahalo* for everything, my friend."

Reluctant to release his friend's hand, Mano gripped it tightly. "Hang in there, Tomi. This will all be sorted out."

"All thanks to you." Tomi let go of Mano's hand, then pulled him into a hug and slapped him on the back. "Talk to you soon." He went out the door with his head held high.

Mano hoped Annie and her father would take the news of Tomi's apprehension as well.

Wilson barked and ran in circles around Annie's feet, then raced up the wall and back down again. "What's with you?" she asked. The mongoose ran to the door and barked again. Someone must be here. Her hand went to her throat. Was Tomi's interview over? The doorbell rang, and she quickly stepped to throw open the door.

"Hi," Mano said. His eyes were bright above the royal blue and white aloha short he wore.

"Where's Tomi?" She opened the door for him.

He stepped inside. "He's in navy custody, Annie. Only until this is sorted out," he added when her eyes filled with tears.

Annie couldn't speak. She nodded and went into the living room. The hope she'd clung to all day ebbed away and left her feeling bereft.

Mano followed her. "It's going to be okay. He'll be home again before you know it." He hesitated. "Be prepared for a dishonorable discharge though."

She pressed her fingers to a pain at her temple. "I don't even want to hear what Father says about it."

"Where's Leilani?"

"Out with friends." If he kept staring at her like that, she was going to melt. There was a new awareness between them, so many things left unsaid. She longed to hear them, but the thought made her catch her breath at the same time. "I'd better get dinner started."

"I'll help you."

She never before realized how delicious anticipation could be. They walked together to the kitchen, and she let herself imagine doing this with him every night in their own home. *Don't go there.* She jerked back from the thought as if from a river of lava. She set him to chopping vegetables.

Mano set the table, then plopped onto a stool at the counter and watched her fix the beef stir-fry. "Smells good."

"I don't know where Father is," Annie said, glancing at the clock on the wall. "He should be home by now."

"Maybe he heard about Tomi in town." He looked around. "Are you safe here?"

Annie tried to smile. "For now. But the lava is moving this way. There's no telling if it will pass us by or destroy the land. But it looks like we'll be moving on to another home regardless. We'll be okay. God is in control." She went to the phone. "I'll call Father." She dialed her father's cell phone number, and her father answered. "Father, dinner is ready."

He sounded flustered and annoyed. "You're interrupting my research, Annie. I had a pizza delivered."

She took a deep breath. It was time she made her stand. "Fine, we'll eat without you. But I'd appreciate it if next time you'll be delayed you give me the courtesy of a phone call."

From the silence on the other end of the phone, she knew he was taken aback by her rebuke. "I may be gone when you get back. Mano's here, and we may go for a drive or something."

Her father began to sputter, but Annie said good-bye and clicked off the phone. "I did it," she said. Her shoulders straightened as twenty pounds—maybe fifty—rolled off. "Let's eat."

Mano's grin spread across his face. "I am Annie, hear me roar."

She laughed. "Or at least meow."

He squeezed her fingers and pulled her chair out for her. She was conscious of his gaze on her throughout the meal. "You're staring," she finally said as they had their coffee.

"You're so beautiful."

She was beginning to believe he saw her that way, miraculous as it was. No snappy answer came to mind, so she just stayed quiet.

"Let's walk down by the water," Mano said. "I have something I want to say to you."

Was she ready to hear it? Her heart told her yes, but her head was still afraid of disappointing him. He deserved so much more than she could give him. His warm hand enveloped hers, and he led her toward the door. Wilson zipped out under her feet and ran ahead of them to the water.

They walked down to what Annie thought of as "their rock." She perched on it, then patted the spot beside her. Wilson took her invitation and hopped up onto her lap, then burrowed under her shirt. Mano knelt in front of her. Her pulse began to gallop. Was he going to propose? If he did, what would she say?

But instead of speaking, his big hands touched her right foot. He pulled her shoe off and cradled her foot in his hand. His hand was so large, her foot lay perfectly in his palm. She tried to pull it away out of sight, but he shook his head and held tightly. A shock as profound as if she'd touched a live current of electricity raced through her when his fingers traced the scars on her instep.

Then he leaned down and pressed his lips to the scars. "Even your feet are beautiful," he whispered. "Don't ever be ashamed of all that you are, Annie. I know in our lives we may disappoint one another, but it is all to make us grow together. You're the finest, most beautiful woman I've ever met. I love every part of you, every knock and hard spot that made you the person you are today. I'm never letting you go. Say you'll marry me. I'm not sure what job I'll be doing, but I'll always take care of you."

What could a woman say to a proposal like that except the word that sprang to her lips? "Yes," she whispered. Mano's arms drew her into an embrace, and Wilson poked his head out of her shirt. Annie thought he'd growl or bark to see Mano crowding his space, but the mongoose licked Mano's face. "I think he approves," she whispered. "That's a kiss."

"Yours are the only kisses I want," Mano murmured as his lips found hers.

Words used in this series

aloha (ah-LOW-hah): a warm Hawaiian greeting or parting; love, grace, sentiment, compassion, sympathy, kindness, affection, friendship; to show kindness or to remember with affection.

haole (hah-OH-lay): white person. Can be a slur depending on tone.

keiki (KAY-kee): child.

ki'i (Kee-ee): the stone statues similar to tiki.

'ohana (Oh-HAH-nah): family.

onolicious (oh-no-LI-cious): A variation of *ofono,* the Hawaiian word for good.

mahalo (mah-HAH-low): thank you. Heard everywhere in the islands, even when something is announced on the loudspeaker in Kmart.

makuahine (mah-koo-ah-HEE-nay): mother.

makuakane (mah-koo-ah-KAH-nay): father.

tûtû (too-too): grandma.

tûtû kâne (too-too KAH-nay): grandpa.

Reading Group Guide Available
at www.thomasnelson.com

Acknowledgements

I had some great help with my research for this book, though as always, any errors are mine. The Big Island of Hawai'i is a fascinating place with so many different climates and areas. Some wonderful establishments gave us lodging at a reduced rate.

We loved the Hilo Hawaiian Hotel. In fact, Hilo was my favorite city on the Big Island. It's very laid back and the people were friendly. The hotel looked out on a beautiful lagoon, and we stood on the balcony and just drank in the view. We highly recommend it. And while you're there, stop next door at Uncle Billy's restaurant. It feels like a place straight out of an Elvis movie with thatched cabanas.

Jessica Ferracane at The Fairmont Orchid welcomed us to our first stop on the west side. The Fairmont Orchid is this glorious, old-world kind of place with lavish rooms and grounds and a bed to die for. The beach area is great for kids, and outside huts boast enjoyable spa treatments. Heaven! I highly recommend it.

Leanne Pletcher made our stay at the Hilton Waikoloa a delight! It's a destination unto itself! A tram takes visitors around the extensive grounds, and there's so much to do, you may never want to leave. (Resist the temptation, though, and make sure you explore *all* of Hawai'i.) The room was fabulous, and Leanne presented us with a chocolate concoction that looked like a flower. We loved our stay there and highly recommend it.

There is one activity at the Hilton Waikoloa you won't want to miss—Dolphin Quest. We actually swam with the dolphins and saw how they are trained. One of the dolphins I met was named Nani! I asked to have my picture taken with her, and you can find that photo on my Web site. Being with the dolphins was an almost spiritual experience. Patrick McLain Jr. answered my many questions about dolphins and was a great help in the research for this book.

David Warganich welcomed us to the Chalet Kilauea. We stayed in the Lokahi Lodge, a charming bed-and-breakfast in the rain forest at the volcanoes. It was a home away from home, and our hosts were very gracious. Highly recommended.

My research at the volcanoes was fascinating! The men and women who study volcanoes are dedicated and brave.

Steve Brantley at the Hawaiian Volcano Observatory took an entire morning to answer my questions and show me around the observatory. It was so captivating, I didn't want to leave! Thanks so much, Steve.

He also put me in touch with Gordon Tribble, who has done some underwater research at the volcanoes. Gordon gave me tons of information about diving to the volcanoes and the hazards involved in that. Thanks, Gordon!

Several writer friends proofed Hawaiian details for me. Special thanks to Hawaii resident Malia Spencer and former resident Carrie Turansky.

No story reaches its potential without good editors. Much as we'd like to think we can do it ourselves, the truth is that if you read a great story, it's because that author had great editors. I have the best out there. Ami McConnell at Thomas Nelson has a great eye for characterization and the deeper meaning behind so many things in the finished product—from the cover to the narrative. She helps me dig deeper and strengthen the theme and characters. I'm also blessed to work with Erin Healy, who catches *everything* and helps me make sure the plot and characterization hang together right. I don't know how she does it, but I'm so grateful.

I'm so blessed to be part of the entire Thomas Nelson team: Allen Arnold, Ami McConnell, Jenny Baumgartner, Amanda Bostic, Lisa Young, Scott Harris, Jennifer Deshler, and Caroline Craddock. Thanks, everyone!

My agent, Karen Solem, is many things in my life—friend, mentor, seat-of-the-pants-kicker, and cheerleader. Thanks, Karen!

My family has been a huge part of the Aloha Reef series. We have gone on two research trips to Hawai'i, and my children, David Jr. and Kara, are my sources for details about diving and fish. My husband, David, is my biggest fan and patiently researches with me and helps in my writing from editing to plotting. Love you all!

Writing used to be a lonely business. My critique buddies and friends, Kristin Billerbeck, Diann Hunt, Denise Hunter, and Carol Cox are my confidantes, encouragers, and brainstormers extraordinaire. I couldn't do without them. Thanks, girls!

I can't believe all that God has done in my life, and I praise him for it. This has been a journey so worth taking with him at my side.

Alaska
Twilight

COLLEEN COBLE

AN EXCERPT FROM

Alaska Twilight

Stalwart, Alaska. Population 301. Haley Walsh laid down her itinerary and looked down from the small plane in which she flew to see its shadow moving over the treetops—a forest of spruce, birch, and alder. Snow melted in puddles and revealed muddy land springing to new life in the lengthening days. Then the shadow caressed Stalwart, a tiny collection of cabins and storefronts. Even though it was April, the temperature wasn't more than forty degrees in this Land of the Midnight Sun, though she'd heard tomorrow would be warmer.

"It says here that Alaska has ten million lakes and a hundred thousand glaciers," Haley's grandmother said. At seventy years of age, Augusta Walsh's blue eyes sparkled with warm liveliness and curiosity. Most people guessed her age to be in the fifties, and her blond pageboy made her look like an older Doris Day, a resemblance she generally played to the hilt. "There are immense areas that have never had a human footprint, and thousands of mountains that have never been climbed."

Augusta's awed pronouncements just served to deepen Haley's fear. She swallowed hard and tried not to look down at the vast wilderness that yawned below her. The plane dipped, and the lake below grew closer, then the tiny craft touched the water. The plane glided to a stop beside a rickety pier that jutted into the water like an accusing finger.

"Let's go, go, go," Kipp Nowak bellowed. Everyone in the plane jumped at the sound of his foghorn voice, but he either didn't notice or didn't care. Only five feet five, his voice was the only large thing about him. Bruno Magli boots encased his small, slender feet, and his dark hair had been spiked into a careless style that would have suited a twenty-year-old but just deepened the lines around Kipp's blue eyes. He looked better on film than in real life.

Haley had watched his documentaries on TV for years. His antics with bears in Yellowstone had captured the American imagination for nearly a decade. Now she was going to take pictures of his next adventure herself. He'd maintained his adventurer's image by picking them up in Anchorage and piloting them out here himself. She settled back against the seat and pulled her camera, a Nikon f/5, up to her face. She adjusted the aperture to compensate for the glare of the glass, then snapped a few shots at the wilderness outside the plane. The familiar whir and click of the camera made her feel less out of her element, though her hands were still clammy.

"That's it, boys and girls. Your last glimpse of civilization for now." Kipp rubbed his hands together. "For the next few weeks, bears will be your companions. I've been here for a month with Tank Lassiter to get the lay of the land as the bears emerged from their dens. Now that the wildflowers are ready to bloom, it's time to shoot. There are a couple of bears I'm eager to show you yet today."

No one said anything. They all knew better than to get Kipp started on his hobbyhorse. Haley shivered. Was she strong enough for this? Staring out the window at a wilderness that seemed to go on forever, she struggled not to give in to her doubts. She lifted her chin, then moved to get out of the plane.

Haley had consulted several Web sites before purchasing Seven jeans, a long-sleeved Rebecca Beeson T-shirt, and a Timberland wool shirt and jacket. The layered outfit was supposed to keep her comfortable no matter what the weather might do. She wore rubber Wellington boots, and though they weren't as stylish as she would have liked, they would keep her dry. She wore a pair of thin wool socks over her regular socks as well, because a local in Anchorage told her the temperature might well drop to the teens tonight. She liked fashion, but she knew better than to let it dictate her choices totally. Functionality was key in Alaska. She remembered that much.

"I thought we'd land in town," Augusta said. She looked around the clearing. "This is nowhere."

Kipp swung open his door. "We have plenty of supplies, so I didn't want to waste time in town. It's to our north, and the bears are to our south. This area is sheltered, and our plane can float here with no problem. We're in a good central location." He got out of the plane and moored it to the dock.

The rest of the crew began to clamber out of the plane. Haley rubbed slick palms against her jeans. She turned her head and felt the blood drain from her face, leaving her vision swimming. The barren trees were still devoid of leaves, and the starkness struck her with an ominous sense of lifelessness. She clawed at her camera and brought it up to her eyes. *Adjust the aperture, focus, center the photo.* The familiar tasks gave her perspective. The camera whirred as she snapped too many pictures to count. The action gained her enough emotional distance to ease her ragged breathing.

Augusta touched her hand. "Don't look at it yet," she whispered.

Easier said than done. Her hands shaking, Haley lowered the camera. "I'll be okay in a minute. It just caught me by surprise."

Augusta cupped Haley's face in her hands and looked deep into her eyes. "I'm so proud of you. You're brave enough to face it now."

She was in her Doris Day encouragement mode. Haley was in no mood for it. "I'm not being brave," she said. "I want my movies, my friends, the malls, and especially my powdered donuts. This is not my idea of a good time. I'm only here because my shrink said this would help bring closure, so I'm going to see it through. If I reconnect with Chloe, maybe the nightmares will stop."

Augusta's brilliant smile faded, and she dropped her hands. "God would help you more than ten shrinks."

They'd been over this a thousand times. Haley decided not to make it one thousand and one. She began to gather up her belongings. She slung her knapsack of photographic equipment over her shoulder, then grabbed her single suitcase and the carrier that held her dapple dachshund, Oscar.

Oscar yelped at the sudden movement and began to bark to be let out. Haley soothed the dog. She was thankful when Augusta grabbed her suitcase and exited onto the weathered pier without saying another word. Haley followed. Uneven ground was difficult for her to navigate, and the mud didn't help as she struggled to exit the plane.

She found her balance, though, and took in the scene. The lake was surreally blue, as blue as Augusta's eyes. Haley stared at the amazing sight and the stand of spruce on the other side. Such a wild, untamed place. She shivered again. The lake and river drained into Cook Inlet to their south, and this airy forest with new moss and sprouting ferns appeared to be the end of the world. She opened the carrier and let Oscar out to do his business. The miniature dachshund dashed out and went to nose a patch of green breaking through a dwindling patch of snow.

Haley listened. The sound of rushing water and the chatter of birds overhead roared louder than any freeway noise. It pressed down on her like a heavy blanket. Vaguely familiar scents assaulted her as well—the last vestiges of melting snow, mud, wet moss, and the decay of last year's vegetation. It might appeal to some people, but for her, it just drove home the truth that she didn't belong here. She'd rather smell other humans and hear the sounds of civilization. She hurried to join the others among the litter of suitcases and boxes of supplies at the end of the dock.

"Ah, it's good to be back," said the producer-cameraman, Denny Saumik. "I grew up in Alaska, you know." His voice held a trace of Alaskan accent, an almost toneless quality. It looked like someone had put a bowl on his black hair, then cut it with jagged scissors. The small, smile-shaped scar above his left eye made him look like he was on the verge of asking a question at any moment. A tiny bear carved from some kind of bone hung from a rawhide string around his neck.

She hadn't known what to make of Denny at first. He never shut up. Her ears still rang from listening to him all the way from the Anchorage airport. But he was friendly, and had immediately made her feel part of the team.

She dared to invite more conversation. "When were you here last?"

"About two months ago. My base is here, though I'm gone much of the year. I pop back now and again."

Haley nodded, then turned to look again at the pristine wilderness, though staring at the place made her feel like a no-see-um caught on flypaper. No place could be this beautiful—and remote. Rugged, snow-covered mountains looked as though they held up a blue sky that stretched to eternity and back. Water gurgled over rocks, a festive marching band of sound as spring thaw began its parade across the land. Timber crowded along the edge of the water and reflected in the broad pool.

It was the familiar place of nightmares.